THE IMMIGRATION LAW DEATH PENALTY

The Immigration Law Death Penalty

Aggravated Felonies, Deportation, and Legal Resistance

Sarah Tosh

NEW YORK UNIVERSITY PRESS
New York

NEW YORK UNIVERSITY PRESS
New York
www.nyupress.org

© 2023 by New York University
All rights reserved

Please contact the Library of Congress for Cataloging-in-Publication data.
ISBN: 9781479816279 (hardback)
ISBN: 9781479816286 (paperback)
ISBN: 9781479816316 (library ebook)
ISBN: 9781479816309 (consumer ebook)

This book is printed on acid-free paper, and its binding materials are chosen for strength and durability. We strive to use environmentally responsible suppliers and materials to the greatest extent possible in publishing our books.

Manufactured in the United States of America

10 9 8 7 6 5 4 3 2 1

Also available as an ebook

In memory of my grandma, Norma Becker, a teacher and a freedom fighter, who taught me that where there is injustice, there will always be resistance.

I don't think the immigration system has come to as sophisticated of a conversation around understanding [the role of] policing in the immigration context. You know I think very often the rhetoric goes to . . . good versus bad immigrant, and there's a real lack of significant understanding of the policing that goes on, the communities that people are embarking from, that people may in fact have criminal convictions, but what is that about? And where is it coming from?
—New York City–based immigration attorney

The commission of an aggravated felony is the most conclusive proof of a public safety threat.
—US Immigration and Customs Enforcement spokesperson, February 2021

CONTENTS

Introduction

From Criminalization to Deportation

Born out of drug policy, administered through immigration law, and triggered by criminal offenses, the aggravated felony legal category penalizes immigrants with criminal convictions more than any other category of law. Invoking well-known criminal system designations in its name, the classification denotes a concrete severity largely unquestioned by policymakers or the public. In reality, the "aggravated felony" is not some long-established criminal category, or even a specific criminal category at all. Instead, it is an immigration law designation created within the past thirty-five years—a period during which the United States has deported unprecedented numbers of people, with the removal of so-called criminal aliens a consistent priority. Introduced in 1988 and expanded over the following decade, the aggravated felony demarcates a range of crimes for which noncitizens, both documented and undocumented, can be deported. Limited to murder, arms trafficking, and drug trafficking when first conceived, this immigration classification now includes thirty-five offense types, together encompassing thousands of state- and federal-level criminal convictions. Convictions in this category need not be "aggravated" nor "felonies" at all, but instead comprise a wide gamut of offenses—including misdemeanors—ranging from check fraud and shoplifting to arms trafficking and murder. The aggravated felony is known to lawyers as the "immigration law death penalty" because noncitizens convicted of aggravated felonies are subject to mandatory detention and almost certain deportation as they are made ineligible for nearly all forms of legal relief from removal. Contextualized by the most expansive system of criminal justice enforcement and incarceration in the world, which is known for doling out punishment in patently unequal and discriminatory ways, the aggravated felony is a determinative entry point to a pipeline that funnels criminalized immigrants toward deportation.

This book traces the development of the aggravated felony over the course of the 1980s and 1990s, to its everyday outcomes in the modern deportation regime. A socio-legal history of the category is followed by an in-depth exploration of its contemporary outcomes for migrants facing expulsion. Drawing on two years of ethnographic research in New York City's detained immigration court—including regular observation of aggravated-felony-based deportation proceedings, as well as in-depth interviews with the legal practitioners and advocates who work on these cases—my findings underscore the severe, expansive, and unequal outcomes of the aggravated felony while also highlighting innovative legal strategies that oppose its harshest effects. Demonstrating how immigration enforcement and deportation work to doubly punish groups already targeted by systems of criminal justice, this book provides an illustrative example of how inequality in the criminal legal system is reproduced through immigration law. Yet even while invoking the most punitive outcomes of any designation in the immigration system, the aggravated felony also serves as a point of resistance. In NYC, networks of progressive lawyers, legal rights advocates, and community-based activists fight for local policy protective of immigrants with criminal records while contesting a broader criminalization-to-deportation pipeline and the systems and ideologies that guide its flow. Though rooted in a particular context, this "crimmigration" resistance holds key lessons for those concerned with creating equal systems of justice and protecting the rights of immigrants nationwide.

The "Criminal Alien" and the Modern Deportation Regime

The exclusion and expulsion of bodies from sovereign countries is a tool that has been invoked throughout history and all over the world.[1] In the United States, immigrant removal and repatriation have been used to varying degrees since the early years of the nation.[2] Still, the deportation regime that has emerged here and in other migrant-receiving countries in recent decades is unique in both its scale and its techniques. Before 1990, deportation rates in the United States never surpassed 40,000 removals per year, with an average of 18,275 removals per year from 1900 to 1990.[3] These numbers stand in stark juxtaposition to the hundreds of thousands of immigrants removed each year in the twenty-first century,

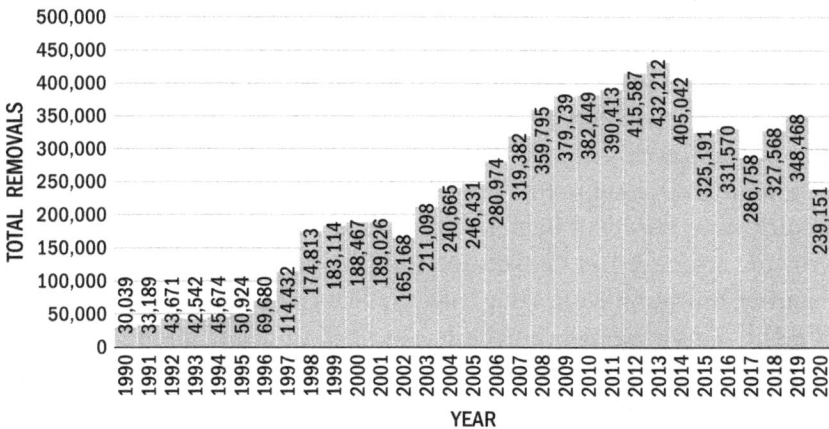

Figure I.1. Total Removals from the United States by Fiscal Year (1990–2020).
Source: US Department of Homeland Security, "Yearbook of Immigration Statistics: 2020" (Washington, DC: US Department of Homeland Security, Office of Immigration Statistics, 2022), www.dhs.gov/immigration-statistics/yearbook/2020.

as seen in figure I.1. While the United States is the world leader in rates of deportation, recent decades have also seen renewed anti-immigrant sentiment, punitive immigration enforcement, and increased deportation in immigration-receiving countries worldwide.[4]

The astronomical deportation rates of the first decades of the twenty-first century are one result of a late twentieth-century shift toward increasingly retributive laws and militarized enforcement surrounding drugs, crime, and migration. This "punitive turn" manifested in the rapid expansion of the War on Drugs, "tough-on-crime" policing, and mass incarceration throughout the 1980s and 1990s.[5] In the immigration context, a decade of policy harshening culminated in the Illegal Immigration Reform and Immigrant Responsibility Act (IIRIRA) and Antiterrorism and Effective Death Penalty Act (AEDPA) of 1996, wide-sweepingly punitive laws that set the stage for massive increases in deportation in the years to come—with a pointed focus on immigrants with criminal records.[6] From 2000 to 2008, using the tools of the 1996 reforms, as well as discriminatory and exclusionary laws passed post-9/11,[7] President George W. Bush set the record for most removals of immigrants under any president up to that time. In 2008, his administration enacted Secure Communities, a massive data-sharing program that continues to facilitate the sharing of arrest data between local criminal justice systems and federal immigration enforcement today.[8] The expansion of this program under the subsequent Obama administration contributed to the deportation of more than two million people within his eight-year term, leading immigration rights advocates to nickname President Barack Obama "Deporter in Chief."[9] Faced with growing criticism from advocates, the Obama administration replaced Secure Communities in 2014 with the Priority Enforcement Program (PEP).[10] This program contributed to a dip in deportation rates overall by making noncitizens convicted of crimes the central targets of enforcement and removal.

Deportation rates continued to fall during 2017—the first year of the vocally xenophobic Trump presidency—an unexpected lag attributed to decreased border-crossing attempts due to migrants' fear of punitive treatment as well as invigorated advocates and volunteers providing legal support to noncitizens facing deportation.[11] By 2018, rates of removal began to rise again, as the Trump administration's aggressive enforcement directives and cuts to asylum protections contributed to a "widening of the net" where all removable noncitizens were at risk. Still, even as the detention and deportation of asylum seekers with no criminal record became more and more commonplace, noncitizens with criminal system involvement remained a priority. In addition to other measures targeting this group, President Donald Trump renewed Secure Communities (and disbanded PEP) in one of his first executive orders,[12] and he directed federal agencies to use "all lawful means" against "all removable aliens"—not only noncitizens who had already been convicted but also those who had been charged with a crime, and even those with no criminal charge, but deemed by ICE to have engaged in illegal behavior or to pose a "public safety threat."[13]

In 2021, under first-year president Joe Biden, Trump-era net widening was eschewed for "sensible enforcement priorities," reminiscent of the late Obama era, and promises to restore human rights and reduce deportation.[14] Early Biden administration actions—like the cancellation of Trump's more insidious executive orders and attempts to reinstate Deferred Action for Childhood Arrivals (DACA)—demonstrate a more humanitarian face toward migrants more generally. Yet advocates continue to urge the president to make good on campaign promises to end Secure Communities and other programs that entangle local criminal justice systems in immigration enforcement.[15] Noncitizens with aggravated felonies have repeatedly been singled out by the current administration—alongside those who are "gang-affiliated" or have a history of "institutionalized violence"—as particularly dangerous factions who newly humanitarian policies will not apply to. Speaking to these groups' exemption from President Biden's (ultimately unsuccessful) one-hundred-day moratorium on deportations, Immigration and Customs Enforcement spokesperson Jenny Burke said in a statement, "The commission of an aggravated felony is the most conclusive proof of a public safety threat."[16]

Developed and sustained by Republican and Democrat lawmakers alike, the modern deportation regime is at its weakest when targeting politically popular groups like DACA recipients or families detained at the border—actions that have drawn widespread opposition from the public. There is less controversy when it comes to the treatment of so-called criminal aliens—or worse, "aggravated felons." In many ways, the lack of political support for these groups allows for the sustenance of systems of mass detention and deportation as a whole, with legislators and advocates on both sides of the aisle continually playing on unfounded stereotypes that link immigrants with crime. The trope of immigrant criminality was hypervisible in President Trump's efforts to expand immigration enforcement, increase deportation, and build a wall on our southern border, as well as his infamous campaign-trail assertions that Mexican immigrants are "bringing drugs," "bringing crime," and are "rapists."[17] Yet the trope is also visible in liberal proposals for immigration reform that call for the amnesty of migrants deemed deserving (like families, children, and students) by contrasting them to those deemed undeserving (like "criminal aliens"). President Obama, whose administration presided over more deportations than any before, emphasized the need to remove "criminals, gang bangers, people who are hurting the community, not . . . folks who are just here because they're trying to figure out how to feed their families."[18]

This false dichotomy between good and bad immigrants not only relies on the idea that those deemed criminal could not possibly have positive ties to their families and communities, but it also combines all migrants with any type of criminal history into one monolithic category: "criminal aliens" deserving of deportation. With criminal justice system inequality on the forefront of the national conversation, and immigrant criminality continually touted as a political priority, there is a need for critical research that seeks to better understand the complex legal processes through which immigrants are marked as criminal and therefore disposable. Legal scholars have written extensively on the disproportionate severity and unequal outcomes related to aggravated felonies and other deportable convictions.[19] Though there is a growing body of sociological literature on the ways that immigrant enforcement and deportation criminalize and punish undocumented migrants and their families,[20] and a wide body of criminological research that describes the disparate outcomes of various criminal justice system processes,[21] there has been less attention to the topic of criminal-conviction-based deportation.[22] By failing to deeply engage with immigration outcomes for noncitizens with non-immigration-related criminal convictions, our fields run the risk of strengthening the false "good immigrant, bad immigrant" binary that upholds the broader criminalization-to-deportation pipeline—giving further power to criminal system markers well-known to reflect and uphold inequality.

I aim to resist these processes through an in-depth examination of the evolution and outcomes of the category of criminal offenses with the most serious consequences in the immigration system—those deemed aggravated felonies. Using tools and concepts from critical criminology and the sociology of law, this book presents an in-depth qualitative study of the aggravated felony's particular history and its modern-day consequences. What are the social forces that shaped the construction and durability of this vague yet vilified legal distinction? Who are the "bad immigrants" it targets? What are its real-world impacts, and how do they relate to existing inequality? And, finally, how do networks of impacted communities, lawyers, and advocates work to disrupt the category's severe and unequal results?

Crimmigration, Inequality, and Resistance

The aggravated felony—which was greatly expanded in both consequences and scope by the immigration laws of 1996—straddles the criminal and immigration systems and is thus impacted by the increased punitiveness of both. Due to the administrative, or civil, status of immigration law, deportation proceedings are not subject to the same due process requirements as criminal law. Therefore, immigrants convicted of aggravated felonies can be detained for months or even years without bond, are not guaranteed lawyers, and can even be deported without an opportunity to plead their case in court.[23] It is the federal government's burden to prove that an immigrant's conviction actually qualifies as an aggravated felony in order for it to serve as a ground of deportability. However, this deportability usually goes uncontested, since only 14 percent of detained noncitizens manage to secure legal representation for their removal proceedings.[24] Once deported for an aggravated felony, individuals are barred from ever returning to the United States and are subject to enhanced criminal penalties for attempted reentry.[25]

Scholars have used the concept of "crimmigration" to describe how the increased intertwining of criminal and immigration law over the past few decades has expanded the punitive and exclusionary potential of both systems.[26] The development of aggravated-felony-based detention and deportation is a clear example of the crimmigration nexus. Though ostensibly created to combat drug trafficking and other criminal offenses, the aggravated felony legal category has effectively enhanced the punitive capabilities of immigration law and, simultaneously, has made certain criminal offenders (noncitizens) subject to enhanced punishment (extended imprisonment and likely deportation) and exempt from the normal protections of criminal law (such as the right to bail and guaranteed legal counsel). By defining the detention and deportation of immigrant offenders as an administrative function of immigration law, our legal system has concurrently harshened punishment for a wide variety of criminal offenses and made the legal standing of immigrants—both lawful permanent residents and the undocumented—deeply tenuous.

Despite the utility of "crimmigration" as a concept, there is concern that the term's popular usage may lead to further crystallization of untrue stereotypes linking immigration and crime.[27] Thus, recent scholarship in the field has urged researchers to critically examine specific practices that allow for the criminalization and punishment of immigrants,[28] and it has urged them to couch such studies in broader theories of race and racialization.[29] While avoiding attempts to distance immigrants from crime in a way that further crystallizes criminal system markers, this book examines the aggravated felony as a specific legal mechanism that contributes to the funneling of racially and economically marginalized migrants toward deportation. By focusing on the aggravated felony, I aim to better understand one specific aspect of a broader web of crimmigration processes that directly enhances state power to punish and exclude. In addition to the effects on immigrants who are made deportable, the uncritical use of criminal legal system determinations in enforcing aggravated-felony-based detention and deportation—despite widespread evidence of racially unequal enforcement and decision-making processes throughout every level of the criminal justice system[30]—only serves to reinforce these determinations. In the process of adding additional punishment to criminal sentences already served, the immigration system reifies criminal markers and the inequality they rationalize.

This analysis draws from a long-standing line of critical theory on the social construction of law, crime, and criminality and the use of these tools to uphold an unequal social order.[31] Critical scholars of migration have followed this tradition and moved beyond traditional theories of immigrant exclusion and deportation that employ a lens of state sovereignty and social membership,[32] instead identifying migrant "illegality" and "deportability" as tools used by neoliberal governments to control a vulnerable surplus population of migrant workers.[33] With regard to criminal deportation in particular, dominant theories in the sociology of migration frame immigrant criminality as the result of "downward" assimilation, used to describe under-resourced groups' assimilation into a criminal "underclass" rather than mainstream society.[34] Contesting this, the critical criminological concept of "social bulimia" describes the "inclusion/exclusion" inherent in contemporary immigration-receiving societies. Jock Young argues that late modern societies consume and culturally assimilate immigrants and other "underclass" groups through education, the media, and participation in the marketplace, indoctrinating them with the "image of what is a normal lifestyle, what goods and level of comfort can be expected if we play the game."[35] At the same time, these groups are systematically excluded in various ways from the structural means of reaching these goals—a long-theorized recipe for crime.[36] From this perspective, criminal deportation, especially that of long-term and lawful permanent residents—as many of those deported based on aggravated felonies are—is actually a story of successful cultural assimilation combined with simultaneous structural exclusion.[37]

This book also follows the work of critical race theorists, who have examined the intersections between race, law, and power with an emphasis on the way in which the law works to maintain white supremacy.[38] Working from the assertions that race itself is socially constructed, and racism is an ordinary, everyday experience for people of color, critical race theory demonstrates how a justice system that claims to be neutral will inevitably reinforce and maintain inequality.[39] Kimberlé Crenshaw's concept of intersectionality is a key contribution of this literature as it speaks to the conflating potential within social identities and the need to recognize the unique impacts of overlapping oppressions on those who experience them. Women of color, for example, are affected not only by racism and sexism, but also by forms of discrimination and exclusion specific to those positioned at the nexus of the two.[40] Overlapping with critical race theory, a large interdisciplinary body of scholarship on the relationships between race and the law materialized in response to the punitive policy shift of the 1980s and 1990s. This literature emphasizes on how the War on Drugs and mass incarceration have disproportionately targeted economically marginalized Black men in particular, contributing to a symbolic construction of Black male criminality that rationalizes inequality and upholds white supremacist racial hierarchies.[41]

While "explicitly colorblind" assimilationist theories have long reigned in the sociology of migration, a growing field of critical scholarship centralizes "race, racism, and racial domination as significant determinants of non-White im/migrant incorporation."[42] Researchers have pointed to the historical role of punitive immigration policy in race-making[43]—most recently in the development of a racialized "illegal" identity, primarily associated with immigrants from Mexico and elsewhere in Latin America.[44] With regard to crimmigration connections in particular, Amada Armenta demonstrates how local law enforcement downplay their role in punitive immigration enforcement and normalize the disproportionate criminalization of Latinx people through professed adherence to a "colorblind" ideology.[45] Martha D. Escobar portrays the intersectional oppression of noncitizen Latinas who navigate the overlapping impacts of militarized borders and mass incarceration alongside systemic race and gender-based hierarchies.[46] Others have described the targeting of Latinx noncitizens through intertwined criminal legal and immigration processes as a "racial project,"[47] a system of "gendered and racial removal,"[48] and a reflection of "white-supremacist capitalist patriarchy."[49] This book draws on these critical fields of scholarship in examining how intersecting oppressions related to race, gender, nationality, and criminal record combined to shape the historical development of the aggravated felony, and are reproduced through its modern-day results.

Despite a growing literature on the role of crimmigration connections in the unequal treatment of Latinx immigrants, there is far less written on the experience of Black immigrants—a group that has drawn relatively scant social scientific attention while accounting for around 10 percent of the US foreign-born population.[50] With the majority of contemporary immigration to the United States coming from Latin America and Asia, immigrants are likely to identify, or be identified as, Hispanic, Latino, or Latinx. Still, noncitizens are affected by the targeting and discrimination experienced by Black populations in the United States as well, due to the racial diversity in Latin America combined with the fact that immigrants from the Caribbean and Sub-Saharan Africa account for 10 percent and 4 percent of the foreign-born population, respectively. In fact, the Black immigrant population increased fivefold from 1980 to 2016, making it so that one out of every ten Black individuals in the United States is now foreign-born.[51] Yet despite making up only 7 percent of the noncitizen immigrant population, this group accounts for more than 20 percent of those who face removal based on criminal convictions.[52]

Rather than engaging with the impacts of policing and criminalization on Black immigrants in a racially unequal system of mass incarceration, the mainstream sociology of migration has largely described a cultural distinctness of African and Caribbean migrants that prevents their assimilation into the American Black "underclass"—where immigrant criminality is said to be acculturated. Relying on thinly veiled "culture-of-poverty" theories to explain crime, such arguments uphold anti-Black racial hierarchies and erase structural factors known to shape inequality.[53] In response, critical research in the field emphasizes the important role of anti-Blackness in deciding national conceptions of who belongs as well as the centrality of race in the experience of Black immigrants.[54] Speaking to these points, qualitative research has documented the overpolicing and profiling experienced by Black immigrants and their children.[55] Considering the disproportional funneling of this group toward criminal deportation, and the breadth of scholarship and advocacy speaking to the anti-Blackness that plagues US systems of criminal justice, there is a need for critical research on the impacts of crimmigration connections on Black immigrants. This book contributes to this literature by examining the racially disparate impacts of the aggravated felony, which is the most determinate driver of criminal-conviction-based removal, as well as intersectional "crimmigration" resistance, both led by Black immigrants and in collaboration with broader Black-led movements for racial justice.[56]

In detailing opposition to the aggravated felony alongside its punitive outcomes, this book speaks to the dual nature of law, recognized in scholarship as a key force for inequality that can—at times—become a potent tool for resistance. By documenting the way the distinctive power of law is successfully harnessed by communities in struggle against persecution and injustice, researchers have demonstrated the oppositional capacity of the law—directly related to its hegemonic power as a culturally legitimate institution.[57] To this point, the concept of crimmigration has largely been employed to describe the punitive and exclusionary outcomes of the intertwining of immigration and criminal law. In depicting how the same bodies of law that create the punitive and unequal effects of the aggravated felony category are drawn on by lawyers and advocates working to defend the rights of immigrants with criminal records, this research demonstrates how the crimmigration nexus also creates opportunities for resistance. This includes innovative legal responses to the aggravated felony and the protective policies that uphold them, developed by attorneys and advocates straddling the worlds of criminal and immigration law. It also includes the ongoing fight by impacted communities to tear down the "good immigrant, bad immigrant" binary and the pipeline that funnels non-citizens from criminalization to deportation.

Observing the Impacts of the Aggravated Felony

This book draws from my 2017–2018 ethnographic study examining the impacts of aggravated felony convictions on the cases of noncitizens facing deportation. This research was conducted at New York City's Varick Street court, where the cases of detained immigrants facing deportation from the city are held. Varick is one of sixty-six immigration courts in the United States, which, along with the appellate Board of Immigration Appeals (BIA), are overseen by the Executive Office for Immigration Review (EOIR), an agency of the Department of Justice (DOJ).[58] Also relevant to removal proceedings are the three Department of Homeland Security (DHS) agencies that were created in 2003 to replace the now-defunct Immigration and Naturalization Service (INS): The first, US Citizenship and Immigration Services (USCIS), is responsible for services such as visa applications, naturalization petitions, and affirmative asylum applications. The second, US Customs and Border Protection (CBP), carries out inspections in border regions. And the third, Immigration and Customs Enforcement (ICE), is responsible for all interior enforcement. In addition to deportation proceedings— officially termed removal proceedings—immigration courts can grant noncitizens lawful permanent residency (green cards) and hear appeals related to claims of asylum, among other functions.

This book is focused on removal proceedings in particular, since aggravated felonies are a ground of deportability, despite other consequences. However, it is important to note that removal proceedings in immigration court are not the only forum through which immigrants are deported from this country. The 1996 immigration reforms made undocumented immigrants convicted of aggravated felonies eligible for administrative processes of expedited removal—through which they can be deported by an immigration officer without seeing a judge at all. Over the next several years, such processes were expanded to other undocumented individuals apprehended at or near the border.[59] By 2014, these "removals in the shadows of immigration court" made up the majority of deportations from the United States.[60] While remaining mindful of these disturbing closed-door processes, this book focuses on the removal proceedings that occur in immigration court which provide an observable opportunity to assess the impacts and responses elicited by the aggravated felony.

The majority of deportation proceedings in NYC are held at 26 Federal Plaza, one of the largest immigration courts in the country with thirty-eight sitting judges. Yet the city's detained immigration cases are held at Varick Street, where there are twelve sitting judges and only a few courtrooms. With NYC jails banned from contracting with ICE, noncitizens on the detained docket are imprisoned in contracted jails and detention centers in New Jersey and upstate New York. This includes most cases having to do with aggravated felonies, which trigger mandatory detention. Despite its size difference with Federal Plaza, Varick Street is one of the most active detained immigration courts in the country, deporting more than one thousand people a year, the majority of them to Latin America and the Caribbean.[61] Although immigration court proceedings are technically open to the public, Varick Street is an isolated and largely unnoticed court, on the eleventh floor of a government building in Manhattan's West Village—a former bohemian bastion and now one of the city's most expensive neighborhoods. (Before engaging with this research, I had walked past the building many times without realizing its content.) Throughout 2017 and 2018, I visited the court regularly, making my way through a security screening and metal detector, often with a long line, before taking an elevator to the eleventh floor, and following a winding industrial hallway to the windowless and drab waiting room. This usually required an 8:00 a.m. arrival for an 8:30 a.m. start time. Still, things rarely started on time at Varick, and there were often breaks in hearings, so part of my time was always spent in the waiting room, where families and lawyers discussed cases and court developments.

At the time of this research, Varick's waiting room and courtrooms—the latter behind a closed door with a large "DO NOT KNOCK" sign on it—were manned by privately contracted security guards. ICE officers were often present, particularly when they still transported respondents to court from spaces of detention,[62] although they did not usually remain in the courtroom or waiting room for long. The three courtrooms behind the closed door at Varick Street are small, usually with two short rows of wooden bench seats facing the raised desk where the judge,

DHS prosecutor, and translator (in most cases) would be joined by a shackled noncitizen wearing a jumpsuit facing deportation and—if they had one—their defense attorney. At most, the court rooms also contain another small desk for a clerk and one or two short benches along the sides of the room where security guards sit and, at times, other detained immigrants wait for their hearings—all with shackles on their wrists and wearing orange jumpsuits. Despite the court being officially open to the public, there were rarely many observers, and I was often the only one. While not always brought into the courtroom for the entire hearing, family—including young children—of the person facing deportation were frequently present. The other most common group were volunteers from the New Sanctuary Coalition, a local immigrant rights organization. Observers were most often placed in the second row of bench seats, although at times we were moved to the front row, where waiting defense attorneys usually sit. Since my aim was to observe hearings of respondents with aggravated felony allegations, I often attended specific cases at the invitation of lawyers or other practitioners. However, on occasion, I attended on my own to observe whatever cases were being heard that day. Cases at Varick Street, like at other immigration courts, are frequently continued or postponed, with detained respondents appearing in front of the judge on several occasions, often with months between each. I followed certain cases over the course of a few hearings, and others I only observed on one day. While at court, I took detailed field notes on proceedings and interactions between court actors, which I transcribed and expanded on once I returned home. During this period, I also attended and observed two large immigration law conferences focused on strategies and skills for defending immigrants with and without criminal records, as well as several smaller workshops and events for lawyers, researchers, and activists related to various aspects of immigration policy and enforcement.

Much of the information presented in this book is gleaned from in-depth interviews conducted with legal practitioners and advocates as part of this research—most with current or recent experience representing noncitizens facing deportation at Varick Street court. Scholars of law and society have long stressed the importance of examining the everyday decisions of legal actors in order to understand the way in which laws are developed and enforced.[63] In this case, lawyers' specific positionality between the state and detained migrants make them uniquely situated to report on broader immigration law processes related to the aggravated felony as well as to speak to the real-world impacts on clients' lived experience. While defense attorneys' voices are in no way a replacement for those of immigrants facing deportation, lawyers are part of the very limited contact detained noncitizens are allowed with the outside world and often possess in-depth knowledge of their clients' trajectories through the immigration system—information that is hard to obtain firsthand due to the difficulties of gaining access to detention centers. Further, the complexities of immigration law—and that related to criminal convictions in particular—are infamously difficult to comprehend, even for skilled and experienced attorneys in other fields of law. By interviewing practitioners who regularly represent noncitizens with criminal records, I was able to learn about legal responses to the aggravated felony that could not be understood simply by observing them as a social scientific researcher with no background in the law.

I conducted interviews with a total of forty participants, including thirty-one immigration lawyers, four criminal lawyers, four advocates, and one social worker (with a few of the immigration lawyers having also transitioned into roles related to advocacy or education). Most interviewed lawyers practiced at public defender organizations or other nonprofits that offered free legal services to qualifying immigrants—a total of twenty-four "public" attorneys, as I refer to them throughout this book. Only five lawyers working at private practices were interviewed as part of this study. However, this is fairly representative for the site of research, with the majority of represented cases on the Varick Street docket handled by public attorneys.[64] Recruited through personal and professional networks, connections made in immigration court, online mailing-lists, and organizational email directories—followed by snowball sampling—participants had an average of eleven years of experience related to immigration law at the time of research, with the overall range spanning from two to thirty years. Following national trends among immigration lawyers, participants skewed female and white. The total sample included twenty-eight women, eleven men, and one nonbinary person. Twenty-three participants identified as white; six, as Latinx; six, as Black; and five, as Asian. Analyses of census data indicate 60 percent of immigration attorneys nationwide are female and 80 percent are white.[65]

Interviews were in-depth and semistructured, and each lasted about sixty to ninety minutes. In order to fit into busy schedules, I offered the option of being interviewed over the phone, which about half of my participants opted for. In-person interviews were conducted at cafés, restaurants, and lawyers' offices. All interviews were recorded and later transcribed, with participants' full knowledge and consent. Upon transcription, names and other identifying information were removed and participants were assigned pseudonyms, which are used throughout this book. The ethnographic work documented in this book is supplemented by an expansive review of legislation, federal rules, precedential court decisions, and organizational resources related to the aggravated felony.

The Case of New York City

Scholars have, up to this point, largely examined "crimmigration" enforcement in locales where there are official relationships between immigration and local law enforcement.[66] This study contributes to a nascent body of work examining the relationship between criminal justice and immigration enforcement in a so-called sanctuary city.[67] Unlike in many jurisdictions around the country, New York City law enforcement agencies are officially prohibited from engaging in, or assisting with, federal immigration enforcement, and the city refuses to honor detainers (requests by ICE to hold noncitizens charged or convicted of crimes).

Yet sanctuary policies only do so much for the city's immigrants, especially those with criminal records. NYC—whose 8.6 million residents include 3.1 million immigrants—is home to one of the busiest immigration courts in the country, with several thousand people ordered deported from the city each year.[68] ICE—a federal agency—is free to make immigration arrests throughout the city, and enforcement initiatives have increasingly targeted noncitizens through raids of their homes and communities, actions which increased under the Trump administration with the stated aim of removing immigrants with criminal convictions.[69] Additionally, the standing refusal to honor detainer requests from city jails only applies to immigrants who have not been convicted of any crime from an expansive list of 170 "serious crimes,"[70] and while the New York Police Department (NYPD) is prohibited from directly engaging in immigration enforcement, the city maintains its participation in Secure Communities, which facilitates the sharing of arrest data and fingerprints between local law enforcement and ICE.[71]

From the targeted policing of the War on Drugs—almost exclusively focused on the city's Black and Latinx communities[72]—to violent enforcement and mass arrests in response to Black-led protests against police brutality, the NYPD has long been criticized for racially disparate levels and tactics of enforcement. With a force of thirty-six thousand officers, the largest in the country, the city has consistently been used as a testing ground for aggressive crime control strategies that result in the targeting of Black and Latinx New Yorkers—enforcement tactics reproduced throughout the country and beyond.[73] Yet these are the same policies and practices that shape the apprehensions and convictions that funnel noncitizens toward deportation. Therefore, while NYC's sanctuary status may help us better understand crimmigration connections and opportunities for resistance in other "immigration-friendly" cities around the country, the mechanisms of its criminal justice system are even more generalizable, providing an important glimpse into the impact of policies and practices popularized throughout the world. Furthermore, as the metropolitan area with the highest concentration of Black immigrants in the country—comprising a full 20 percent of the statewide foreign-born population (as opposed to 10 percent nationwide)—NYC provides a window into immigration enforcement and deportation among this understudied population.[74]

Finally, New York is unique in its provision of legal representation for detained immigrants facing deportation. While legal representation has been shown to play an important role in determining immigration court outcomes, only 37 percent of all immigrants, and just 14 percent of detained immigrants, are able to secure representation for their removal proceedings nationwide.[75] Beginning in 2013, NYC has guaranteed legal representation for detained immigrants in deportation proceedings through the New York Immigrant Family Unity Project (NYIFUP), the first universal representation program for noncitizens facing removal.[76] This allows for a unique look into the complexities of criminal-conviction-based mandatory detention and deportation—cases which largely go unrepresented throughout the country—through the expertise of lawyers who work widely in these areas. Universal representation in immigration court is especially important for nonciti-zens with criminal records as they are more likely to be detained and are less likely to be represented by existing legal service providers.

In some ways, by studying NYC, this book looks at the "best case scenario" for immigrants with aggravated felony cases, who are man-datorily detained and far less likely to secure legal representation in other contexts. In part, this is a limitation of this study, and comparative research in places without a universal representation model would cer-tainly yield important results. Yet, from a law and society perspective, NYC presents a unique opportunity to examine the ways that legal ac-tors understand and respond to a legal category with far-reaching and punitive consequences. Furthermore, the fact that the observed effects of the aggravated felony category are still so expansive, severe, and unequal in NYC, despite its contextual advantages, speaks to injustice inherent in the law itself. Finally, observed strategies of legal resistance—an un-expected area of findings that arose as I conducted this research—are developed and implemented, in part, due to the universal representa-tion model and other key policy and organizational developments in NYC. Therefore, this case study has key implications for all who resist the pipeline that funnels criminalized migrants toward deportation, re-producing the severe inequalities of our criminal legal system with in-tensely punitive results.

Overview of the Book

Following this introduction, the book's first chapter traces the historical development of the aggravated felony category from early laws regarding immigrant criminality to the category's official inception in the Anti-Drug Abuse Act of 1988 and its extreme expansion in the immigration overhaul of 1996. The category's evolution is linked to broader punitive turns in drug, crime, and immigration policy, as well as to a racialized moral panic about immigrant criminality stoked by insecurity in a time of growing multiculturalism and neoliberal economic restructuring. Weaving critical theory with findings gleaned from archival research and secondary accounts, this chapter provides an illustrative account of the human actors and social forces that contributed to the creation and growth of the aggravated felony.

Chapter 2 draws from immigration court ethnography and interviews with lawyers and advocates to examine the everyday outcomes of the aggravated felony. It begins by describing the expansiveness of the category and its perceived overuse in immigration court. This is followed by an assessment of aggravated felonies' effects on immigrants' chances for deportation, an exploration of due process violations related to the aggravated felony, and an overview of changes during the Trump era (when this research was conducted). The chapter argues that the expansive and severe effects of the aggravated felony—even in the "best case scenario" of NYC—underscore injustice inherent in the law itself and illustrate the power of moral panic to influence policy in lasting ways.

Also drawing from in-depth interviews and ethnographic observation of immigration court, chapter 3 begins with a discussion of the aggravated felony in relation to the practical intertwining of immigration and criminal justice policy and enforcement—the "crimmigration" nexus. The chapter goes on to describe how the aggravated felony's entrenchment in the criminal justice system, combined with its harsh immigration outcomes, results in the reproduction and exacerbation of existing criminal system disparities. Finally, the chapter explains how immigration court processes and outcomes related to the aggravated felony serve to erase such structural considerations, demonize immigrants with criminal records, and reinforce a racialized image of the "bad immigrant." Findings demonstrate the punitive power of crimmigration connections, as well as the role of law and legal processes in the reproduction of inequality.

Chapter 4 draws on interviews with lawyers and legal workers, courtroom ethnography, observations of legal conferences and workshops, and analysis of court decisions to describe intriguing strategies of "legal resistance" to the harshest effects of the aggravated felony. After conceptualizing legal resistance and demonstrating its applicability to observed responses, this chapter outlines tactics of resistance to the aggravated felony that are executed through both immigration and criminal law. Findings contribute to scholarly debates on the role of law in social change and expand the concept of "crimmigration"—mostly used to describe the punitive results of the intertwining of criminal and immigration law—by demonstrating the ways that this intertwining also creates opportunities for resistance.

Chapter 5 focuses on the central roles of context, organizing, and activism for strategies of legal resistance related to the aggravated felony. Drawing from my interviews and supplemented by the analysis of organizational literature, this chapter describes protective policies and practices constructed and upheld by NYC's networks of progressive lawyers and advocates, who continue to push for reform in terms of access to justice for immigrants with criminal records. Further, this chapter speaks to the organizing and activism led by impacted communities, who have continually fought to bring attention to the impacts of the criminalization-to-deportation pipeline and to deconstruct the false "good immigrant, bad immigrant" binary on which it is based.

The conclusion summarizes the book's major findings and arguments and expands on suggestions for policy and scholarship. Mainly, it contends that the aggravated felony category, and processes of criminal-conviction-based deportation more generally, are born from racist and unfounded stereotypes about immigrant criminality, invoke severe and unjust penalties on immigrants with criminal records, and reproduce disparities well-known in the criminal justice system. Still, just as law has often served to reify inequality, it can also serve as a tool for resistance, as seen in the unique policy environment supported by community-based advocacy and activism in New York City. The successes, as well as shortcomings, described in this book suggest key implications for those concerned with protecting the rights of immigrants nationwide.

1

"Savaging Our Society"

The Legal Construction of Immigrant as Criminal

It is now generally conceded that the most insidious and
dangerous enemies to the State are not the armed foes who
invade our territory, but those alien races who are incapable
of assimilation, and come among us to debase our labor and
poison the health and morals of the communities in which
they locate.
—US Solicitor General, 1893

Alien felons are rapidly becoming the most violent network
of organized criminals in the country.
—Florida senator Lawton Chiles, 1988

We opened the doors, they came in, and they sought to destroy us. Why shouldn't we send them back?
—New York City mayor Edward Koch, 1988

The severe and unequal impacts of the aggravated felony for immigrants
today are shaped by long-standing racial hierarchies in the United States
and rooted in the specific historical context from which the category
emerged. This chapter examines the social and political forces that
allowed for the enactment and expansion of the aggravated felony in the
1980s and 1990s and their relationship to broader societal panic linking
Black and Latinx immigrants with drugs and crime. A brief history of
immigration law focused on noncitizens with criminal records sets the
stage for the creation of the aggravated felony in 1988 and its intense
expansion in the decade that followed. The evolution of this policy is
couched in a broader punitive turn in the final decades of the twentieth century, when increased public and political attention to the issues

of drugs, crime, and immigration ushered in expansive and severe systems of social control that would shape policy for years to come. To better understand the rapid evolution of the aggravated felony and the intertwined policy shifts of which it was a part, I apply the critical criminological concept of moral panic. The concept of moral panic is useful for researchers aiming to understand the development and entrenchment of punitive policies—in particular, punitive policies that emerge in response to apparently overstated problems and which often have no proven ability to ameliorate the supposed harms at hand.

Though "moral panic" is at times used in popular culture to describe any case of increased societal attention to a given issue, the theoretical formulation of moral panic emphasizes how the panics draw power from personified scapegoats—or "folk devils"—with specific symbolic salience in the context from which they emerge. Drawing on historical accounts and analyses, I explain how the long-standing scapegoat of immigrant as criminal—held up by entrenched racial hierarchies that go back to slavery and the colonization of the Americas[1]—was reinvigorated as a pervasive societal trope in the 1980s and 1990s and invoked by legislators and advocates in the passage of the laws that created and evolved the aggravated felony. Personifying fears about drugs, immigration, crime, and the assumed links between them, this folk devil held specific symbolic power in an era of increasing diversity, inequality, and neoliberal social ideology. It is the salience of this image in this particular context that helped facilitate the creation and expansion of the aggravated felony amid a spiral of retributive lawmaking that has now shaped social policy in the United States for more than three decades. Through these intertwined structures of punitive drug, crime, and immigration policy targeting the fabled Black or Brown "criminal alien," our system creates what it claims to counteract: criminalizing, detaining, and deporting hundreds of thousands of Black and Latinx immigrants each year.

The Historical Evolution of the Aggravated Felony

Although the aggravated felony category was first introduced in 1988, criminal activity as a basis for immigrant inadmissibility or deportation is not a new development in the United States. Since the late 1700s, even before the federal government took any part in regulating immigration, states began barring entry of individuals convicted of crimes.[2] Once the Supreme Court ruled that Congress and the executive branch have "plenary" (absolute) power over immigration in the late 1800s,[3] the federal government's first efforts toward controlling immigration placed a heavy weight on criminal history as a basis for inadmissibility, with laws banning convicts exiled from their countries of origin, as well as "idiots," "lunatics," and "persons likely to become public charges."[4] In 1891, Congress passed a law to include individuals who had committed crimes exhibiting "moral turpitude" to those denied admission into the country. Legal scholar Diana Podgorny explains:

> Courts have never clearly defined the term "moral turpitude." However, the term is generally understood to connote something more than mere illegality or criminality, and consequently, it is evaluated based on moral, rather than legal, standards. Courts have described moral turpitude as "an act of baseness, vileness, or depravity in the private and social duties which a man owes to his fellow men or to society in general, contrary to the accepted and customary rule of right and duty between man and man."[5]

The term's ambiguous definition made it a useful tool in early efforts of the federal government to restrict immigration by "undesirable" potential citizens. While crimes of moral turpitude were used to exclude noncitizens throughout the turn of the century, it was not until 1917 that the federal government put in place its first official deportation policy, and by 1938, immigrants could be deported for felonies or crimes involving moral turpitude if they were committed within five years of admission into the country.[6]

Throughout the twentieth century, increasingly prohibitive drug laws brought with them additional grounds of criminal deportation. The Narcotic Drugs Import and Export Act of 1922 both criminalized narcotics importation and simultaneously deemed it a deportable offense if committed by a noncitizen. The Immigration and Nationality Act—enacted in 1952 and the enduring legal foundation of today's immigration system—made it so that deportable drug offenders included any "drug abuser or addict" or anyone the government had "reason to believe" was an "illicit trafficker."[7] These provisions were amended soon after to make the possession of *any* controlled substance a deportable offense—standards that remain in place today. (This standard is only not applicable to those with a single simple possession conviction for less than thirty grams of marijuana.)[8]

These early policies resulted in the deportation of forty-eight thousand people between 1908 and 1980 for criminal and narcotics violations. Yet it wasn't until the final decades of the twentieth century that criminal deportation moved toward the levels we see today. During this period, societal shifts around drugs, crime, and immigration bolstered increasingly punitive measures of social control. David Garland refers to a "culture of control" which emerged in the late 1970s and early 1980s as the prominent American ideology regarding criminal justice shifted from the aim of rehabilitation to the aim of punitive retribution.[9] Research shows an intensified focus on crime by the media in the later decades of the twentieth century,[10] with drugs in particular the focus of a great deal of journalistic and public attention, especially with the arrival of crack cocaine in the mid-1980s.[11] Throughout the late 1980s and early 1990s, the proportion of news articles dedicated to drugs increased, along with the use of sensational graphics, numbers, and frames that exaggerated the severity of drug-related problems.[12] As the subject of drugs overtook the media, public attention to the topic also increased.[13] Between 1986 and 1989, the proportion of Americans who rated drug abuse as the country's most important problem shot from 3 percent to 64 percent.[14]

Supported by (and supporting) this cultural shift was the ramping up of the US War on Drugs and "tough-on-crime" criminal justice policy more generally. From the mid-1980s to the mid-1990s, the country witnessed the continuous induction of increasingly punitive drug legislation focused on criminalization and enforcement over prevention and treatment. This decisive shift in policy was manifest in laws like the Anti-Drug Abuse Acts of 1986 and 1988, which ushered in harsher penalties and mandatory minimum sentences for drug offenders.[15] President George H. W. Bush's $7.8 billion National Drug Control Strategy of 1989 continued in this vein, with an emphasis on stronger law enforcement, mandatory sentencing, and increased arrests and incarceration.[16]

At the same time, in response to growing calls for a federal response to the dual "crises" of undocumented immigration and immigrant criminality, Congress passed a slate of legislation that expanded the state's ability to investigate and deport immigrants for criminal offenses. Some of these laws were passed in the immigration context—like the Immigration Reform and Control Act of 1986, which allowed for expedited deportation of so-called criminal aliens by the attorney general. Yet these laws also included laws in the burgeoning War on Drugs—like the aforementioned Anti-Drug Abuse Act (ADAA) of 1986, which required the (now-defunct) Immigration and Naturalization Service (INS) to coordinate with local law enforcement officials to investigate drug cases involving noncitizens.[17] Even more pivotal was the ADAA of 1988, which set the stage for the massive expansion of deportation for criminal offenses in the years to come. With a stated aim of fighting drug trafficking, the ADAA of 1988 amended the Immigration and Nationality Act (INA) of 1965 with language specifically aimed at allowing for more severely punitive treatment of criminal aliens, through the creation of the aggravated felony legal category.[18]

As seen in table 1.1, the aggravated felony's original manifestation in the ADAA of 1988 made it so that noncitizens (both documented and undocumented) convicted of murder, weapons trafficking, or drug trafficking became subject to deportation. Based on the ADAA, noncitizens with convictions deemed aggravated felonies were subject to mandatory detention without bond while awaiting trial for deportation, and for those with prison sentences of at least five years, deportation was mandated. Once deported, noncitizens with aggravated felony convictions were barred from returning to the United States for ten years.[19] Due in a large part to these new provisions, thirty thousand people were deported over the course of the 1980s alone for criminal or narcotics violations, as compared to less than fifty thousand over seven decades prior.[20]

Just two years after its creation, the aggravated felony category was expanded by the Immigration Act of 1990 to include violent crimes with prison sentences of at least five years and state- and federal-level drug offenses with sentences of at least one year—offenses "far less serious than the crimes denoted in the ADAA."[21] The 1990 act also made it so that those deported based on aggravated felony convictions could not

TABLE 1.1. Major Laws Shaping the Development of the Aggravated Felony Category (1988–1996)

Year	Legislation	Implications Relevant to Aggravated Felony
1988	Anti-Drug Abuse Act (ADAA)	- Creation of aggravated felony category including murder, drug trafficking, weapons trafficking - Deportation, mandatory detention, and ten-year reentry bar
1990	Immigration Act	- Includes lesser drug crimes and all violent crimes with prison sentences of at least five years - Twenty-year reentry bar - Bars 212(c) waiver for those imprisoned at least five years
1991	The Miscellaneous and Technical Immigration and Naturalization Amendments	- Noncitizens can be deported for aggravated felony convictions still under appeal in criminal court
1994	Violent Crime Control and Law Enforcement Act	- Creates processes of expedited administrative removal for non-LPRs with aggravated felonies
1994	Immigration and Technical Corrections Act	- Includes more offenses, such as those related to weapons, theft, burglary, fraud, and prostitution
1996	Antiterrorism and Effective Death Penalty Act (AEDPA)	- Includes variety of less serious crimes - Excludes all immigrants with aggravated felonies from 212(c) waiver of deportation
1996	Illegal Immigration Reform and Immigrant Responsibility Act (IIRIRA)	- Includes wide variety of minor crimes - Mandatory detention without bail - Removal of virtually all judicial discretion and options for relief from deportation - Applies retroactively - Permanent ban on reentry

return to the United States for twenty years after their conviction, as opposed to the previous ten, and, perhaps most importantly, it began the erosion of judicial discretion that would only intensify over the next several years. Before 1990, lawful permanent residents (LPRs) in the United States who had been convicted of crimes, including aggravated felonies, could apply for a 212(c) waiver of deportation. In order to qualify for 212(c) waiver, a noncitizen had to demonstrate that deportation would cause "extreme hardship" to their self or their family, that they had accrued at least seven years of continuous residence in the United States, that their individual absences from the United States were "brief, casual, and innocent," and that they had good moral character.[22] These factors made it easier for immigrants with strong family ties to the United States to escape deportation. Under the Immigration Act of 1990, noncitizens convicted of aggravated felonies who were imprisoned for at least five years became ineligible for this waiver, removing the discretion of the attorney general to consider mitigating factors for a whole category of deportation cases.[23] Continuing the punitive evolution of the law, the Miscellaneous and Technical Immigration and Naturalization Amendments of 1991 made it so immigration authorities were not required to stay the deportation of an immigrant convicted of an aggravated felony while their criminal case was being appealed unless the court specified otherwise.[24]

At the same time, the United States became entrenched in the era of "get-tough-on-crime" criminal justice policy, characterized by retributive laws, increased enforcement, and astronomical levels of incarceration. Between 1972 and 1988, government funding for criminal justice increased fivefold.[25] The "get-tough" paradigm became the ruling American crime control framework, and subsequent administrations continued to throw more and more money into law enforcement and criminal justice. The Crime Control Act of 1993 and the Violent Crime Control Act of 1994, both passed by the Clinton administration, pledged $23 billion and $30 billion, respectively, making the 1994 act the most expensive crime bill in American history.[26] Increased funding for law enforcement and prisons, extensive mandatory minimum sentencing laws, three-strikes provisions requiring extended or life sentences after three felonies, and extremely aggressive policing tactics all contributed to unprecedented increases in incarceration. From 1980 to 2000, the United States quadrupled its prison population and became the country with the highest incarceration rate in the world. The laws of the War on Drugs played a key role in this increase.[27]

The aggravated felony continued its evolution through some of these same laws. The Violent Crime Control and Law Enforcement Act of 1994 (largely drafted by then senator Joe Biden) gave the attorney general new authority to deport undocumented immigrants with aggravated felonies outside of immigration court through administrative processes known as "expedited removal."[28] The category was further expanded in 1994 to include additional firearms and explosives offenses, more theft and burglary offenses, and additional types of fraud and prostitution, among other convictions.[29] Moreover, throughout the 1990s, several federal rules were enacted to either preclude immigrants with aggravated felony convictions from receiving special visas and other affirmative benefits or to more efficiently facilitate their removal from the United States.

Meanwhile, the "get-tough" outlook on drugs and crime was paralleled by a shift in public sentiment around immigration. Despite a long tradition of negative media and societal stereotyping of newcomers to the United States,[30] throughout the 1960s, 1970s, and early 1980s, public policy on immigration demonstrated at least a nominal focus on humanitarian values—in a large part due to an official move away from the racial quota systems that dictated legal immigration in the pre–civil rights era.[31] During this period, priorities included family reunification for naturalized citizens and lawful permanent residents, the admittance of—and the provision of public welfare benefits for—refugees, and respect for the natural rights of migrants. However, in the early 1980s, public opinion on immigration moved, "from a willingness to absorb and generously resettle refugees and a tolerance of illegal immigration to a growing sense of crisis that the United States had 'lost control of its borders' and that US immigration policy was dangerously adrift."[32] Analyses of public opinion surveys taken from the early to mid-1990s reflect this evolution, reporting predominantly negative views of immigrants during this period.[33]

Growing public fears about immigration during this era were manifest in the Antiterrorism and Effective Death Penalty Act (AEDPA) and the Illegal Immigration Reform and Immigrant Responsibility Act (IIRIRA) of 1996—acts that together broadened the scope of the aggravated felony category in unprecedented ways.[34] This expansion was among a slew of far-reaching impacts that continue to shape our punitive immigration system.[35] AEDPA "expand[ed] the aggravated 'grab-bag of convictions' to include less serious crimes, such as bribery, counterfeiting or mutilating a passport, obstruction of justice, gambling offenses, and transportation for purposes of prostitution."[36] Furthermore, this act made it so that *all* noncitizens with previous aggravated felony convictions, not just those with prison sentences of five years or more, were ineligible for 212(c) discretionary relief. IIRIRA, passed just six months after AEDPA, further expanded the list of crimes that qualify as aggravated felonies to include petty larceny, assault, second-degree theft, burglary, sexual abuse, and the transport of an "illegal alien" into the United States, along with other offenses. It also greatly reduced the monetary minimums for convictions of fraud, deceit, money laundering, and tax evasion, and it reduced the sentence length that caused less serious crimes to be defined as aggravated felonies from five years to one year. Furthermore, it made it so that an individual did not actually need to be convicted of any crime in order to be considered an aggravated felon; along with AEDPA, IIRIRA "mandated that potential aggravated felony adjudications deferred by judges, regardless of the absence of sentencing, were still to count as convictions warranting deportation from the US if immigration authorities could find sufficient evidence that a crime was committed—such as an initial admission of guilt or some finding excluded from the courtroom. . . . The result was that individuals could be identified as aggravated felons without an explicit conviction for an aggravated felony."[37] IIRIRA also expanded "expedited removal," which is controversial for its repudiation of due process, since it makes it so that noncitizens convicted of aggravated felonies can be deported without ever being granted an appearance in front of an immigration judge. Furthermore, the punishment associated with aggravated felonies became much more severe, as the law mandated the detention of "virtually all criminal aliens subject to deportation, regardless of family ties, dependent children, or the extensiveness of the alien's ties to his community,"[38] and it made it so that once deported, noncitizens with aggravated felonies are permanently barred from returning to United States.

Not only did IIRIRA intensely expand the definition of what could be considered an aggravated felony and dramatically increase the severity of punishment, it also further limited judicial ability to take mitigating factors into account in deportation decisions. The act completely repealed the 212(c) provision of the INA and supplanted it with new language which excludes any and all noncitizens facing removal due to aggravated felonies from being entitled to discretionary relief from deportation by the attorney general. Therefore, "With IIRIRA, Congress effectively made conviction of a crime grounds for removal without any real possibility of relief, by vesting the power of expedited removal in individual immigration officers whose decisions are subject to neither judicial nor administrative review."[39] This cutting away of judicial discretion was intensified by provisions which kept judges from applying shorter jail sentences to prevent convictions from being considered aggravated felonies. In order to preclude this discretionary practice, "IIRIRA provides that any reference in the INA to 'term of imprisonment' includes any period of time that the sentence is suspended."[40] Therefore, criminal courts could no longer suspend sentences in order to avoid aggravated felony convictions in cases where they did not believe that deportation was justified.

Despite the draconian nature of the changes made by the 1996 Acts, perhaps most controversial is the retroactivity of these changes. Under IIRIRA, any noncitizen with a previous conviction (and as mentioned, the term "conviction" is loosely defined under this law) for an offense that is considered an aggravated felony under the 1996 Acts is considered an "aggravated felon" and is therefore subject to deportation. This retroactive punishment for past criminal behavior appears to be in direct conflict with the ex post facto clause of the Constitution. However, the Supreme Court has consistently upheld the constitutionality of the law's retroactivity because the ex post facto clause only applies to criminal proceedings and deportation is "a purely civil action."[41] Constitutional or not, the retroactivity provision of IIRIRA has had remarkably punitive consequences, making it so noncitizens, including lawful permanent residents and other long-term residents, often with fairly minor criminal histories, can be deported "with virtually no legal recourse, for past offenses that were not deportable crimes at the time of conviction."[42] Combined with new limits on judicial discretion, the retroactivity of IIRIRA effectively removed the potential for rehabilitation to be taken into consideration during the detention and deportation of immigrants with previous aggravated felony convictions. As the following chapters will illustrate, these changes continue to have severe and expansive effects.

"Moral Panic" and Punitive Social Control

The punitive responses that emerged from the 1980s and 1990s have now shaped drug, crime, and immigration policy for over three decades—despite little to no evidence of their ability to ameliorate the social harms they claim to address. The escalation of the War on Drugs came at a time when American drug use was actually in a state of decline,[43] and although crime rates in the United States had been rising since the 1960s, many researchers have shown that punitive drug control and crime control policy frameworks were introduced and continued despite little to no evidence of their ability to achieve purported aims of curbing drug use, drug trafficking, and violent crime.[44] Furthermore, while immigration to the United States was certainly on the rise during the 1980s and 1990s, research going all the way back to the Chicago school of the 1930s has demonstrated that the supposed link between immigration and crime is groundless as well.[45] Despite this, the United States has continued to deal with immigration in more and more punitive ways, with an ongoing focus on so-called criminal aliens—exemplified in the ongoing impacts of the aggravated felony.

Popularized by critical criminologists Jock Young and Stanley Cohen,[46] "moral panic" theory is a useful tool for those who seek to understand the development and entrenchment of punitive policies—in particular those that emerge in response to apparently overstated problems, often with no proven ability to ameliorate the supposed harms at hand. According to Cohen, a moral panic occurs when "A condition, episode, person or group of persons emerges to become defined as a threat to societal values and interests; its nature is presented in a stylized and stereotypical fashion by the mass media; the moral barricades are manned by editors, bishops, politicians and other right-thinking people; socially accredited experts pronounce their diagnoses and solutions; ways of coping are evolved or (more often) resorted to; the condition then disappears, submerges, or deteriorates and becomes more visible."[47] Though first used by media theorist Marshall McLuhan,[48] Young introduced the concept of moral panic to the sociology of deviance with his study examining the public condemnation of drug use by "hippies" in Notting Hill, London.[49] He saw mass media attention to the issue as condemning and seducing at the same time, creating a "spiral of public fear and indignation that pushes for the action of control agencies."[50] Drawing from Howard Becker's *Outsiders*,[51] Young explained how "moral crusaders" fanned the flames of public indignation about drugs toward an end goal of harsher rules and enforcement.[52] Most importantly, he found that the panic was not about the drugs themselves, but rather about the people who were using them and the culture they represented.

In the seminal work *Folk Devils and Moral Panics*, Cohen further developed moral panic theory with his case study of the intense societal outcry provoked by the 1964 conflicts between "Mods" and "Rockers," two British youth subcultures of the era.[53] In the panic studied by Cohen, a series of relatively minor bouts of teenage fighting and vandalism in seaside resort towns resulted in an outpouring of media sensationalism, public indignation, and social control measures aimed toward dealing with the problem of youth violence and "hooliganism." Furthermore, the subcultural groups involved came to be villainized and persecuted as dangerous delinquents. For Cohen, the creation of "folk devils," or deviant stereotypes that are used to identify and demonize the human source of the supposed problem, is essential to the creation of a moral panic. Like the hippies who became a personified symbol of drug use in Young's study, Mods became a symbol of youth delinquency and violence.

In Cohen's formulation, moral panics often begin with an initial escalation of media attention to an issue, which is followed by a process of "sensitization" among the public. He explains, "Any item of news thrust into the individual's consciousness has the effect of increasing the awareness of items of similar nature which he might have otherwise ignored."[54] In this process, people begin to see outcomes and behaviors that they would give little attention to under normal circumstances as negative effects or deviant acts attributable to the subject of the moral panic and the groups associated with it. In the case studied by Cohen, a media uproar about youth hooliganism led people to define all kinds of normal rule breaking by youth as being part of the "Mods and Rockers phenomenon."[55]

This sensitization in the public is exploited by "moral entrepreneurs" and interest groups as they vie for support for their cause and work to shift policy.[56] Attention to the issue is "diffused" to jurisdictions beyond the locality where the initial problem occurred, as politicians and social control agencies become involved in efforts to control the deviant behavior under focus. Enforcement is "escalated" and the whole culture of control becomes more stringent in order to respond to what has been framed as an urgently dangerous phenomenon. Finally, new methods of control are "innovated" as lawmakers expand current policy or create new rules with regard to the behaviors and groups implicated by the moral panic. Such measures often have adverse effects as stigmatization and criminalization end up increasing the amount of social harm linked with what began as a fairly minor problem.[57]

Although the original conceptualization of moral panic was theoretically precise and based in a particular historical context of social transformation and cultural conflict, it has since been diluted to a catchphrase, of sorts, used in reference to any issue that attracts even a minor flurry of media attention or public outrage.[58] Young warns against this expansion of the moral panic concept beyond its theoretical boundaries and emphasizes that, in assessing the power of a moral panic, one must look for specific criteria concerning the panic itself and also for particular cultural and social conditions in the context in which the panic occurs.[59] By contextualizing the moral panics that they studied in the societal transformations of their time, the original formulations of moral panic theory put forth by Young and Cohen show how the deviance of emergent youth subcultures and the societal indignation with which they were met both stem from the same cultural transformations and structural strains. More generally, they demonstrate that rather than viewing moral panics as the spontaneous accumulation of societal attention to a random issue, we must see them as important symbolic events, which often have very real consequences.

The "Criminal Alien" Folk Devil and the Political Construction of the Aggravated Felony

Through this contextualized lens, the aggravated felony—and the extreme and lasting policy shifts of which it is a product—cannot be explained solely by increased public and political attention to drugs, crime, and immigration throughout the latter decades of the twentieth century. Instead, this panic drew power from the symbolic salience of these topics in that specific place and time—symbolic salience most clearly depicted in the racialized folk devil of the "criminal alien." Drawing its power from long-standing and fallacious tropes painting migrants as criminal—both in the United States and around the world[60]—this symbolic scapegoat was reinvigorated throughout the 1980s and 1990s as part of a broader panic linking immigrants with drugs and crime. Throughout this era, the racialized figure of the "criminal alien" was strategically used by moral entrepreneurs in support of punitive policy—including that which created and developed the aggravated felony.

From the Chinese Exclusion Act of 1882, which drew on racist societal attitudes linking Chinese immigrants with opium, to the prohibition of marijuana in the 1930s with the support of inflammatory campaigns associating the drug with "dangerous" Mexican immigrants, this country has a well-established history of passing legislation based on unfounded connections between immigrants, drugs, and crime.[61] While few immigrant groups to the United States have remained untouched by such stereotypes, those racialized as Hispanic and Black have borne the brunt of these tropes—tropes that are distinctly shaped by broader white supremacist hierarchies. Mexicans and other Latin American migrants—many of them with ancestry indigenous to the region—have continually been subjugated and vilified as a "threat" to the so-called American way of life.[62] Black migrants—largely hailing from Africa, Latin America, and the Caribbean—are impacted by the same criminalizing stigmatization placed on African Americans and their antecedents since slavery.[63] Both groups have also historically been marginalized in an immigration system constructed through laws like the Naturalization Act of 1790, which limited citizenship to "free White persons" with "good character,"[64] and the racial quotas of the National Origins Act of 1924, which was passed—as stated by one congressional report at the time—"to preserve, as nearly as possible, the racial status quo in the United States."[65]

In line with this historical and ongoing stigmatization, the racialized figure of immigrant as criminal was revitalized in the late 1970s and early 1980s in response to an influx of asylum seekers from the Caribbean. Largely made up of Haitian refugees and "Mariel" Cubans—a group with lower socioeconomic status and more members of African descent—these newcomers were treated differently from ongoing streams of wealthier (and "whiter") Cubans fleeing communism.[66] Derogatively termed "boat people," the new arrivals were branded as criminals and freeloaders by the media and public, attracting a rise in far-right advocacy and riots led by white supremacist organizations like the Ku Klux Klan.[67] They were also met with early federal programs and policies—both punitive and patently discriminatory—foundational to the system of detention and deportation that was expanded over the following few decades.[68] This growth was directly related to a flurry of attention to the emergent "criminal alien"—a term popularized by media and public officials throughout the latter half of the 1980s.

Despite growing claims of criminality targeting Caribbean boat arrivals in particular, in the mid-1980s, the majority of national attention to immigration remained focused on the issue of unauthorized ("illegal") immigration, rather than identifying those who had committed non-immigration-related crimes. Republican senator Alfonse D'Amato of New York was one of the first major politicians to push the issue of immigrant criminality during this period, requesting in 1985 that the US Government Accounting Office (GAO) inspect the performance of the Immigration and Naturalization Service (INS) in removing noncitizens with criminal convictions in the New York City area. Playing off the fears of his conservative constituents during a period of intensified racial tensions and crime in the city, D'Amato claimed that "criminal aliens"— including Haitian refugees and Cuban "Marielitos"—were "savaging our society."[69]

The requested GAO report, published in 1986, was the first of many in this period to identify the "deportable criminal alien" as a central concern for immigration policy.[70] D'Amato continued to push for further action by Congress regarding the "criminal alien problem," deriding INS for "bureaucratic laziness" that "practically invites repeated re-entry into this country by precisely those undesirables that we have already determined to be dangerous to our community."[71] Democratic senator Lawton Chiles, from Florida—another state with a large Caribbean immigrant population—stood by D'Amato in his crusade against immigrant criminality, claiming that "Alien felons are rapidly becoming the most violent network of organized criminals in the country."[72] Chiles organized 1987 and 1988 hearings on INS's failure to effectively remove immigrants with criminal convictions, and he proposed the legislation that the Anti-Drug Abuse Act (ADAA) of 1988, the law that created the aggravated felony category, was largely based on.[73]

The racialized scapegoat of the immigrant offender continued as a popular media image from the 1980s into the 1990s, serving as fodder for spiraling fear and indignation in support of increasingly punitive policy. As legal scholar Ira Kurzban explains, "The antidrug and anti-crime rhetoric . . . could be dragged out and used or reused to keep people in a state of fear and anxiety by recalling specific cases of noncitizens who may have been dangerous and/or engaged in criminal conduct. Often one story, repeated endlessly in the corporate media, was sufficient to demonstrate how necessary undemocratic measures were to protect we the people."[74] As the initial influx of Caribbean arrivals subsided, Mexican and Central American immigrants were brought under focus, the southern US border was painted as a "war zone" which must be contained by militarized action,[75] and the stereotype of the Latino "criminal alien"—often tied with drug trafficking—was commonly invoked by entertainment and news media.[76]

Furthermore, the punitive frameworks supported by such imagery have, since their inception, had vastly unequal effects—thus reinforcing the racist tropes by which they are supported. Domestically, the policing and enforcement of the War on Drugs (and "tough-on-crime" criminal justice more generally) disproportionately targets poor Black and Latinx communities,[77] while internationally, there is a heavy focus on the interdiction of drugs from Mexico, Latin America, and the Caribbean.[78] Hence, both major fronts of the highly publicized US War on Drugs have helped further solidify assumed connections between Black and Latinx immigrants, drugs, and criminality. An increased focus on criminal deportation, the militarization of country's southern border, intensified and discriminatory policing of immigrant communities, and expanded incarceration for immigration offenses further reinforced a racialized image of the criminal alien.[79]

As the issue of immigrant criminality became an increasingly relevant factor in policymaking, the aggravated felony category expanded and became more and more stringent in its effects—culminating in the aforementioned landmark immigration reforms of 1996. In her book, *Illegal, Alien, or Immigrant*, political scientist Lina Newton compares the symbols and imagery present in the legislative development of IIRIRA with that of the Immigration Reform and Control Act of 1986 through discourse analysis of the *Congressional Record*.[80] She found a nuanced discussion in the mid-1980s of the complex push and pull factors driving "illegal immigration." By the mid-1990s, the conversation had shifted to paint immigrants as unlawful and undeserving. Two important storylines that emerged in congressional hearings leading to the passage of IIRIRA were what Newton refers to as "The Criminal Alien Narrative," which labeled immigrants, and especially those who are undocumented, as inherently criminal, and "The Lawless Border Narrative," which painted the border as a "breeding ground for smugglers, drugs, violence, and generalized chaos."[81] These narratives were exemplified in statements like, "We look at the drugs coming across the flow, and on those drug ride-alongs, 99 percent have involved illegal aliens," and with regard to the border, "Smuggling is organized crime, both the smuggling of people and drugs. You have certain parts of turf that are staked out by these criminals. You don't just move from Tijuana over to Mexicali for example without getting your kneecaps blown off."[82]

Organizations like the Federation for American Immigration Reform (FAIR)—founded in 1979 by a eugenicist who viewed immigration as a threat to "White America," and since classified as a white supremacist hate group by the Southern Poverty Law Center[83]—gained power and influence throughout the era as they "fueled and echoed" concerns about the links between immigration and crime.[84] By the mid-1990s, organizations which only drew "meager support" during the 1980s were working directly with policymakers to shape punitive legislation.[85] Kurzban reflects on the central role of anti-immigrant advocacy in the drafting and passage of IIRIRA:

> Lamar Smith, who was the Chairman of the House Immigration Sub-committee at the time, rewrote the immigration laws by hiring lawyers from FAIR (Federation for Immigration Reform), an anti-immigration group. He knew he could not simply eliminate all waivers so he and his staff rewrote the waivers to make them far less useful to most people. The Republican members of Congress deferred to Smith and the Democrats were only provided the IIRIRA legislation less than 72 hours before there was a vote.
>
> As an author on immigration law, it took me several months to go through the legislation. It is unimaginable that anyone except Lamar Smith and the lawyers who worked with him had any idea of the depth and breadth of changes they proposed and rammed through Congress.[86]

In support of the eventual AEDPA provisions that expanded the aggravated felony category and "streamlined" the deportation process, Smith argued that these actions were necessary to "counter the escalation of crime robbing Americans of the freedom to walk their streets, the right to feel secure in their homes, and the ability to feel confident that their children are safe in their schools."[87] The impacts of spiraling fear around "criminal aliens" can also be seen in the actions of the Clinton administration and other Democratic lawmakers who saw passing and enforcing the harsh 1996 immigration laws as an opportunity to demonstrate their lack of leniency for "criminal aliens" and undocumented immigrants.[88]

The Context of Neoliberal Late Modernity

This history shows how the demonized figure of immigrant as criminal—long-entrenched in the US imagination—was reinvigorated in the 1980s and 1990s at the center of growing public and political attention to the issues of drugs, crime, and immigration. "Moral entrepreneurs," including advocates and lawmakers on both sides of the political spectrum, drew on the symbolic salience of the "criminal alien" folk devil to pass increasingly punitive laws—including those that created and expanded the aggravated felony. Yet, what gave this familiar scapegoat, and a corresponding moral panic linking immigrants with drugs and crime, such symbolic salience in this time? What is it about *this* panic that allowed for such an unprecedented rise in punitive policy, despite centuries of societal blaming of immigrants for crime? Key to moral panic theory—and a point sometimes lost in the theory's modern use—is the central role of *context* in determining the power of a panic to invoke punitive social responses. Young and Cohen both emphasize that the content of moral panics and the folk devils which they persecute are symbolic points of focus that obtain their strength from anxieties and tensions within the greater cultural and structural context.[89] Thus, it is only through an examination of the broad societal conditions that give a given panic its symbolic power that we can we begin to understand the real, and often lasting, effects it can have.

In more recent work, Young describes the contemporary roots of racist and nationalist "othering" as "a vertigo of insecurity" based in the "disembeddedness of late modern society, the shock of pluralism, the fear of the ever possible loss of status or of downward mobility."[90] In the case at hand, the othering of migrants racialized as Black and Hispanic through the reinforcement of the "criminal alien" folk devil was particularly powerful in the context of the late-1980s and early-1990s United

States—a time which was characterized by economic shifts that increased social inequality, ideological shifts concerning the government's place in dealing with social problems, and demographic shifts toward an increasingly diverse nation.

During the last three decades of the twentieth century, ruling economic doctrine around the world underwent a radical shift. Drawing its roots from Austrian economist Friedrich von Hayek's 1944 treatise, *The Road to Serfdom*, and elaborated by American economist Milton Friedman and his University of Chicago colleagues in the 1950s and 1960s, neoliberalism is the dominant economic doctrine today. Yet it ran directly in the face of the ruling economic ideology at the time of its emergence. Contrary to the state-centered, Keynesian policies popular in the postwar period, Hayek, Friedman, and their acolytes called for a system that would ensure individual freedom through the achievement of completely unfettered economic markets.[91] Policy based on this utopian dogma of freedom and choice is characterized by "the three trademark demands" of "privatization, government deregulation and deep cuts to social spending."[92] Neoliberal policy was instituted with a vengeance throughout the global South beginning in the 1970s, especially in South America, where it was backed intellectually by Friedman and other Chicago school economists and militarily by the United States government. However, it wasn't until the 1980s that this economic framework came to dominate policy in the United States, when the fervently neoliberal Reagan administration worked to deregulate the markets and dismantle governmentally provided social programs, contributing to increased economic inequality and insecurity.[93]

Jamie Peck and Adam Tickell explain the way in which this period of "roll-back neoliberalism" in the 1980s was followed by the "roll-out neoliberalism" of the 1990s, a period of statecraft during which pervasive systems of neoliberal regulation and control were constructed, systems "concerned specifically with the aggressive reregulation, disciplining, and containment of those marginalized or dispossessed by the neoliberalization of the 1980s."[94] By linking a move toward more punitive frameworks around drugs, crime, and immigration with a need to protect the country from criminal aliens, a moral panic about immigrant criminality lent important support to policies which may have seemed oppressive and cruel if they were seen as negatively affecting white American citizens instead of nonwhite immigrant others. Furthermore, from this viewpoint, middle- and lower-class economic insecurity (exacerbated by neoliberal deregulation and removal of social programs) could be blamed on an undeserving immigrant other rather than on structural inadequacies or elite power. The growing power of corporate media made it even easier to frame the "deterioration of everyday life" felt by the middle classes as something to be blamed on a "criminal alien" folk devil.[95]

Such viewpoints were further supported by the ideological shifts that undergirded neoliberal economic restructuring. According to David Garland, the punitive turn in American criminal justice policy can largely be attributed to changing societal perspectives concerning the place of the government in relation to social problems.[96] Over the course of the 1970s, American public opinion decisively shifted away from the welfare-state economic policy of the postwar era and toward a neoliberal belief in individualism and free-market competition, a philosophical transformation which culminated in Reagan's 1980 election. The Reagan administration quickly discarded any remnants of a criminal legal framework which privileged government-funded social programs and offender rehabilitation as important tools in crime prevention, and it instead pushed for retributive policy that moved the onus of blame away from societal problems and onto individual offenders.[97]

Finally, demographic shifts that became more pronounced in the United States of the 1980s and 1990s contributed cultural fear and insecurity to a context where panic about immigrant criminality could flourish. Doug Massey explains how, after the United States went through a "long hiatus" from about 1931 to 1970 during which immigration was fairly limited, a "new regime" of large-scale, non-European (mainly from Latin America and Asia) immigration began, which continued through the end of the century.[98] By 1998, Mexico was the largest single source of migrants to the United States.[99] The foreign-born Black-identifying population also burgeoned during this period, doubling from about 816,000 in 1980 to 2,435,000 in 2000[100]—with the majority hailing from the Caribbean.[101] The historical subjugation and demonization of those racialized as Hispanic and Black in the United States—legacies tracing all the way to the colonization of the Americas through Indigenous genocide and the institution of the transatlantic slave trade—gave substance to cultural insecurities manifest in nativism and the racist othering of immigrants.

Conclusion

Despite drawing on racial hierarchies and tropes older than this country itself, the "criminal alien" folk devil had a specific salience in the United States during the 1980s and 1990s, contributing to the proliferation of punitive policy that would shape social control in this country for decades to come. In a context of intensified economic inequality, neoliberal victim blaming, and growing cultural diversity, societal fears around drugs, crime, and immigration were enflamed in distinctly racialized ways by media, advocates, and politicians, reinforcing the trope of immigrant criminality with increasingly punitive policy. It is this juncture—where distinctly modern conditions allowed for the reinvigoration and political implementation of long-standing and unfounded stereotypes—from which the aggravated felony emerged and expanded. And it is this specific background that has allowed for the endurance of the category—alongside similarly punitive policy—over the past thirty years.

2

The "Immigration Law Death Penalty"

Everyday Court Impacts

Aggravated felonies are a huge indicator of the outcome of the case. If someone has committed an aggravated felony, it is going to negatively impact every step of the immigration process. It will be a thing that makes them subject to removal proceedings in the first place. It will be the thing that makes them fall within mandatory detention . . . it's a huge indicator of whether they can ultimately prove their case and stay here.
—Jess, immigration lawyer

These broad definitions are really leading to the mass deportation and detention of individuals.
—Pia, immigration lawyer

Until now, scholarly analyses of the aggravated felony category have almost exclusively appeared in law journals, where legal scholars have interpreted and critiqued the written policy and its inconsistencies with dominant legal doctrine.[1] This literature is key in understanding the development of the law as well as its procedural implications. Emphasizing the aggravated felony's everyday impacts on immigration court processes—and drawing from interviews with lawyers and other legal actors as well as ethnographic observation of New York City's Varick Street immigration court—this chapter confirms, illustrates, and expands on existing critiques of the aggravated felony. Guided by prominent themes in the legal literature, the chapter begins with a description of the expansiveness of the category and its perceived overuse in immigration court. This description is followed by an assessment of the effects of aggravated felony convictions on immigrants' chances for relief from deportation, an exploration of observed and reported due process violations related to the category, and a brief description of developments during the Trump era (when this research was completed). Ultimately, I argue that the continually expansive, severe, and legally questionable effects of the aggravated felony—even in the "best case scenario" of New York City—underscore injustice inherent in the law itself and illustrate the power of moral panic to influence policy in lasting ways.

"Doesn't Have to Be Aggravated or a Felony"

One recurring theme in the legal literature on the aggravated felony category is the expansiveness of the category.[2] Of all the criminal grounds that make immigrants deportable—which also include crimes involving moral turpitude, as well as controlled substance, firearm, and domestic violence offenses—the aggravated felony applies to the widest range of offenses. Today, the Immigration and Nationality Act (INA) definition of an aggravated felony is based on a list of offense types that were decided on in the immigration reforms of 1996.[3] Yet, while immigration law is federal, criminal offenses are defined at both the state and federal level. Therefore, each of the thirty-five offense types listed in the INA can be applied to a corresponding federal conviction as well as hundreds of state-level offenses. The resulting breadth is summed up in a practice advisory issued by a major immigration law organization, advising attorneys that "Because so many offenses are unexpectedly classed as aggravated felonies, advocates need to examine each offense carefully to make sure that it is not an aggravated felony" (emphasis in original).[4]

Throughout my interviews, lawyers discussed what they saw as a disconnect between the "aggravated felony" label and the myriad convictions that it encompasses. George, who had worked as a public immigration lawyer and advocate for over thirty years, discussed the importance of the expansion in the 1996 laws, remarking, "The first sort of contradiction or almost oxymoron is that something doesn't have to be aggravated or a felony to be an aggravated felony." He explained how since 1996, "A theft crime with a one-year sentence is an aggravated felony, and a suspended sentence, which is where you don't have to serve your time, counts as a sentence for the purpose of the aggravated felony laws." Brianna, a private immigration lawyer who had been working in the field for ten years, said the "broadening of the category" has "caught a lot of people in the crosshairs." She deemed the name "misleading" as it implies "supervillain" despite the wide variety of state-level offenses included. Brianna explained, "Let's say it's a misdemeanor or a low felony in your state, but in front of immigration, they consider it [an aggravated] felony. It could just be a violation in your state, but let's say how you get charged or how you get sentenced or whatever, it becomes [an aggravated] felony." May, a public immigration lawyer for five years, felt reform was needed to at least make the category fit its title. She joked, "It would be nice if we could have a case being like, 'the phrase aggravated felony means something, right?' Like it has to be a felony. Or there has to be some aggravating factor."

Several lawyers spoke to disproportionality in the aggravated felony definition, citing its inclusion of crimes they believed to vary greatly in terms of harm caused. Seth, a public defender and immigration lawyer for almost twenty-five years, said, "I think some of the crimes are things that probably most people would think should be in the aggravated felony, like slavery, like murder, like rape." He continued,

> I think the public starts—to the extent that they think about it—starts wondering [in cases when] the rape is statutory rape and it involves like an eighteen-year-old guy with his sixteen-year-old girlfriend, and it's consensual to the extent that a sixteen-year-old can give consent, I think people think, "Hmm, should that really bar all immigration relief and make you mandatorily deportable?" But then I think things like shoplifting, for which someone happened to get a year in jail, I think most people would probably say that's not something that should lead to you being barred from all forms of relief.

May said, "It's so ridiculous and disproportionate, like if you read the list. It's like, 'Okay murder, rape, sexual abuse of a minor, drug trafficking—okay that sounds pretty bad, that sounds like, okay maybe there should be some consequences,'" At this point she paused to say, laughingly, "If you're buying into the validity of the whole system, which I don't, but I can get why people would think that." She continued, "But then you're like, 'Huh, theft ag fel [aggravated felony]? I stole a tiny thing once.'"

The majority of immigration lawyers that I interviewed reported examples of minor crimes technically considered aggravated felonies. Jackie, an immigration lawyer and advocate with eight years of experience, explained how a subway turnstile jump is a theft offense with a maximum sentence of one year in New York State, which—if so-sentenced—constitutes an aggravated felony. She said, "That's how wide and broad it is. . . . Even though it's not likely, you could be convicted of an aggravated felony for not paying $2.75 on the subway." Petty theft offenses, minor drug crimes, and DUIs were among the other examples provided by lawyers to illustrate of the wide variety of convictions that could potentially be deemed aggravated felonies.

Some lawyers also explained how certain types of crimes that are included in the INA's definition of the category can sound more severe than the convictions that they are applied to in practice. Jon, a private criminal and immigration lawyer for six years, described a case regarding a client convicted of a child pornography misdemeanor, classified as an aggravated felony, based on the "attempted possession" of internet pornography which turned out to include a sixteen-year-old girl. Marco, a public immigration lawyer for five years, explained how in New York, "Any sort of possession with intent to distribute pretty much qualifies as a drug trafficking conviction, even though possession with intent to distribute is sometimes without intent of being remunerated by any financial gain." He felt it was "absolutely insane" that someone could just be "sharing, I don't know, some like molly [MDMA] with friends and that can be . . . a drug trafficking aggravated felony." The central role of drug crimes was an ongoing theme, which will be discussed further in the following chapter.

Raina, a public immigration lawyer with six years of experience, referred to the fact that fraud offenses "where the loss to the victim is over $10,000" are included as aggravated felonies as particularly "unfortunate," explaining, "If you think about fraud offenses, that could be welfare fraud. That could be [that] I signed up for Medicaid and I didn't necessarily qualify for it the whole time." Raina explained how in cases of welfare fraud, "It's oftentimes when people are making a little bit more than what the threshold amount is, or they were told by whoever was registering them, 'just write that you earn this much so I can register you,' and they kind of know, but it's a very easy thing to kind of get caught up in." She went on to describe a previous client charged with an aggravated felony because she had taken "a couple thousand dollars" from her employer to make her rent and not be evicted. She paid it back soon after, Raina explained, "but had already messed up all the books, and then the employer charged and convicted her, and not only did she get convicted for the small amount that she took, but like for all of the mess ups in the books. So things like that can happen."

The expansiveness of the aggravated felony category as written is further compounded by a perceived overuse by Immigration and Customs Enforcement (ICE). Participants relayed that, particularly in recent years, any noncitizen facing deportation with a previous conviction even tangentially related to one of the thirty-five included offense types was likely to be deemed an "aggravated felon" by ICE. Cally, a public immigration lawyer with four years of experience, said, "They often will charge things that we disagree with being aggravated felonies"—a sentiment that was prevalent among interviewees. Jane, a public immigration lawyer for eight years, explained that "What constitutes an aggravated felony is highly contested between immigrant advocates and attorneys and ICE." She reported, "ICE will always lodge the most serious immigration charges that they possibly can. So they always take an aggressive interpretation of the law. . . . So yeah, we very oftentimes think they have an overly broad interpretation of what constitutes an aggravated felony." George, alongside several others, referred to seminal Supreme Court cases that have overturned certain ICE interpretations surrounding the aggravated felony category (discussed in more detail in chapter 4). He explained, "they're saying everything is an aggravated felony, and their interpretations, which like I said, have often been found to be wrong, are so excessive that even the Supreme Court, which is hardly a neutral arbiter, rejects them, and they go ahead and continue to do it anyway." Despite wins at the Supreme Court level, many migrants facing deportation are without the resources to contest their aggravated felony in immigration court, where the burden of proof falls on the respondent.

The "Immigration Law Death Penalty"

A second major theme in the legal literature on the aggravated felony category is the severity of its effects on noncitizens' chances for avoiding deportation.[5] Despite key innovations by lawyers and advocates in New York City, this severity was emphasized throughout my interviews and ethnography. At an observed immigration law conference panel on "crimmigration law," it was stressed that the aggravated felony is the most important criminal category for noncitizen clients to avoid. Panelists even referred to the aggravated felony as the "immigration law death penalty" since it can have such deleterious effects on migrants' deportation cases. This outlook was reflected in many of my interviews. Jackie posited, "I think it's completely bleak. The number of people who can make some kind of claim that they should be able to stay here after being convicted of an aggravated felony is so low, and the number of people that may have a claim but without the resources to win one of those claims . . . it's ridiculous." Pia, a public immigration lawyer with six years of experience, concurred, describing the consequences that stem from aggravated felonies as "so so so so devastating. . . . very often mandatory detention, mandatory deportation, essentially not eligible for any possible defense, with very limited exception." Jess, a public immigration lawyer working in the field for eleven years, said that an aggravated felony conviction will "negatively impact every step of the immigration process." She went on to explain how an aggravated felony both makes a person deportable and subject to mandatory detention, which negatively affects their ability to argue their case. Among all the effects, Jess felt that limits to relief were the most harmful, saying, "If you are correctly categorized as having committed an aggravated felony, a lot of that stuff will ultimately not matter, because it's going to prevent you from getting any type of relief from removal in the first place."

The concept of "mandatory" deportation was raised in several interviews to explain the extent to which the aggravated felony bars conventional forms of relief from deportation. Barb, a public immigration lawyer and educator with thirty years of experience in the field, stated, "It's just a huge problem to have this category that has such enormous consequences . . . makes you subject to mandatory detention, makes you subject to mandatory deportation. . . . It has all these consequences. So it's a real problem to have that definition to begin with." Marco attributed the label of mandatory deportation to the fact "that you are pretty much ineligible for any sort of immigration relief. There are very, very few forms of immigration relief that you are eligible for." He went on to emphasize limits on relief from deportation as "the most harmful thing that aggravated felonies do." Emily argued that Congress intended the law to trigger "automatic deportation," saying, "When I have clients [with aggravated felonies], I often have to advise them that there are very little options for them to stay." Amy, a public immigration lawyer with ten years of experience, referred to the aggravated felony as the most severe out of the various criminal bars to relief, saying, "Certainly the aggravated felony category is the most serious one that we have to avoid, because it ends up barring so many things."

While aggravated felonies do not actually ensure mandatory deportation, they do cut immigrants off from almost all available forms of legal relief from removal. Though other criminal grounds of deportation also make it difficult to obtain relief from removal, the aggravated felony presents more categorical bars to legal relief than any other category. As seen in table 2.1, noncitizens in removal proceedings based on aggravated felonies are wholly barred from voluntary departure, cancellation of removal, and asylum—some of the most common forms of relief from deportation—and many are also barred from withholding of removal.[6] Although voluntary departure can hardly be considered a form of relief, it does allow many noncitizens to leave "on their own will" without a formal order of deportation. Unlike those facing removal for other criminal grounds, people convicted aggravated felonies are barred from this route, are banned from ever returning to the United States after deportation, and are subject to enhanced criminal penalties upon reentry.

Cancellation of removal is a relatively common form of discretionary relief, available to lawful permanent residents (LPRs, also known as green card holders) made deportable based on criminal grounds (that are not aggravated felonies), as well as to certain undocumented immigrants who can demonstrate lengthy residence and strong ties to the United States.[7] Aggravated-felony-based ineligibility for cancellation of removal makes it so that these discretionary factors cannot be taken into account in immigration court. The Illegal Immigration Reform and Immigrant Responsibility Act (IIRIRA) of 1996 repealed the 212(c) provision of the Immigration and Naturalization Act (INA) which had—until then—provided a key waiver of deportation that noncitizens with criminal records were eligible to apply for. This discretionary waiver allowed immigration judges to consider mitigating factors, such as an

TABLE 2.1. Forms of Relief from Deportation, Numbers Granted in 2018,*
and Availability to People Convicted of Aggravated Felonies†

Relief Type	Total Number Granted in 2018*	Availability to People Convicted of Aggravated Felonies
Voluntary Departure	22,189	Barred
Cancellation of Removal	6,091	Barred
212(c) waiver	368	Available for some with pre-1996 convictions
212(h) waiver	Data unavailable	Available to some who are adjusting to lawful permanent resident status
Asylum	13,248	Barred
Withholding of Removal	1,746	Available to those who have not been convicted of a "particularly serious crime"
Withholding of Removal under the Convention against Torture	1,157	Available to those who have not been convicted of a "particularly serious crime"
Deferral of Removal under the Convention against Torture	177	Available
T Visa	1,278	Available to those who are victims of trafficking and are providing helpful information to law enforcement
U Visa	17,710	Available to those who are victims of serious criminal abuse and are providing helpful information to law enforcement

* As of June 2022, 2018 is the most recent year for which statistics are publicly available from the Executive Office of Immigration Review (EOIR).
† Executive Office for Immigration Review, "Statistics Yearbook Fiscal Year 2018" (Department of Justice, 2019); US Citizenship and Immigration Services, "Number of Form I-918, Petition for U Nonimmigrant Status, by Fiscal Year, Quarter, and Case Status 2009–2018," 2019, www.uscis.gov/sites/default/files/document/data /I918u_visastatistics_fy2018_qtr4.pdf.

individual's LPR status, their length of residence in the United States, and potential impacts of their deportation on their families and communities.[8] IIRIRA replaced this provision with a new form of relief, cancellation of removal, for which noncitizens with aggravated felony convictions are wholly ineligible. This made it so that discretionary factors became mostly irrelevant in their removal proceedings,[9] a problem consistently raised in my interviews with lawyers.

Naomi, a public immigration lawyer with ten years of experience, said, "It's particularly aggravated felonies that both make you deportable and strip the court of any power to look at your equities and decide what your life is like now." Pia said it's "critical" for noncitizens "to avoid at all costs being convicted for something categorized as an aggravated felony, because . . . it takes away really, essentially, all discretion from judges, in most instances, to consider a lot of other factors, for example someone's family, their ties." She went on to say that an aggravated felony conviction "severely limits what form of relief they will be eligible for, and also really means the judges can't consider super compelling humanitarian factors."

Bars to discretionary relief are seen as being particularly problematic in the context of the retroactive application of the aggravated felony— another result of the 1996 reforms—which made it so that noncitizens could be deported for crimes that weren't even considered aggravated felonies at the time of conviction. Seth described the striking combination of retroactivity with the bars on judicial discretion that stemmed from the 1996 laws. This combination caused

> the complete abolition of 212(c) relief and its replacement by cancellation of removal for permanent residents with the ag fel [aggravated felony] bar contained within it. That really was a huge stripping away of discretion from the courts, so it meant that it didn't matter what you had done with your life or what the countervailing equities might be. And then the retroactivity of the definition meant that you could have done something at a very early stage here, led a perfect life since then. And I think for a lot of people who aren't sympathetic to people's criminal convictions, I think that would strike a lot of people as unfair.

In 2001, the Supreme Court ruled that 212(c) waivers must remain available to LPRs in removal proceedings who were eligible at the time of their guilty pleas (prior to 1996). While several lawyers did mention this shift as helpful, it only affects a limited group of noncitizens in removal proceedings, and becomes less and less relevant now, a quarter century past 1996. In 2018, 368 noncitizens received 212(c) relief nationwide compared to 6,091 who were granted relief under cancellation of removal—although none of them with aggravated felonies.[10]

It is common for immigrants to be placed in deportation proceedings based on alleged aggravated felonies years—or even decades—after serving their sentence for the convictions in question. Below, Marco explains the results of this model, emphasizing the way in which limits on discretion affect immigration courts' ability to account for rehabilitation.

> Some of our clients and the families of our clients are so surprised and so shocked that if you had a conviction, no matter how old the conviction is, if this conviction is an aggravated felony . . . it doesn't matter how long you've lived here, the family you have, the rehabilitation, nothing, absolutely nada matters, because in the end they're just statutorily ineligible for that form of relief. I mean it's shocking news that we need to deliver to both the client and the family.

Lawyers often gave examples of cases where they believed discretionary factors should have been taken into account, but were not, due to aggravated felony bars. These were usually removals based on older aggravated felony convictions, where community ties and rehabilitation were obvious. Cori, a public immigration lawyer with twelve years of experience, described one client who would be an "excellent candidate" for cancellation of removal if it weren't for one old conviction from the 1990s. She said that "He's been out of trouble for several years," and that "He's an older man, is disabled, has a young baby. . . . But he's really precluded from every sort of relief whatsoever by this conviction that occurred in '95." Marco described a similar case: a client who had recently been placed in deportation proceedings based on a 1997 conviction, for which he had served a five-year probation, "after this person had been completely giving back to the community, had a family, had multiple jobs, had an absolutely stable life." Despite several years of immigration law experience, Marco expressed incredulity at the situation, continuing, "The fact that he has completely rehabilitated, reintegrated, is not taken into account at all, because his old conviction automatically triggers what is pretty much called mandatory deportation."

The inability of immigration judges to account for discretionary factors in these cases is further problematized by the fact that many noncitizens in removal proceedings related to aggravated felonies are actually green card holders—legal residents—with deeply entrenched relationships with families, communities, and other institutions in the United States.[11] As a ground of deportability, the aggravated felony category is most often applied to people who have already been admitted to the United States at a port of entry, either as a visitor or resident. Furthermore, the use of expedited administrative removal processes for certain undocumented people with aggravated felony convictions makes it so that those who actually make it to immigration court are even more likely to be LPRs.[12] Although the Department of Homeland Security (DHS) does not release data on the number of LPRs deported, a study out of the University of California, Berkeley School of Law reported an average of 8,700 green card holders deported each year on criminal bases between April 1997 and August 2007, close to 10 percent of total deportations at the time. The authors primarily attributed these numbers to aggravated felonies and their negative effects on discretion.[13]

The impacts on LPRs also came up in several of my interviews with lawyers. For example, May explained that the typical aggravated felony case that they receive at the public legal providers is a green card holder "who has lived here for a long time and has a lot of ties to the community." She said such cases are both "emotionally very difficult" and "legally very difficult" due to "the fact that you are barred for all forms of relief by an ag fel [aggravated felony]." May found it especially problematic that aggravated felonies bar cancellation of removal, which she identified as "most of our lawful permanent residents' best option for relief."

In terms of fear-based relief, noncitizens convicted of aggravated felonies are made ineligible for asylum, and those with sentences longer than five years, or others with so-called "particularly serious crimes," are ineligible for withholding of removal.[14] Asylum is a key international protection, for which an applicant must show that they have suffered past persecution in their home country or that they possess a well-founded fear of persecution if returned—persecution based on one of the five protected grounds of race, religion, nationality, political opinion, or membership in a particular social group. In order to be granted asylum, applicants must apply within one year of entering the United States and must establish that their likelihood of persecution is 10 percent or higher. Once granted, asylum allows immigrants the opportunity to apply for lawful permanent residency or, if already an LPR, the reinstatement of their green card. Withholding of removal has no time limit and is based on the same grounds of persecution as asylum. However, while a grant of withholding of removal prevents a person from being deported and allows them to work legally within the United States, it does not allow them to apply for legal permanent residency. Furthermore, the burden of evidence is higher, as applicants for withholding of removal must prove that it is more likely than not that they will be persecuted upon return. Therefore, it is statistically far less common for a person to be granted withholding of removal than for a person to be granted asylum. As seen in table 2.1, 13,248 people were granted asylum by US immigration courts in 2018—33 percent of decided asylum applications. That same year, just 1,746 people were granted withholding of removal—a mere 6 percent of decided applications for that form of relief.[15]

While asylum is barred for all noncitizens with aggravated felony convictions, withholding of removal is also barred for many due to wide use of the "particularly serious crime" classification within the aggravated felony category. In my interviews, Barb referred to this classification as one "that has been vastly overread by the government." Seth discussed the classification's expansion and explained how even "small drug trafficking offenses" like "selling ten dollars' worth of crack" are often categorized as "particularly serious crimes" that make immigrants ineligible for withholding of removal. Lawyers also pointed out that criminal bars to fear-based protections are inconsistent with their stated purpose and make it more difficult for those seeking refuge from persecution. For example, Pia referred to aggravated felony bars on asylum as harmful to noncitizens "who may be able to show fear of prosecution on protected grounds—you know, due to race, national origin—things that we've decided are really, really important to protect and preserve."

The only forms of fear-based relief available to many people convicted of aggravated felonies are those related to the Convention against Torture. The United Nations Convention against Torture and Other Cruel, Inhumane, or Degrading Treatment or Punishment was enacted into US law in 1998. The convention states that "No State Party shall expel, return, or extradite a person to another state where there are substantial grounds for believing that he would be in danger of being subjected to torture."[16] There are two types of relief under the Convention against Torture (CAT): withholding of removal and deferral of removal. Like the withholding of removal explained above, both forms of CAT relief are based on a "more likely than not" standard. However, while general withholding of removal can be founded on various forms of persecution, CAT requires a respondent to establish that there is more than a 50 percent chance that they will be tortured or otherwise injured upon return to their home country either at the hands of the government or with government acquiescence. Furthermore, withholding of removal under CAT is also like general withholding of removal in that it prevents future deportation, and is limited to those who have not been convicted of offenses deemed to be "particularly serious crimes." The many who are unable to prove that their conviction is not "particularly serious" are limited to deferral of removal under CAT—a tenuous form of relief which affords no real status and can even be reversed at a later date if home country conditions shift. As seen in table 2.1, only 1,157 people were granted withholding of removal under CAT in 2017—4 percent of decided cases—while just 177 were granted deferral of removal under CAT—a grant rate of less than 1 percent of decided cases.[17]

The difficulties of meeting the standard for relief under CAT was a common thread throughout my interviews and court observation. It was widely agreed on by participants that the best chance to win CAT relief cases is through the use of an expert witness—an additional expense that is out of reach for many nonprofit organizations and privately paying immigrant families. In general, lawyers did not regard CAT relief as a very hopeful option. Marco explained,

> The problem with this form of relief is that it is incredibly, incredibly hard to get, and the burden can be so high, that one, of course not everyone is afraid of going back to their home country, so they are simply not applying for that form of relief, and second, it's so, so hard to get, so even if you're afraid of going back and you have valid reasons, and valid concerns that you will be tortured if you go back, our experience is that most of our clients get deported at the end regardless of their eligibility for that form of relief.

Seth had a similar perspective. He referred to the intense burden of evidence in such cases, arguing, "I would say it's almost impossible to win a CAT claim without an expert witness, unless you're a well-known figure in your country who is fleeing, who has been clearly tortured by government officials, and there are Amnesty International reports out about you or someone in exactly the same situation as you, and then you might be able to rely on country reports." He said perhaps with official reports specifically speaking to your case or your exact case characteristics, as well as medical documentation of the torture and violence you'd experienced, "You could possibly win without an expert witness, although it would probably be good to have a doctor come testify on your injuries as well." While it is common knowledge that many immigrants to the United States are fleeing violence, it is not the type of violence that CAT relief is designed to protect from. Gang violence in the Northern Triangle (Guatemala, Honduras, and El Salvador) or narco-cartel power in Mexico and the Dominican Republic are not easily framed as grounds for relief under the Convention against Torture. Thus, many migrants removed from the United States are sent directly to dangerous conditions where deportees—and especially those with criminal records—are particularly stigmatized and vulnerable.[18]

The bars that the aggravated felony creates on more apt forms of relief for people seeking protection from such circumstances are made even more ironic when the crimes triggering these bars are also shaped by the power of gangs and cartels. In one hearing I observed, a forty-year-old man from Guatemala had come to the United States in his early twenties, fleeing the control of a powerful gang he was forced to join at the age of fourteen. However, after building a life here—including a young family and small business—he is cut off from all forms of relief besides CAT, which he is unlikely to receive, based on serious crimes he committed under gang coercion in his youth. Similarly, Marco described a client who had fled violence in his home country by way of drug trafficking. The client was caught at the border with drugs in his suitcase—a crime which would most likely end up cutting him off from the protection he was seeking. Marco explained that this man "was kind of taking a separate shot to get here, because he was in danger in his home country, and it was like a risky, foolish way to try to get safe and have a way to start his life over again here." Marco continued that because the client was discovered with drugs, "what would otherwise be a pretty straightforward asylum case is a likely losing Convention against Torture case, because the standard is so high."

In many of the cases I observed, the crime that made the respondent deportable was related to the conditions in the country they were fleeing (conditions that the United States often played an important part in creating). Furthermore, there were several cases where respondents' fears of return were based on them having cooperated with the US government to indict transnational criminal organization higher-ups after their original conviction. Certain immigrants who cooperate with law enforcement, and who have also been victims of trafficking or other serious abuse, are eligible, along with immediate family members, for protection through the T visa or U visa.[19] While these forms of relief from deportation are technically available to people convicted of aggravated felonies, in practice, they are difficult to obtain. By the end of fiscal year 2018, the two visas had a combined backlog of more than two hundred thousand applications.[20]

Throughout my visits to immigration court, I regularly observed cases where immigrants had cooperated with law enforcement yet were not eligible for the T or U visas. In one case, a man had been convicted of a few robberies in the early 2000s while working small-time for a transnational drug gang. He had then cooperated with US law enforcement, and quite a few people were picked up because of him—including gang higher-ups. After cooperating, he was threatened through his lawyer, and then there was an attack on his family home in the Dominican Republic, where his brother was shot. Another man in a similar situation was asked by his lawyer in court, "What will happen to you if you are deported?" The man answered, "They will torture and kill me," referring to the drug gang he had worked for, who he had cooperated against with US federal authorities. A third case was that of a sailor who had climbed to the high rungs of a narco-organization and had trafficked drugs throughout the region and then, once caught, gave vital information to a grand jury, leading to several arrests. In court, he described threats from the organization, and claimed, "There is a stamp on my life if I return."

Although at times these arguments can prove successful, they are extremely difficult in the CAT context, which is designed to protect from torture at the hands of, or with the knowledge of, government officials—and not necessarily to protect from the violence of criminal organizations. Even in successful cases—which, as noted, are extremely rare—withholding and deferral of removal under CAT only provide a tenuous form of "liminal legality" with no formal legal status or path to citizenship.[21] Thus, unlike in cases of asylum or cancellation of removal, a later determination of changed country conditions by the court can easily reverse such protections and trigger deportation.

"Certainly a Due Process Violation"

A third key theme in the existing literature on the aggravated felony is the category's effects on immigrants' legal rights. Courts have consistently upheld that noncitizens, even those without lawful status, are entitled to constitutional protections of due process—rights and court procedures outlined by US law. Yet in practice, as a body of administrative (civil) law, immigration law is not held to the same due process requirements as criminal law—for example, there is no compulsory federal provision of legal representation in immigration law.[22] Furthermore, legal scholars have credited the aggravated felony category with the further erosion of the due process that does exist in immigration law through mechanisms such as administrative removal and detention without bail.[23] In my interviews, processes related to the aggravated felony category were frequently cited as infringing on immigrants' due process rights.

While there is universal legal representation for detained immigrants in New York City through the New York Immigrant Family Unity Project (NYIFUP), only 14 percent of detained immigrants nationwide are represented in their deportation proceedings.[24] In spite of the favorable locale, lack of representation was often mentioned by participants as a key due process concern in immigration law—a concern further compounded by detention. When asked how the aggravated felony has affected due process, Pam, a public immigration lawyer with three years of experience, said, "I think it usually is in the context of not having an attorney. . . . Because it's such a complicated area of law [and] you don't have anyone to raise these arguments for you." This was echoed by numerous other interviewees. Lisa, an immigration lawyer and advocate working in the field for more than twenty years, said, "The idea of, you know, civilly detaining them, denying them liberty, and then putting them through this banishment process without council just doesn't seem to make a lot of sense based on what we consider to be a fair and just system."

The specific difficulty of winning the forms of relief that are not barred by aggravated felonies, such as withholding of removal and deferral of removal under the CAT, was cited as making the lack of guaranteed legal representation particularly unjust. Jackie gave an example of a recent case that illustrates this concern.

> I just ended with a client who had been convicted of an aggravated felony drug sale offense, and we put on a withholding case for him. . . . And my brief to the court was over six hundred pages. . . . It was helpful that he had me to do that, because it was very unlikely that he would have been able to. . . . He has a claim basically that he was going to be retaliated against by drug dealers in Jamaica who are powerful enough to evade any kind of lawful sanctuary that he'd be able to get from the government there. So I had to do things like prove that a specific person had been deported to Jamaica already, right? That's not anything that he could've done by himself. I ordered all of these records. . . . We hired two experts for his case. So he couldn't have done that without an attorney. And most people, the vast majority of people who are detained, have no council."

Greg, a private immigration lawyer for eight years, claimed to enjoy crimmigration work specifically because of its legal difficulty, and said "If you don't have a lawyer, you can't do a withholding or a CAT case or really even an asylum case. It's virtually impossible."

The difficulty—or virtual impossibility—of obtaining legal relief without a lawyer and with an aggravated felony is further compounded by detention, which is made mandatory when facing removal for most criminal offenses. Created with the aggravated felony as part of the Anti-Drug Abuse Act of 1988, mandatory detention was expanded to also include those convicted of terrorism, drug crimes, and crimes of moral turpitude as part of the 1996 immigration laws.[25] Yet, it is lengthy and complex to fight aggravated-felony-based deportation—whether arguing for fear-based relief or contesting removability—especially when factoring in court backlog and including appeals. This is not an easy undertaking while mandatorily detained. Jackie explained how either way, aggravated felony cases "are going to be the most legally complicated, factually complicated to prove" and expressed dismay at the fact that "everybody's doing that from detention and without any opportunity to leave." Not surprisingly, migrants detained throughout their deportation proceedings are less likely to secure legal representation, less likely to win relief from deportation, and more likely to self-deport.[26]

Thus, many lawyers felt that detention, and mandatory detention in particular, is not only an impediment to justice but also works as a deterrent to keep migrants from fighting their deportation at all. Cecy, a public immigration lawyer for two years, explained how in cases involving aggravated felonies, in addition to having such limited relief already, "The fact that they're going to be in detention throughout the entirety of their immigration court proceedings, without any hope in sight, . . . does discourage people sometimes from even trying to seek relief under the Convention against Torture." She found this to be "really problematic" not only due to families being separated by detention but also because people may want to pursue "legitimate forms of relief that they're eligible for and they might meet the standards for, but the idea of jail is too much." Barb also saw detention as a key obstruction to winning aggravated-felony-based removal cases. She said, "It's this lengthy process. People have to be willing to endure detention. . . . A lot of people will do it because they're permanent residents and their whole life is here and they can't imagine being deported. But I think a lot of people, even when they can't imagine that, they think, you know, 'It's gotta be better to be out and not be locked up.'"

Several participants maintained that this effect of detention is no coincidence, and that the system is set up to purposely deter migrants from contesting their removal. George said, "Where a person has to be locked up to vindicate their rights, that's a very effective tool to give up their rights." Jackie called mandatory detention "a coercive measure that tries to get people to not fight their cases." When asked if long periods of detention may be a tactic to deter people from fighting deportation, Barb said, "Yeah, and the government has almost said that. Because in detained cases they always say, 'Well the person is only detained because they're not accepting their deportation order.'" The harsh conditions of immigration detention further compound this deterrent effect. Cecy describes,

> It's so interesting because "detained" is supposed to mean in a detention facility, not a jail, but when you talk to people who have been, let's say

they've been in federal prison after being sentenced, they talk about the differences between the ICE detention facilities and how much worse they are, just in terms of the quality of life, and just the way that they're treated, which just makes it really difficult. . . . So for people who might not necessarily have been in jail for a long time or ever before, now they're faced with these really terrible conditions, and even people who have been transferred to those detention facilities from other places, there's a stark difference in that the conditions are pretty terrible, in terms of just like food and privacy and everything.

While officially deemed nonpunitive "administrative detention," migrants detained throughout their removal proceedings are imprisoned throughout more than two hundred jails and privately run facilities around the country. Researchers have reported extensively on the conditions at these facilities, emphasizing unsafe infrastructure, poor medical care, lack of oversight, profit-seeking management, and the punitive treatment of detained populations.[27] Internal investigations conducted by the Department of Homeland Security (DHS)—ICE's parent agency—and the inspector general have also repeatedly raised concerns about conditions and safety at these facilities,[28] including health and medical problems that were further exacerbated during the COVID-19 pandemic,[29] when immigrants with criminal records were deprioritized for release.[30]

The unjust nature of mandatory detention without bail, as triggered by the aggravated felony, was a particular area of concern for many of my participants. This issue became more prominent about halfway through the study, in February 2018, when the *Jennings v. Rodriguez* decision by the Supreme Court ruled that detained immigrants do not have a constitutional right to periodic bond hearings. This overturned a 2015 decision by the United States Court of Appeals for the Second Circuit (which encompasses New York, Connecticut, and Vermont) that held that immigrants who are mandatorily detained must be given a bail hearing after six months of detention. The 2015 decision *Lora v. Shanahan* was an important win for mandatorily detained immigrants in New York City and the rest of the second circuit. Still, some lawyers said the ruling's helpfulness for people convicted of aggravated felonies was limited. Speaking before *Lora* was overturned, Jon explained how the demonization of immigrants with many of the crimes that are classified as aggravated felonies made it so the required bond hearing only meant so much.

> If the crime involved violence of any kind, or actual drug sales, you know you're going to have a tough time convincing a judge to let you out, even when you get to that *Lora* hearing, where it's supposed to be the government's burden to prove that you're a danger to the community, but a lot of judges sort of say, "Well, I consider drug dealing to be a dangerous offense" [or] "Y'know, this happened recently, so no. I find the government has met its burden," so you're going to remain in for the majority of your proceedings.

Speaking after *Lora* was usurped by *Jennings*, Laura, a public immigration lawyer for three years, admitted, "What was good about *Lora* was that . . . people were able to get bond hearings." However, she went on to qualify that while "a really old aggravated felony might have actually been able to get out on bond" under *Lora*, for people with more recent aggravated felonies, "if you get a bond hearing but you don't have really good facts in your case, it doesn't matter, because the judge is going to deny you bond or set it prohibitively high anyway."

Still, the *Jennings* decision was seen as a major blow to the rights of immigrants who are subject to mandatory detention, like those with convictions alleged to be aggravated felonies. Cori said, "Now that *Jennings* came down the Supreme Court, and *Lora* has been reversed, we're back to a world where someone with an aggravated felony or some other conviction that makes mandatory detention . . . where those people, because they want to fight their case, they want to appeal it, and like keep it going, they could be looking at years in detention." Pia agreed, saying, "In practice, unfortunately, it's a huge setback, where people were getting these automatic hearings and they're not anymore." Especially considering that so many people are detained based on convictions that are quite old, she found it "extremely unfair that the judge can't even look at whether you deserve to be detained or not." Laura agreed that the system was unjust. She identified immigration detention, and especially mandatory detention without bail, as an intrusion on due process. Laura elaborated, "First of all, you get detained, you don't even see a judge usually for like a month, right? And you're just sitting there. And you can lose your job, you can lose your apartment. You miss your kid's first birthday, all of that is completely awful, and the thing is that you're not even eligible to get a bond hearing because you have a certain criminal conviction. . . . I think that's certainly a due process violation." Jane also saw detention without bail as a violation of migrants' legal rights and explained how another area of litigation pursued by immigration lawyers with clients who are mandatorily detained is "arguing that it is unconstitutional to hold people for prolonged periods of time without giving them a bond hearing."

Though the argument that prolonged detention is unconstitutional is successful at times on the individual level, additional Supreme Court decisions since the time of research have further concretized the systemic use of indefinite detention for immigrants with criminal convictions. In *Nielson v. Preap* (2019), the court ruled that the language in IIRIRA of 1996 that states that a noncitizen convicted of a deportable crime "shall be taken into custody" by immigration authorities "when the alien is released" does not preclude the detention of individuals years after finishing their criminal sentence—even if they have lived safely in the community throughout that period. In *Johnson v. Arteaga-Martinez* (2022), the court overturned a lower court decision that mandated bond hearings after six months of detention for individuals fighting deportation based on fear of persecution in their home countries, and in *Garland v. Aleman Gonzalez* (2022), the court overturned another circuit court decision allowing federal courts to impose "class-wide injunctive relief" for noncitizens with similar cases against deportation who had been detained more than six months. Collectively, such cases have confirmed the legality of mandatory detention without bail in the immigration system—further eroding the limited due process protections for noncitizens facing deportation based on criminal records.

While indefinite detention and lack of representation were the due process violations most commonly mentioned in interviews, they were not the only ones encountered in this research. Ethnographic observation at Varick Street was an ever-changing experience, with new apparent injustices surfacing at each visit. One week, early in the research, a group of angry defense lawyers in the court waiting room discussed the unconstitutionality of a new move by DHS in New York City immigration courts. Beginning that week, government trial attorneys had begun forcing respondents to "plead to" (admit or deny) alleged grounds for deportation before making them privy to any actual allegations or evidence. On this day, I had been invited to observe by Nicole, a public immigration lawyer with fifteen years of experience. In court, she argued that the government must present their evidence. The DHS attorney contended that they had no burden of evidence until pleading is complete. Nicole told the court it was a "grave injustice" that her client has been detained for a month with no evidence presented. However, the month of detention was enough for her client. He pled guilty that day and was deported to Mexico, waiving his right to appeal—with no grounds of deportation ever demonstrated.

Another of Nicole's cases I observed was an instance of wrongful deportation. Her client had been prematurely sent back to the Dominican Republic while in the midst of fighting for CAT relief from removal. The respondent's fear-based claim was based on having cooperated with US federal law enforcement to indict drug cartel higher-ups after his original aggravated felony conviction. After his wrongful deportation, the man had spent six months in his home country before Dominican authorities agreed to facilitate his return to the United States. During this time, he had been threatened and violently attacked by associates of the drug dealers he had implicated. Upon his return to the United States, the man had already spent eight more months in detention by the time I began to observe his case. Ten months later, at the end of my ethnography, the man was still detained and his case still undecided. Such lengthy detention was in part due to long periods between each hearing (usually about three months, due to backlog) but also to the amount of time spent by Nicole arguing against various due process violations that could have had important influences on the case.

In one particularly contentious hearing, she objected to the fact that there were plainclothes ICE officers present in the courtroom—an unusual occurrence, with court security provided by private contractors. Nicole asked for a reason for this additional security (which the DHS attorney refused to provide) and objected to the presence of these unknown actors for the sensitive testimonies scheduled that day. She explained that, given the history of the case, where the respondent was lied to and wrongfully removed by ICE deportation officers, this was creating a clear environment of intimidation in the courtroom. The DHS attorney and judge expressed annoyance at Nicole's objections, and ultimately, the officers were allowed to stay.

An ongoing due process concern throughout my research was translation—every hearing I observed had a translator working in some capacity. This is representative of the norm across the country; the vast majority of immigration court hearings use language interpreters. In 2015, only 11 percent of immigration hearings were conducted solely in English.[31] Federal law requires courts to provide "meaningful access" for respondents with limited proficiency in English. ("Meaningful access" is defined by the Department of Justice (DOJ) as the provision of interpreters during hearings, screening of translators, training about translation for judges and other court personnel, and translation of all "vital documents.") Despite the DOJ enforcing such standards in other types of courts around the country, research has found immigration courts—which are run by the DOJ directly—to be inadequate in their adherence to the department's own regulations.[32]

A long-standing complaint of immigrant advocates is the fact that interpreters are often only asked to translate questions or statements directly addressed to the respondent as opposed to the entirety of proceedings. In 1989, a federal judge in Southern California ruled that this type of partial translation violated immigrants' due process rights, but this precedent has not been enforced.[33] Incomplete translation is particularly harmful in the cases of migrants without legal representation—which make up the vast majority of detained aggravated felony cases nationwide—where respondents without English proficiency have even less chance of fighting deportation.[34] In my research, I only observed one hearing where the interpreter appeared to be translating all proceedings, even sitting beside the respondent on the bench while other witnesses were on the stand. My feeling of surprise at this instance speaks to how normalized partial translation was in the immigration court I observed. Lengthy and complex legal arguments and testimonies regarding respondents' cases would go completely untranslated, with respondents sitting quietly, looking down at their hands, almost as if they were props in their own trials. In the rare instance when a lawyer would request that the entire hearing be translated, judges and government attorneys were outwardly annoyed with the extra time it took and, invariably, proceedings would devolve back into partial translation.

Another issue in this area is the inconsistent quality of immigration court interpreters, who are not required to undergo any specific training or certification. Instead, they are screened internally by private contractors and by the Executive Office of Immigration Review (EOIR), the department of the DOJ that is responsible for running immigration courts. These screening processes are not transparent and have been critiqued by state court systems for being inadequate.[35] Research has found a great deal of variance among translation quality in immigration courts, including the observation of egregious errors and the inappropriate insertion of personal opinions by translators.[36]

In my own research, translator quality seemed to vary greatly, and, on several occasions, translation errors were noticed by Spanish-speaking or Spanish-proficient defense attorneys—errors which likely would not have been picked up in cases where immigrants go unrepresented. There was also the problem of regional language differences, as interpreters were often from different countries than respondents. On one occasion, a respondent repeatedly referred to the "*banda*" or "gang" whom he feared persecution from if returned to his home country. The interpreter repeatedly translated the word as "band," another possible meaning of the Spanish word, until the defense lawyer finally picked up on the discrepancy. Such issues of translation were especially prevalent in CAT cases, where interpreters were vital to providing full understandings of telephonic testimonies made by internationally based witnesses describing home country conditions.

A development that occurred within the later months of my research compounded difficulties of translation further, while also presenting new due process concerns of its own. In June 2019, ICE announced that they would no longer be physically bringing detained individuals to Varick Street for their court appearances, and detained individuals would therefore have to appear from the detention center using video-conferencing technology.[37] This was purportedly in response to a brief anti-ICE occupation staged outside the Varick Street court, but several interviewees felt that ICE was using the protest as an excuse for changes they were already planning to implement. Although the use of video-conferencing is common in detained immigration courts around the country, it has been critiqued by advocates and scholars for violating due process, interfering with judges' ability to assess respondent credibility, and obstructing immigrants' ability to fully participate in the judicial process.[38]

In the several hearings I observed that used videoconferencing, there was a noticeable impact. First, there were delays due to technical issues and backlogs which were further exacerbated on days when multiple immigrants detained at the same jail were scheduled for court at the same time. In court, migrants facing deportation—appearing on a large television screen set up in the courtroom—seemed even more detached and isolated, and even less of the proceedings were translated. In addition, lawyers expressed intensified concern that respondents with sensitive cases would fear divulging key facts due to the possibility of being overheard by guards and other detained people.

A later hearing of Nicole's client who had been wrongfully deported occurred soon after the introduction of videoconferencing. Nicole argued that continuing court proceedings without her client present was a clear violation of his due process rights, but after quite a bit of back and forth on this issue, the hearing commenced, albeit at a snail's pace, as the judge, in response to Nicole's concerns, had the interpreter translate far more than she usually would—although still not all of the proceedings. In addition, the videoconferencing made it even more difficult for the respondent to understand the interpreter, who was already from a different country than he. The respondent appeared confused, the translator was visibly overwhelmed, and the judge seemed harried as she tried to limit speakers to two sentences at a time.

Lawyers at Varick Street found the new policy to be additionally harmful to due process in that it prevented them from meeting with their clients before or after their hearings. Having meetings around the hearings was common practice at the detained court before the introduction of videoconferencing due to the difficulties of meeting with clients at detention centers. In addition to intense security screening and limited visiting hours at jails, most respondents at Varick Street at this time were detained in New Jersey or Upstate New York—trips to which were made even more difficult by public lawyers' heavy caseloads. By the spring of 2020, when the COVID-19 pandemic led to the expanded use of remote and semiremote hearings throughout the country, ICE had refused to bring detained individuals to Varick Street for their hearings for close to a year. In an investigation of the early COVID-19 pandemic response in New Jersey detention centers, colleagues and I found additional due process concerns that were created by the increased use of tele-video and lawyers' inability to meet face to face with their clients.[39] There is concern that the expanded use of remote technology during the pandemic may outlast its public health necessity and continue to erode the rights of migrants facing deportation.[40] As stated in a joint lawsuit filed by NYIFUP providers and clients in 2019, official reasons for videoconferencing are "merely pretext for the true reasoning behind the policy—limiting due process, access to the courts and counsel for immigrants in an effort to rush deportations and deport more people."[41]

"This is Not Anything New": Aggravated Felonies in the Trump Era

A general push "to rush deportations and deport more people" was a common theme that came up in response to interview questions regarding changes under the Trump administration. The aggravated felony and the problems associated with it are not new developments, as chapter 1 makes clear. However, doing this research when I did—in the context of an administration vocal and active in its fight to intensify immigration enforcement and increase deportation, with a supposed focus on immigrants with criminal records—required the timely documentation of related changes.

Despite Trump's continual invoking of the "criminal alien" stereotype,[42] the outcomes of his immigration enforcement agenda, as described by interviewees, actually served to deprioritize immigrants with previous convictions. Lawyers described ramped-up enforcement and a "widening of the net" which resulted in the increased detention and deportation of individuals with no criminal records at all. Jon explained, "There are more and more people being detained. Community enforcement is up significantly. We're seeing way, way more people being taken into custody than we were." Lisa described a return to "universal enforcement"—a move away from the Obama administration's prioritization of "felons not families." This expanded enforcement was seen as stoking widespread fear among immigrant communities. At the same time, lawyers saw immigration courts working to process more cases more quickly. Nicole explained how judges were overbooking hearings with increased regularity amid intensified pressure to get through cases. A few lawyers referred to new DOJ instructions or quotas for immigration court judges to move cases and relayed that such accelerated movement would inevitably have a negative effect on due process and respondents' ability to put forth complicated aggravated felony cases.

Matter of Castro-Tum, a May 2018 decision by the attorney general to no longer administratively close cases—and to "recalendar" (reopen) those that were already administratively closed—was also seen as harmful for people with aggravated felony convictions. Administrative closure was encouraged by the Obama administration, as a way that DHS could use their prosecutorial discretion to indefinitely suspend cases where it was clear that the respondent was not a danger to the community.[43] Before *Castro-Tum*, a few interviewees identified administrative closure as a single way that discretion could play a role in cases based on aggravated felonies. After *Castro-Tum*, attorneys immediately began to feel its effects.

Cori mentioned that her client with a 1995 drug sale "would have been an excellent candidate for prosecutorial discretion" if it were not for the recent change. Working at one of the major NYIFUP legal providers and interviewed soon after the decision, she went on to say, "In the last week, we and other providers have seen a waterfall of motions to recalendar cases like that, and I bet a lot of them are people with aggravated felonies." Raina described an aggravated felony case of hers that had recently been recalendared. It had been administratively closed "because the underlying offense was a single offense that was kind of bogus." Brianna spoke of two elderly clients of hers—pastors from Trinidad—whose cases had recently been reopened years after being administratively closed. She was shocked that these clients had been recalendared despite having no criminal records and felt it did not bode well for people who did.

While most lawyers did feel tangible effects of the Trump administration's push for intensified enforcement and increased deportation, a few were keen to point out that most of what went on under Trump was a continuation of former presidents' policies. Nora, a public defender and immigration advocate for eight years, said, "Trump has definitely empowered ICE to do more, to be more brazen. But them grabbing our clients and taking them from court is not new, it's just they're doing it with a little bit more frequency now and little bit more boldness." She felt that people began paying more attention with Trump as president, and remarked, "Hopefully they don't go to sleep after we elect a Democrat." Alisa, a public immigration lawyer for six years, concurred, saying,

> Yes, the immigration climate is horrible right now, but I think that some-thing that's important to highlight is the fact that a lot of things that are outraging people right now have been going on for years. They went on under Obama. . . . It's great that people are finally waking up and realizing this, but this is not anything new. People have been dying in detention centers for the longest . . . people have been separated from family. . . . This was happening under other presidents and no one really seemed to care, and now people are really outraged.

Advocates have largely been disappointed by what is seen as a lack of progressive movement on immigration reforms during the first year of the Biden administration—though several Trump-era changes, includ-ing the barring of administrative closure in *Castro-Tum*, have been reversed.[44] Still, the Biden administration's stated focus on immigrants with serious crimes, and especially aggravated felonies, makes it so these cases remain unlikely candidates for this form of relief. As stated by Emily, "It really frustrates me when everyone is like, 'Oh Trump, Trump, Trump, he's so awful.' He's enforcing the laws that Congress passed under the Clinton administration, who's a Democrat." She said Congress needs to "do their job" and pass major immigration legislation, referring to the fact that there has not been meaningful reform since 1996—reform that created the laws that expanded and harshened the aggravated felony category.

Conclusion

The existing legal literature on the aggravated felony emphasizes the expansiveness of the category, the severity of its effects on immigrants' chances for relief from deportation, and its effects on due process in immigration law.[45] Based on ethnographic observation of court pro-ceedings and interviews with legal actors, this chapter has described the everyday impacts of the aggravated felony in immigration court with particular attention to these three areas. Findings show that not only is the category expansive as written—including many crimes that do not live up to the harsh "aggravated felony" label—but it is also overused by ICE in immigration proceedings, further extending its reach. In terms of severity, the aggravated-felony-related bars to immigration relief that are written into the law are shown to be even harsher once the difficulty of attaining available forms of relief is made clear. Major problems include the lack of judicial discretion—despite many cases involving old crimes or LPRs, or both—and the difficulty of arguing for relief under the CAT, which is the only form of relief many people convicted of aggravated felonies are eligible for.

Following the literature, interview participants described nonguaranteed legal representation and mandatory detention without bail to be the most important impediments to due process related to the aggravated felony. Other due process issues that came up in this research included inconsistent translation, videoconferencing in lieu of bringing detained individuals to court, intimidation, and wrongful deportation. Finally, while participants reported intensified enforcement and a widespread sentiment of fear under the Trump administration, most changes were seen as not particularly affecting immigrants with aggravated felonies, and several interviewees emphasized that the biggest problems for this population have been ongoing since 1996.

Even in the "best case scenario" of New York City—a sanctuary city with guaranteed legal representation for detained immigrants facing deportation—the harsh and expansive effects of the aggravated felony are evident. While immigrant detention and removal are technically administrative processes, their clear punitive force is only intensified by the indiscriminate yet decisive outcomes of the aggravated felony category. That the category's massive enlargement and intensification by the immigration reforms of 1996 has not received a serious legislative reevaluation since speaks to the strength of the moral panic described in the previous chapter, as well as the ongoing salience of the "criminal alien" folk devil. Further, the endurance of the aggravated felony demonstrates the power of criminal justice system markers in our society and demonstrates the historic and ongoing marginalization of the societal groups who the designation most deeply affects.

3

Marking the "Bad Immigrant"

Crimmigration Enforcement and Inequality

I feel like there has been more of a recognition in recent years that there are racial disparities in policing, but there's not this recognition in immigration law—I mean most immigrants I'm representing who are indigent are immigrants of color, and they're in these same communities, or being policed in a way, that we sort of acknowledge, from the criminal side, how disproportionately it affects people of color, but then somehow, well, the immigration system is completely unforgiving.
—Pia, immigration lawyer

People have often differentiated between "good immigrants" and "bad immigrants," that false dichotomy which ignores the role of racial bias in the criminal justice system.
—George, immigration lawyer and advocate

To fully grasp the everyday impacts of the aggravated felony, we must consider the category's place at the juncture between criminal and immigration law—the "crimmigration" nexus. While "crimmigration law" is also used more generally to designate expertise and practices involving the two legal bodies, the concept's original theoretical formulation emphasizes how the entangling of the two systems grows the punitive and exclusionary potential of both.[1] Scholars of crimmigration have demonstrated the increased intertwining of immigration and criminal legal systems over the past thirty years—a period during which both legal bodies have become more expansive and retributive—resulting in a variety of negative outcomes for immigrants ensnared at the crux of the two in the United States and other migrant-receiving countries around the world.[2] The aggravated felony—an immigration law category that is based on unfounded beliefs about immigrant criminality, born out of drug policy, and triggered by criminal convictions—is a key example of the crimmigration nexus. From the enforcement strategies through which migrants are apprehended in the first place to the convictions that permanently mark them as subjects for mandatory detention and almost certain removal, criminal justice system processes, decisions, and categorizations play a central role in aggravated-felony-based deportation. Yet despite a long-standing and extensive body of research documenting the pervasive disparities, racial and otherwise, plaguing US systems of criminal justice[3]—and an increasing societal attention to such inequality—official criminal markers are continually taken at face value and used to invoke enhanced punishment and exclusion in the immigration context.

Drawing on interviews with lawyers and ethnographic observation of New York City's detained immigration court, this chapter examines the way that well-documented inequities existing in the criminal justice system are reproduced through the crimmigration processes surrounding the aggravated felony. The chapter begins by recounting the fundamental role played by local law enforcement in the apprehension of noncitizens targeted for aggravated-felony-based deportation, even in a "sanctuary city" where municipal police are officially banned from engaging in immigration enforcement. This is followed by a discussion of the ongoing contributions of the US War on Drugs to aggravated-felony-based deportation despite wider societal movement away from drug criminalization and prohibition. Next, qualitative research findings are complemented by existing statistics to demonstrate how the aggravated felony's entrenchment in the criminal legal system, combined with its harsh immigration outcomes, results in the reification and enhancement of systemic inequality. Findings demonstrate the role of the aggravated felony (and the crimmigration processes and policies that surround it) in the reproduction and rationalization of pervasive disparities around race, class, gender, and citizenship status—funneling marginalized Black and Latinx noncitizens in particular toward deportation. I argue that immigration court processes and outcomes related to the aggravated felony reinforce a racialized "good immigrant, bad immigrant" binary, which erases structural considerations and stigmatizes noncitizens with criminal records—thus rationalizing their mistreatment and exclusion. In doing so, the immigration system crystallizes socially constructed designations of who is "criminal," further validating criminal justice system practices and categorizations that have been shown to produce and uphold oppressive social hierarchies.

Crimmigration in a Sanctuary City

An important development that has emerged alongside the contemporary union of criminal law and immigration law is the devolution of immigration law enforcement to local jurisdictions.[4] For most of US history, immigration was almost exclusively a federal matter, and local law enforcement bodies dealt mainly with matters of criminal law. Over the past thirty years—an era characterized by the neoliberal "hollowing out" of the federal government—the emergence of policies that increasingly link deportation to criminal offenses and the growing treatment of unauthorized immigration itself as a criminal offense have further contributed to an influx in local police departments' attention to immigration enforcement.[5] Federal immigration policies put in place during the past few decades—like 287(g) agreements and the Secure Communities program—officially place immigration enforcement capabilities into the hands of local police departments.[6]

Created by the Illegal Immigration Reform and Immigrant Responsibility Act (IIRIRA) of 1996, the 287(g) program allows state, county, and municipal police officers to be trained and deputized as immigration agents by Immigration and Customs Enforcement (ICE), capable of making immigration arrests, taking custody of immigrants for federal authorities, and transporting immigration prisoners. Secure Communities is a program established in 2008 that facilitates the sharing of arrest data and fingerprints between local law enforcement agencies and ICE. Widely used in the early years of the Obama administration, both programs received intense criticism, most notably for their stirring distrust in law enforcement and government authorities among immigrant communities, as well as their enabling of racial profiling and other civil rights abuses.[7] In the face of this criticism, both programs went through overhauls in the later years of the Obama presidency; the 287(g) program was diluted and minimized between 2009 and 2016, and

Secure Communities was replaced by the Priority Enforcement Program (PEP) in 2015. In January 2017, in his first executive orders as president, Trump called for the expansion of 287(g) and the reinstatement of Secure Communities—terminating PEP.[8] According to ICE, by 2018, the agency had 287(g) agreements in place with seventy-eight law enforcement agencies across twenty states and the program had "trained and certified more than 1,514 state and local officers to enforce immigration law."[9] At the same time, Secure Communities had been reimplemented in "all 3,181 jurisdictions within 50 states, the District of Columbia, and five U.S. Territories" and, since its reinstatement in 2017, had resulted in the deportation of "more than 43,000 convicted criminal aliens"— also according to ICE.[10] (While President Biden distanced himself rhetorically from these enforcement programs throughout his campaign against Trump, at the time of writing this book, he had yet to discontinue the use of 287[g] or Secure Communities, despite the urging of activists.[11])

To this point, scholars have largely examined "crimmigration" enforcement in locales where there are official relationships between immigration and local law enforcement.[12] This research expands on a nascent body of work that has looked at the continued role of immigration enforcement in locales with protective, "sanctuary" policies.[13] As a so-called sanctuary city, New York City law prohibits municipal law enforcement from participating in or cooperating with 287(g) agreements. Furthermore, the city refuses to honor detainers—requests by ICE to hold noncitizens charged or convicted of crimes, usually based on information received through Secure Communities—and has removed ICE's official access to Rikers Island, the city's largest jail. Still, these measures only do so much for the city's immigrants, and especially for those with potential aggravated felonies. ICE and other immigration enforcement entities can still make arrests throughout the city, and they have increasingly targeted noncitizens in NYC in their homes and communities.[14] Furthermore, the standing refusal to honor detainer requests only applies to those who have not been convicted of an expansive list of 170 "serious" crimes[15]—many of which would be considered aggravated felonies—although, even for those with a conviction for one of these crimes, ICE must present a judicial warrant. Additionally, the city maintains its participation in Secure Communities.

Local criminal justice system involvement in immigration enforcement came up in various ways throughout my research. While NYC law enforcement is prohibited from engaging in immigration enforcement, this was not the case throughout the rest of the state at the time of study. Without a local immigration court, noncitizens detained by ICE in the nearby Long Island suburbs are sent to NYC immigration courts and are eligible to be represented by the public lawyers provided by the city through the New York Immigrant Family Unity Project (NYIFUP). Lawyers often spoke of the intense involvement of Long Island law enforcement with ICE throughout my interviews and ethnography, and though a federal judge has since ruled that New York State law enforcement agencies can no longer hold immigrants for purposes of immigration enforcement without a judicial warrant,[16] a 2020 report by the New York Immigration Council shows continued cooperation with immigration authorities by Long Island police departments.[17] In one hearing I observed, Nicole, a public immigration lawyer for fifteen years, expressed confusion at the DHS lawyer's contradicting assertions that her client had refused to speak with ICE, yet that he had told them his immigration status. Nicole declared that Suffolk County (Long Island) jail officers are asking the immigration status of inmates, and she requested that the internal policies of the jail in question be subpoenaed. Later, she told me that her organization was "seeing a substantial amount of cases coming out of Suffolk County" at the time, which she thought had "a lot to do with Suffolk County's law enforcement cooperation with ICE." In this case, after being picked up for a traffic stop, her client—who was already on probation—had been brought to jail. There, as the client eventually relayed to Nicole, officers hit him with a flashlight to get him to disclose his immigration status.

Jane, a public immigration attorney for ten years, said she represented "a lot of Long Island residents" and said that the area jails "still have agreements with ICE where they just turn people over directly." Elena, a public immigration lawyer with eight years of experience, also worked with many clients from Long Island, and she emphasized the amount of racial profiling that went on in the local policing of immigrants— especially related to gang enforcement. Lisa, who had twenty years of experience as an immigration attorney and advocate throughout New York State, confirmed that local law enforcement passing migrants directly over to ICE—as has become common practice throughout the country—raises concerns in terms of constitutional protections against racial profiling. She said, "Now, [racial] profiling could exist without anyone ever finding out about it because they could stop the individual and give them right over to immigration authorities. And nobody would know about it because the due process protections that would kick in if that person was criminally charged wouldn't because we're in civil immigration court." Here, we see how crimmigration processes erode the effectiveness of existing protections in criminal law as well as immigration law.

Instated in 2014 at the urging of community-based advocates, NYC's detainer policy prevents municipal jails and police from honoring ICE requests to hold non-citizens released from criminal custody. While several lawyers saw this as an important win for local immigrants with criminal records, most agreed that ICE had evolved their apprehension methods to the new circumstances. Nora, a public defender for eight years, thought that the detainer policy was an important victory, saying, "It's better, in a sense because we've challenged the law on that." However, she went on to qualify, "But obviously things are much worse in that we've seen like a 900 percent increase of ICE just grabbing our clients after their case is called, because they don't need an ICE detainer or an ICE hold. They physically just grab them anytime they are coming and going from their court dates. So that's the negative. They're finding another way." Soon after Trump came into office, ICE became particularly vocal about their displeasure with the NYC's detainer policy, issuing detainers they knew would be turned down in an attempt to shame the city for releasing "dangerous criminals."[18] The agency also turned to more intrusive and expansive enforcement methods and blamed them on NYC's refusal to honor detainers.[19] ICE arrests in NYC increased by 88 percent in between fiscal year 2016 and fiscal year 2018—the third-highest increase of arrests of all ICE field offices.[20] This included what was actually a 1,700 percent increase in ICE arrests and attempted arrests at New York State courthouses between January 2017 and December 2018.[21] When asked how her NYC-based clients with aggravated felonies usually entered deportation proceedings, Jane explained, "Because NYC Department of Corrections will not turn people over directly to ICE, those people are mostly arrested at their homes, at their jobs, and with increasing frequency at court dates, or outside of courts in NYC." Although some participants expressed hope at the possibility of court arrests being outlawed as well—a federal court win that eventually came in June of 2020[22]—the sentiment usually came with assurances that ICE would find other ways to target and pick up noncitizens with potentially deportable convictions, especially aggravated felonies.

For many affected immigrants, these pickups come years after the conviction that makes them deportable. Pia, a public immigration attorney with seven years of experience, spoke of one client who was arrested by ICE in a home raid a few years after his aggravated felony conviction. She said, "By the time I met him . . . he had been serving probation for three years, doing great on probation, was almost done. For a single offense, you know, in twenty-something years in the country." She went on to explain that this type of unexpected raid years after the original conviction is "quite common," saying, "And that's three years later. I've had clients ten, fifteen, twenty years later picked up." Although the source of ICE's information is not always clear, several lawyers referred to "lists" of immigrants with criminal records the agency would reference in order to pinpoint targets for raids. Lawyers also described how various forms of contact with law enforcement or immigration authorities trigger searches of Secure Communities–era digitized databases that could identify a long-past aggravated felony. Sometimes unknowing lawful permanent residents (LPRs) come onto the radar of Customs and Border Protection (CBP) when reentering the country after a trip or trying to renew their green card or apply for citizenship—without any hint they may actually be deportable. Raina, a public immigration lawyer for eight years, found these cases particularly upsetting, saying, "They are actually trying to avail themselves of the immigration laws, and then ICE is like, 'Well, you know what? You're subject to mandatory detention. We're going to detain you and basically destroy your life.'"

Still, based on my interviews, one of the most common ways that immigrants are picked up for aggravated felonies—in the context of NYC's detainer laws—is through further interaction with the criminal justice system. Pamela, an immigration attorney with three years of experience, explained that although immigrants with very old aggravated felonies are often picked up at the airport or through other contact with immigration officials, for those that are more recent, it is usually because they are "picked up for a new criminal thing, so then there's a referral for that." Oren, a public defender and immigration lawyer for fifteen years, saw this process also affecting those with old offenses, especially offenses they might not even know are aggravated felonies. He said, "You could be a permanent resident, have a very old conviction that has significant immigration consequences, and you haven't traveled outside of the United States. You haven't been in jail recently or whatever. You haven't applied for citizenship or something. You haven't come to immigration's attention. You get arrested for a new offense, even if it's something minor, then suddenly that offense is flagged during the fingerprinting." Laura, a public immigration lawyer for three years, also felt this was the typical route. She said, "That's very common for our clients. They get picked up on something. When they're fingerprinted at a precinct, ICE gets a data dump that has their address on it, and will often have their immigration status, if they have some sort of status, or ever had it, and then will list their crimes, and if it's an aggravated felony, they'll pick them up." Under Secure Communities, states send fingerprints and information of arrestees to immigration authorities, including those taken in "sanctuary" cities like New York. Laura explained that the city "doesn't have any control over that, because those fingerprints also go to other federal databases, like the FBI and other federal agencies, and they're all connected." Therefore, even in a municipality with a variety of policies put in place to prevent connections between immigration and criminal law enforcement, the criminal justice system plays a crucial role in the apprehension of immigrants for aggravated felony convictions.

Beyond facilitating ICE's identification and detainment of noncitizens with previous convictions that may be aggravated felonies, state and local criminal legal systems also play an obvious role in the original arrests and convictions that make such immigrants deportable. In fact, the limits on judicial discretion inherent to the forms of relief available to migrants facing aggravated-felony-based deportation—as described in the previous chapter—makes it so that criminal legal system decisions are fundamental to the sorting of which noncitizens will be subject the category's harsh outcomes. Since the thirty-five offense types listed in the Immigration and Nationality Act's (INA) definition of the aggravated felony can each be applied to a plethora of state-level offenses, differing criminal laws in each state play a vital role in dictating what might be considered an aggravated felony.

As Zara—an immigration attorney, criminal defender, and advocate with ten years of experience—asserted, "You definitely see these geographic disparities in who is going to be labeled an aggravated felony, but the conduct is no different." Since included misdemeanors require a one-year sentence to constitute an aggravated felony, the impact of sentencing laws was commonly mentioned by lawyers. As an example, Zara explained that while you can get probation without a suspended sentence in New York State, "in a place like Georgia, the criminal procedure law requires a suspended sentence to accompany probation. That's the only way you can get probation. And usually twelve months is the minimum suspended sentence that you get, so if you commit shoplifting in Georgia, and you just get this probationary sentence that's accompanied by a suspended sentence . . . then that's an aggravated felony." Laura, who had previously practiced law in Louisiana, spoke to the harsh sentencing she had seen in their criminal legal system, including an example of a twenty-years-to-life sentence she had witnessed—for the possession of drug paraphernalia containing heroin residue. When I confirmed that while the various immigration courts make a difference, the criminal justice climates and laws that exist in each state or city are key as well, Laura responded, "Yeah, and I would imagine those are pretty correlated too," implying that harsher immigration courts may also be in places with harsher criminal laws. Beyond variation from state to state, more general criminal justice system priorities also play a noticeable role in determining who falls into the aggravated felony dragnet—none more than the War on Drugs.

Deportation and Drug Prohibition

The emergence and development of the aggravated felony was distinctly related to the ramping up of US War on Drugs during the 1980s and 1990s. Despite widespread criticism of the harmful and disproportionate effects of harsh drug laws and enforcement, US drug prohibition and its associated mass incarceration have continued to thrive into the twentieth century.[23] Still, there is some evidence that contemporary drug policy is moving away from the long-standing War on Drugs and toward a more humanistic approach. The widespread decriminalization and legalization of cannabis,[24] public health and harm reduction initiatives in response to the opioid epidemic,[25] and moderate movement away from mass incarceration[26] all seem to indicate an erosion of the punitive prerogatives that have characterized US drug policy and enforcement for more than forty years. Yet, when it comes to law enforcement priorities at the federal, state, and international level, drug offenses remain high on the list—especially for immigrants and other people of color.[27] The idea that migrants are "bringing drugs" into the United States was a key rhetorical tool of Trump's crusade against immigration,[28] and between 2012 and 2017, one out of every five immigrants deported based on Secure Communities data had a nonviolent drug offense as their most serious conviction.[29] Furthermore, the United States continues to fight a futile War on Drugs in Latin America and the Caribbean, which has only exacerbated problems of narco-cartel control and violence.[30]

In my interviews, drugs came up time and time again as the most common type of aggravated felony convictions. Victor—a criminal defender, immigration lawyer, and advocate for almost thirty years—explained, how in the 1980s and 1990s, "A lot of the [War on Drugs] carried over to the immigration area, and a lot of the cases where the federal agency was trying to apply the harsh consequences of the aggravated felony label were in the drug area." May, a NYIFUP attorney for five years, said drug-related offenses are "the most frequent ones we see here." Nicole concurred, saying, "drugs is always the most common. It's very common for our clients to at least have a controlled substance offense." Although she qualified that they were not always aggravated felonies, Nicole said, "It's rare that I have a client that has no controlled substance offense." Marco—a public immigration lawyer for five years at a NYIFUP provider as well as various other locations throughout the country—said, "Absolutely the biggest one is drug-related offenses. Drug-related offenses are the most common aggravated felony that our clients have." When I asked if that was true "across all the places you've worked?" he replied, "Across Arizona, Massachusetts, New York, it's the most common offense."

Some lawyers expressed discontent with outcomes they saw as disproportionate to many of the crimes that are grouped together by the aggravated felony category. Despite their central and original place in the category, drug crimes were often cited as not deserving the harsh outcomes the aggravated felony entails. To underscore this point, several lawyers referred to minor drug crimes they had seen charged as aggravated felonies. Jackie, an immigration lawyer and advocate with eight years of experience, reported that in the early 2000s, "the government was using a theory that upon your second marijuana [possession] conviction, you became an aggravated felon." This has since changed due to the work of lawyers and advocates (as will be discussed in the following chapters). Still, even with trafficking included and not possession, many small-time drug offenses are classified as aggravated felonies. As mentioned in chapter 2, Marco relayed how even "sharing . . . molly with friends" could be considered a drug trafficking aggravated felony, and Seth, a public defender and immigration lawyer for close to twenty-five years, reported how "selling ten dollars' worth of crack" could also make you deportable based on the category. Victor explained how state-level differences in drug-related offense types played a role in minor crimes being defined as aggravated felonies: "Even the offenses that are trafficking offenses, or at least labeled as trafficking offenses by criminal law jurisdictions, some of those offenses are quite minor as well. . . . Here in New York, the lower-level sale offenses can be pretty minor offenses where people receive pretty minor sentences, but even under the now narrower scope of the drug trafficking aggravated felony grounds, a lot of people are still being subjected to mandatory deportation under that ground." After stating that, in her experience, aggravated felonies were usually drug related, Pamela mentioned that she found DHS charging the small-scale sale of marijuana as a drug trafficking aggravated felony to be "pretty egregious."

The particular demonization of drug crimes in the criminal legal system helps in creating the aggravated felony convictions that make people deportable. While some district attorneys (DAs) have proved amenable to working with immigrants and their lawyers to achieve immigration-safe convictions—a strategy that will be discussed in the next chapter—special DAs focused on drug enforcement were seen as being particularly resistant to this tactic. The Office of the Special Narcotics Prosecutor of the City of New York, created by the New York State Legislature in 1971, is "the only prosecutorial agency in the country exclusively dedicated to the investigation and prosecution of narcotics felonies."[31] Nora, a public defender for eight years, explained how DAs in this office were especially harsh and unforgiving in the cases of immigrants who had committed drug crimes. She explained, "Special narcotics is the worst DAs office because they're separate from the Manhattan DAs in a separate prosecutors' office. It's a special narcotics prosecutors' office. And they are just the dirtiest, the worst kind of cops, the worst kind of DAs." Nora went on to describe the case of one client charged for a drug felony where she was confronted by a DA from this office, who "had no empathy for my client whatsoever. She didn't care if he'd be deported." The prosecutor

> blatantly told me my client did not have the right to stay in the country when I tried to tell her that he's not a citizen, he can't plead to the drug felony [or] he'll get deported . . . that he doesn't have family where he is from. And she basically just told me that he didn't have a right to stay here, because he "came to somebody else's house and broke their rules."

Options intended to lessen the punitive effects of drug war policies—like drug court—are not helpful for immigrants with potential aggravated felonies, since these alternatives usually require an original plea and sentence that are vacated once you have completed drug treatment and other requirements. Nora explained, "Immigration doesn't recognize the vacatur of any plea. They're just like, 'Well, you pled originally. You still pled to it, and that's what we go by.'" In the case described above, Nora said that while she tried for several alternatives, including drug court, the man was eventually forced to take a plea that rendered him deportable.

The impossibility of avoiding aggravated-felony-based deportation through drug court or other rehabilitative alternatives to incarceration is an example of how the criminalization of addiction—and mental health more generally—is exacerbated through the immigration system. Oren, a public defender and immigration lawyer for fifteen years, said, "If you're a public defender for any period of time you realize—and I'm just speaking loosely, but—probably two-thirds of clients, a little bit higher, are in the criminal justice system because they're mentally ill, they have a drug problem or they have an alcohol problem." Kayla—a social worker who had spent three years working on criminal and immigration cases at a NYIFUP provider—said how under the current administration, driving under the influence (DUI) and possession of an illegal substance are the two most frequent convictions that ICE makes arrests based on. She felt this spoke to the criminalization of addiction and found it problematic that "One DUI now lands you in this criminal danger zone." In a June 2018 op-ed, Kristin Anderson, an immigration social worker at Bronx Defenders—one of the three NYIFUP legal providers—explains how "The opioid epidemic and our broken immigration system . . . are more connected than many think." Despite the white face of the modern opioid crisis, Anderson reminds readers that "Black and brown people face just as great a risk of addiction and a greater risk of being criminalized for it," and writes, "Among immigrants, the punishment for addiction can mean deportation."[32]

Several lawyers remarked on the disconnect between continuously harsh immigration consequences for drug offenses amid the simultaneous easing of drug prohibition for white Americans. Zara said, "As the War on Drugs is slowly ending, we haven't seen that parallel shift when it comes to immigration." She explained how even conservative politicians have joined the consensus that "mass incarceration was bad, prison sentences should be lowered, and these drug sentences [should be reexamined]," yet "we haven't seen that shift when it comes to immigrants." Zara explained how the federal immigration consequences of cannabis use remain, even in states that have legalized its recreational use:

> In those very states, like Colorado, Washington, California, USCIS [US Customs and Immigration Services] affirmatively, any time someone applies for an immigration benefit, for a green card or for naturalization, they go out of their way to ask them about marijuana use, even if nothing is flagged in their application, specifically looking for ways—and people will often—you know it's not illegal in these states to use medical marijuana or to use a small amount of marijuana, but that's still a ground to deny benefits and to deport people.

Marco felt deportations based on marijuana convictions were especially ironic in a context where decriminalization and legalization are spreading throughout the country. He remarked that while these laws allow drug use for white citizens, for the Black and Brown people in prison and being deported, the new laws "don't seem to apply to them."

Furthermore, not only are immigrants subject to harsher punishment for drug-related offenses, but they also disproportionally experience structural conditions in the United States that make drug convictions more likely—such as poverty and overpolicing. Cori, a public immigration lawyer with ten years of experience, said she saw more controlled substance aggravated felonies than other types, a proportion she attributed to the War on Drugs and the fact that many of her clients "are from low-income communities that have historically had problems with the crack epidemic." She said, "More of my clients have controlled substance convictions, or potentially still have controlled substance addictions, or are in over-policed neighborhoods where if you did have any sort of drugs, or even if you didn't, you're getting stopped and frisked and everyone is getting picked up." With War on Drugs enforcement prerogatives now in place for decades, their impact was seen in cases of aggravated felonies both new and old. Cally, a public immigration lawyer with four years of experience, described a particularly painful case where a client from the Caribbean had been deported based on a drug offense that he was convicted of more than a decade before. She said this client "was an LPR, a green card holder, since he was a teenager." When he was young, "by his own admission—I mean his family was really poor, and the friends in his neighborhood had nicer things and there was a way to get those things, and that way was selling drugs. And so he did that." In his early twenties, Cally's client was arrested for possession of cocaine with intent to sell. After serving time for the offense, he turned his life around. As Cally explained, "He had two US citizen kids, he had fully rehabilitated. He's lovely. He wasn't a threat to the community at all." Still, more than ten years after the original offense, the man was deported based on his aggravated felony conviction, with no chance for relief.

As poverty and overpolicing in the United States serve to exacerbate addiction, incentivize dealing, and intensify enforcement in the communities that many immigrants live in, the regional arms of the War on Drugs also contribute to the likelihood of drug-based aggravated felony deportations. These connections—which are contextualized by a long history of US imperial intrusion in Latin America, as well as intensified

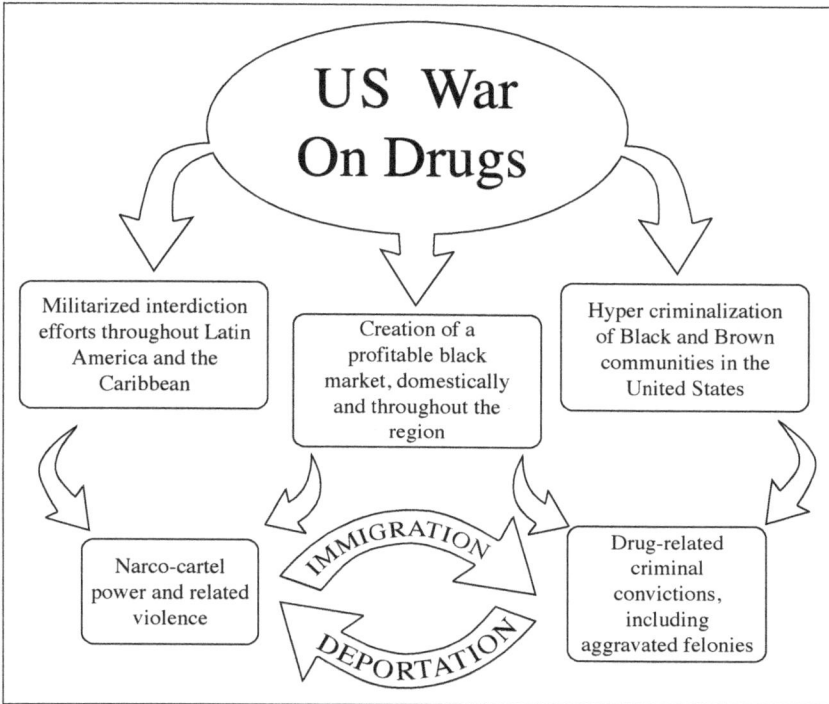

Figure 3.1. The US War on Drugs and Streams of Immigration and Deportation.

inequality in the neoliberal era[33]—are depicted in figure 3.1. While the domestic enforcement of the War on Drugs has disproportionately focused on poor Black and Latinx communities, internationally, the focus has been on the interdiction of drugs from Latin America and the Caribbean.[34] These policies have failed to curtail domestic drug use or stem the flow of drugs into the country. Instead, US drug prohibition—combined with a consistent demand for illicit substances—has served to exacerbate drug-related violence and cartel power in Latin America and the Caribbean, creating important push factors for immigration.[35]

As migrants flee cartels and other drug-related violence in Latin America and the Caribbean, there are some who are forced to transport drugs into the United States, or who agree to do so in order to afford the expensive journey across the border.[36] Although the violent and coercive power of transnational drug cartels is well-known, immigration court has little sympathy for the reasons why people "chose" to smuggle drugs into the country—indicative of the reigning neoliberal ethos of personal responsibility. Even if it was the only option, once in immigration proceedings based on a drug trafficking aggravated felony, immigrants are mandatorily detained and cut off from most forms of relief from deportation. In the previous chapter, I described the example of Marco's client, who was caught with drugs at the border in a last-ditch effort to flee violence in his home country and start a new life in the United States. Marco explained that while the man would otherwise be eligible for asylum, with the drug trafficking aggravated felony, he will most likely be deported. While cases like this came up a few times in my research, cross-border drug-smuggling cases are most often adjudicated in states on the US-Mexico border. After illegal entry and reentry, drug-related offenses are the second most common category of criminal charges among those prosecuted in that region.[37] This category is exemplified by unauthorized migrant "backpackers" who carry drugs into the United States on their backs—often under violent coercion or as part of the crossing fees required by coyotes and cartels.[38]

While it has become more common for unauthorized migrants smuggling insignificant amounts of marijuana to be charged with misdemeanors in order to expedite their removal, those who have additional criminal histories or other aggravating factors are intentionally given sentences of thirteen months, in order to trigger an aggravated felony.[39] Even unaccompanied minors, described as "prime targets for cartels and gangs on the border"[40]—are not safe from the effects of the aggravated felony. Marco, who had previously practiced immigration law near the border in Arizona, explained how his organization would often see the cases of children forced to bring drugs into the country by narco-traffickers—minors who were then processed through the federal criminal legal system and convicted of drug trafficking convictions. Marco explained how, "Those same children were often people who were seeking asylum in the country, and the only reason why they were caught in this trafficking scheme is because they wanted to make it to the other side of the border." He found the application of the aggravated felony category in these situations as particularly unjust, saying, "And now . . . people who needed our protection end up being in deportation proceedings, mandatory detention, mandatory deportation, and sent back often to the same territories where the narco-traffickers control."

In addition to first-time offenders coerced into bringing drugs across the border, some immigrants also end up in US deportation proceedings after previous involvement with the drug trade in their home countries. In certain parts of Latin America and the Caribbean—including Mexico and the Dominican Republic—narco-cartel power, weak or corrupt public institutions, and widespread poverty result in little economic opportunity outside of the drug trade.[41] Once someone is convicted of a drug trafficking aggravated felony, these country conditions are usually only considered in terms of relief under the Convention against Torture (CAT)—the only relief available to most people charged with an aggravated felony—and cannot be viewed as mitigating factors for drug trade involvement. As described in the previous chapter, even those who cooperate with US drug-enforcement authorities and help indict drug organization higher-ups have trouble meeting the burden of evidence for relief under CAT despite rampant threats and obvious danger.

The Reproduction of Criminal Justice System Inequality

To better understand the aggravated felony's role in perpetuating inequality, this book draws on seminal research on socioeconomic inequities inherent in the criminal justice system,[42] as well as the more contemporary contributions of critical theorists studying race, law, and migration.[43] From these fields, I form two presuppositions: that law and social control measures (1) play an important role in the social construction of race, and (2) contribute to the production and reification of various forms of inequality. As seen in the historical development of the aggravated felony—detailed in chapter 1—the societal treatment of Black and Latinx immigrants has long been entwined with a racialized image of the "criminal alien." This socially constructed trope was revitalized during the latter decades of the twentieth century in support of a punitive policy turn in the areas of drugs, crime, and migration—with the decidedly unequal impacts of resultant social control frameworks further reifying the racist stereotypes on which they were based. Yet while there has been a good deal of research into race-based inequalities in mass incarceration and the War on Drugs, there has been less attention paid to the reproduction of these inequalities through processes of criminal deportation.[44] This section examines the role of the aggravated felony in the continued replication of race-based criminal justice system inequalities—as well as those related to socioeconomic status, gender, nationality, and mental health.

Keeping in mind the socially constructed nature of race, critical scholars have examined the way in which racial categorizations and hierarchies are produced and reinforced through the law and its enforcement. In recent decades, researchers have emphasized the extreme racial inequities emerging from the criminal justice system policies and processes implemented during the punitive turn of the 1980s and 1990s[45]—with a focus on racial disproportionality in the War on Drugs.[46] Despite widespread reporting on resulting inequality—and state-level moves toward decarceration and drug decriminalization[47]—the mechanisms and outcomes observed by these scholars remain. The United States continues to imprison more people than any other country in the world—with one in five prisoners incarcerated based on drug convictions[48]—and those racialized as Black and Hispanic are more likely to experience negative outcomes at every level of the criminal justice system.[49] Therefore, migrants placed in these racial and ethnic categories are disadvantaged throughout the criminal justice system processes that generate an aggravated felony conviction. With 40 percent of the United States' foreign-born population hailing from Mexico, Central America, and South America, immigrants are likely to be racialized as Hispanic or Latinx.[50] Noncitizens are also affected by the targeting and discrimination experienced by Black populations in the United State due to racial diversity in Latin America combined with the fact that immigrants from the Caribbean and Sub-Saharan Africa account for 10 percent and 5 percent of the foreign-born population, respectively.[51] In fact, the Black immigrant population increased fivefold from 1980 to 2016, and in 2022, one out of every ten Black individuals in the United States is foreign-born.[52]

From police targeting and higher arrest rates to harsher sentencing and disproportionate incarceration, Black and Latinx immigrants are more likely to be affected throughout the criminal legal system processes that produce aggravated felony convictions—making it so the pool of noncitizens subject to the severe outcomes of this category disproportionately draws from these groups. Racial profiling is an ongoing problem in policing[53]—a problem that is particularly conspicuous in relation to Black and Latinx youth and adolescents, who are more likely than white youth to be the focus of policing priorities.[54] Surveys show Black and Latinx drivers as more likely to be searched and arrested at traffic stops—the most common police interaction in the United States.[55] Official arrest rates are most often tracked by race, but not ethnicity, so nationwide numbers for Latinx people are not clear.[56] Yet Black communities in the United States experience arrests at 2.5 times the rate of their white counterparts, and Black and Latinx arrestees have been found more likely to be placed in pretrial detention than white arrestees.[57]

Furthermore, Black adults are 5.9 times more likely to be incarcerated than white adults, Latinx adults are 3.1 times more likely, and while Black and Latinx people comprise 29 percent of the US population, they account for 57 percent of the US prison population.[58] These populations are also more likely to receive mandatory minimum sentences—in 2011, 31 percent of mandatory minimum sentences were given to Black offenders, and 38 percent to Latinx offenders. Drug prohibition plays an important role in these discrepancies. Despite consistent reports showing that people of different races use drugs at similar rates, Black people—13 percent of the US population—account for 29 percent of drug arrests and 40 percent of those incarcerated based on drug law violations. Latinx people, who comprise 18 percent of the US population, account for 38 percent of people incarcerated in federal prisons for drug offenses and 47 percent of drug-related federal court cases.[59] Even in states that have legalized recreational cannabis use, such as Colorado and Washington—where police traffic stops and searches have decreased greatly—Black and Latinx drivers are still far more likely to be searched for drugs than their white counterparts.[60]

These racial disparities are compounded by related criminal justice system discrepancies around class, gender, and citizenship status. Incarcerated people of all races have lower preincarceration incomes than nonincarcerated people, and incarcerated people are highly concentrated at the lowest end of the national income distribution.[61] Low-income Black and Latinx neighborhoods are the common focus of aggressive policing tactics, and young men in particular from these neighborhoods are consistently targeted by the police.[62] LGBTQ individuals from these communities are also disproportionately criminalized.[63] Research has found that noncitizens convicted of drug offenses are more likely to be sentenced to prison than citizens convicted of drug offenses are—with young, noncitizen Latino men and undocumented immigrants of all genders among the groups that are most likely to receive prison sentences upon conviction.[64] Furthermore, as discussed, criminal legal system checks on racial profiling are sidestepped in the cases of immigrants, as local law enforcement agencies increasingly turn noncitizen arrestees directly over to immigration authorities who are not beholden to regulations against profiling.[65]

In NYC—like many large cities across the country—the entrenchment of "broken windows" policing throughout the 1990s, and its dominance in the decades since, has facilitated the aggressive use of police stops and misdemeanor arrests in Black and Latinx neighborhoods.[66] The "broken windows" theory, introduced by conservative criminologists George Kelling and James Wilson in 1982, rests on the assertion that the existence of neighborhood "disorder"—such as broken windows—leads to further disorder and eventually violent crime.[67] This theory spurred a trend in law enforcement, also known as "order maintenance" or "quality of life" policing, focused on punishing minor offenses with the aim of cutting off more serious crime before it begins.[68] Closely tied to racialized panics about drugs that emerged in the same era, the rise of broken windows policing was buttressed by a criminalized image of young Black and Latino men.[69]

Upon the adoption of broken windows theory by the New York Police Department (NYPD), misdemeanor arrests in the city rose drastically, from 187,385 arrests in 1994—the year order maintenance policing was first implemented under mayor Rudolph Giuliani and NYPD commissioner William Bratton—to 292,219 arrests in 2010.[70] Such arrests can lead to dire consequences for noncitizens. As the previous chapter explained, misdemeanor convictions are often categorized as aggravated felonies. Perhaps more importantly, misdemeanor arrests and other low-level contact with the criminal justice system are a key route through which immigrants with old aggravated felony convictions reemerge on ICE's radar. Increased arrests in NYC were largely concentrated in low-income Black and Latinx neighborhoods and were often accomplished through the controversial (and now-defunct) "stop-and-frisk" program. Police stops increased six-fold between the mid-1990s and ten years later in the mid-2000s, with a heavy focus on marijuana possession and an intensely disproportionate focus on Black and Latino men.[71] Research has also found higher numbers of police stops and arrests in NYC neighborhoods with greater proportions of immigrants—despite lower crime rates in these same areas.[72] The city's LGBTQ populations were also particularly impacted by stop-and-frisk, with trans and nonbinary people in Jackson Heights, a LatinX immigrant enclave, reporting disproportionate stops and harassment by police.[73]

Although street stops decreased dramatically after the NYPD's use of stop-and-frisk was ordered unconstitutional by a federal judge in 2013, over 80 percent of NYPD stops in 2015 still targeted Black or Latinx "suspects."[74] Furthermore, while yearly misdemeanor arrests have decreased since 2010, they still account for about 70 percent of total NYPD arrests. Over 85 percent of people arrested for misdemeanors from 2015 through 2020 were Black or Latinx—with drug arrests playing an important role.[75] In 2019, there were over twenty-one thousand drug arrests and violations in the city—the majority for low-level possession or paraphernalia charges—84 percent of which targeted Black and Latinx New Yorkers.[76] Though marijuana arrests have plummeted since the state legalized recreational use in 2021, the NYPD officially reinvigorated their focus on "quality of life" offenses more generally in early 2022—part of the antiviolence initiatives of first-year mayor Eric Adams, a former officer in the department. Advocates have decried this revival of "broken windows" policing for its inevitable impacts on communities of color, arguing that rising violence in the city would be better combated by addressing underfunded social services and increased poverty.[77]

The targeted policing experienced by Black and Latinx New Yorkers has significant impacts for the city's foreign-born communities of color. Aggressive policing practices reminiscent of stop-and-frisk continually target neighborhoods with large populations of African and Caribbean immigrants.[78] One NYPD precinct in a predominantly Caribbean neighborhood received media attention in 2020 after images of collectible coins sold in an office fundraiser were discovered. The coins identify the area as "Fort Jah" (a play on the Rastafarian word for God) and include imagery of the Jamaican flag with the caption, "For those who like hunting there is no hunting like the hunting of man." Another version, depicting a Black man surrounded by armed NYPD officers, was inscribed, "LET THE GAMES BEGIN."[79] Cases of police brutality against Black and Latinx immigrants have long plagued the city, with the 1992 murder of Amadou Diallou—a twenty-three-year-old Guinean student shot forty-one times by four plainclothes officers while reaching for his wallet—as a high-profile example and a catalyst for ongoing struggles against police brutality and racial discrimination.[80] Other prominent cases include the 1992 killing of Jose Garcia, a twenty-three-year-old Dominican immigrant shot in a Washington Heights building lobby, and the 2012 murder of Ramarley Brown, an eighteen-year-old Jamaican immigrant shot in the apartment where he lived with his grandmother in the Bronx—both at the hands of NYPD officers acting on suspicion of minor drug crimes.[81] The overpolicing of Black and Latinx populations is replicated in the city's Long Island suburbs—also served by NYC immigration courts—with people of color in the area experiencing arrest at close to five times the rate of white people.[82] This problem is exacerbated by racial profiling during immigration enforcement efforts by local police, which has been an ongoing problem in Long Island's Suffolk County.[83]

Another criminal justice system disparity that came up in this research was that related to mental health. With the neoliberal decline in public services and concurrent expansion of crime control, the past forty years have seen extreme increases in the use of criminal justice intervention in relation to mental health. Police are largely the first responders to mental health calls, often leading to arrests of and violence toward those who are mentally ill.[84] Researchers have found that at least 16 percent of those incarcerated in the United States suffer from severe mental illness, and that inmates with mental illness outnumber those remaining in state mental hospitals by more than tenfold—leading some to refer to prisons and jails as the country's "new asylums."[85] The overconcentration of mental illness in the criminal justice system is exacerbated by racial and socioeconomic stratification, as underserved and marginalized communities are the most likely to be funneled into jails or prisons rather than receiving expensive private care.[86] Mental health treatment in prisons has been found to be sporadic at best and, at worst, the cause of further psychological harm.[87]

In NYC, the NYPD receives over 165,000 calls a year to deal with "emotionally disturbed persons." Public criticism has mounted regarding the department's violent response to such calls, including the killing of ten mentally ill individuals between 2015 and 2018.[88] As the nation's third-largest jail, NYC's Rikers Island is "by default, one of the largest mental-health facilities in the country."[89] In 2017, 43 percent of those imprisoned at the Rikers jail complex had a mental illness. Firsthand accounts and investigative reporting have shown rampant abuse, maltreatment, and violence at the facility.[90] In addition to conditions of incarceration, mental health inequities in the criminal legal system are exacerbated by cooccurring substance abuse disorders, the overpolicing and criminalization experienced by communities of color, immigrants' premigration trauma, and immigrants' fears of deportation and experiences of detention in the United States.[91] Therefore, Black and Latinx noncitizens in NYC and surrounding areas—especially young men, LGBTQ people, people with mental health and substance abuse issues, and people living in low-income areas and immigrant enclaves—are disproportionately more likely to experience the low-level criminal justice system contact that may ultimately result in aggravated-felony-based deportation.

Not surprisingly, immigration detention and deportation—and especially criminal deportation—are characterized by the same disparities that plague the US system of criminal justice. Migrants from Latin America experience the vast majority of deportations—over 90 percent—despite only comprising about half of the US foreign-born population.[92] Latinx noncitizens are also more likely to be deported if they live in areas with high-immigrant populations.[93] Black immigrants (who may also be Latinx) account for about 10 percent of the foreign-born population, and only 7 percent of the noncitizen population, yet comprise more than 10 percent of all immigrants placed in deportation proceedings—and they comprise more than 20 percent of those who face removal based on criminal convictions.[94] Ninety-two percent of all deportations are of men, despite women accounting for close to half of the unauthorized immigrant population,[95] and trans and gender nonconforming migrants are particularly susceptible to detention, deportation, and discriminatory treatment.[96] Furthermore, not only are deportees from the United States often sent back to regions of extreme poverty, they are also disproportionately removed from communities that are under- and precariously employed in the United States—in line with analyses by critical scholars who theorize deportation as a tool used by the neoliberal state to control a vulnerable economic surplus population.[97] Finally, it is estimated that 15 percent of people in immigration detention experience mental illness, and people in these circumstances are regularly tried and deported without representation or other due process safeguards in the immigration court system.[98]

Although national trends in the gender and socioeconomic status of deported migrants largely hold in the populations deported from NYC, the city presents an interesting example in terms of the racial and ethnic breakdown of deportees. Due to NYC's large population of undocumented Chinese immigrants, the majority of deportations from the city's immigration courts are to China. Yet, when one looks only at Varick Street—the detained immigration court where criminal deportations are most likely to occur—Chinese immigrants are deported at insignificant rates, far lower than those of immigrants from Mexico, Central America, the Dominican Republic, and Jamaica.[99] While I do not claim a representative sample, all but one of the removal hearings I observed at Varick Street were of Latino men, and my interviewees often referred to a concentration of immigrants from Latin America and the Caribbean among their experience with aggravated felonies—with specific mentions of the Dominican Republic and Jamaica.[100] (Pamela shrugged, saying, "A lot of my clients are just Jamaican men who live in Brooklyn"—implying that this is a group targeted by the NYPD.) Similar patterns are reflected in existing research on the role of systemic racism in the disproportional criminalization and deportation of migrants from the Caribbean.[101]

Several interviewees connected such disparities to existing inequalities in the criminal legal system. Raina explained, "Because of the intersections between the criminal [system] and the immigration system, what you see is there's a disproportional representation of Black and Brown folks, and whatever is being criminalized there, is reflected in immigration proceedings." She went on to emphasize the role of drug prohibition in this process—saying, "A lot of drug crimes come under that." Others commented on the role of socioeconomic status. May, for example, explained the difficulties people with aggravated felonies face in securing legal representation by stating, "People who are targeted by the criminal justice system are people who are low income and can't afford private attorneys." This point is underscored by the fact that the majority of cases at the Varick Street detained immigration court qualify for NYIFUP representation, which has an income limit of 200 percent of the federal poverty rate[102]—totaling $29,160 per year for a single-person household in 2023.

Although most interviewees did not mention race or class specifically, there was definite acknowledgment of the role played by criminal justice targeting of "certain" communities in shaping the characteristics of those facing deportation for aggravated felonies. Cecy, a public immigration attorney with two years of experience, said, "It's just the overpolicing of certain neighborhoods and it kind of leads to them falling eventually into deportation proceedings." Laura concurred, "Working at a public defender's office in New York City I can really see how certain things are—it's basically some things in New York are legal for certain people and not legal for other people." As mentioned, drug policing was referenced as being particularly problematic, considering the different levels of criminalization across racial and socioeconomic lines. Cori asked, "How did these people come into contact with the criminal justice system in the first place? What was going on in their communities that led them to potentially have any involvement in controlled substance use or distribution?" She continued, "Some of my clients maintain that they were just in the wrong place at the right time, and I believe them." When I mentioned the wide use of drugs among different sectors of the population, Cori responded, "Right, and only certain people are actually getting in trouble for it."

The concentration of mentally ill people in the criminal justice—and subsequently, immigration—system was mentioned by several interviewees. Laura explained,

> The other thing with aggravated felonies is I think the swath of people who they encompass include a ton of people who have pretty serious mental illnesses, or substance trauma issues, but it all goes under the mental illness category, which is partially just reflective of our criminal system, but it's also partially like, who are we deporting as a country? And it's often the people who are the most vulnerable and need the most support and help and that's often the people who do have these aggravated felony convictions.

Marco agreed, saying, "A lot of the clients that we serve who have aggravated felony convictions are people that are mentally ill." He believed these are mainly people who "slipped through cracks in the criminal justice system" and "never got some sort of assessment to see whether they were competent to be prosecuted for the crimes that they allegedly committed." He described the case of a mentally ill client who was a green card holder who had lived in the United States for thirty years before being deported for an old aggravated felony. The original conviction was a controlled substance felony in New York State, "possession with intent to sell"—a conviction the client did not remember or understand due to his mental illness. Marco went on to say, "You fast forward to 2016, he was very, very mentally ill, and he ended up going into a bodega in New York because he was hungry and he stole two boxes of sharp cheddar cheese and salami, and that brought him to the attention of the immigration authorities." The man was mandatorily detained and deported to the Dominican Republic.

Through these cases and many others like them, we see the influence of existing criminal legal system inequalities in deportation proceedings related to aggravated felonies. Groups that are targeted by the criminal justice system—such as Black and Latinx men and gender nonconforming people, residents of low-income communities and immigrant enclaves, and the mentally ill—are disproportionately detained and deported. For those with aggravated felonies, intensely punitive outcomes dictated by immigration law (such as mandatory imprisonment without bail and permanent banishment from the country) often come after noncitizens have already served their criminal sentence—amplifying existing inequalities in punishment through the immigration system. Yet, despite my participants' acknowledgment of these processes, existing criminal justice system inequalities are largely brushed aside by the immigration system in favor of an essentialist "good immigrant, bad immigrant" binary.

The "Good Immigrant, Bad Immigrant" Binary

The harsh and unequal effects of the aggravated felony category are upheld by a "good immigrant, bad immigrant" binary that paints migrants with criminal records as a monolithic group undeserving of residence, citizenship, or even basic rights. The aggravated felony supports this false dichotomy by making it so that noncitizens with convictions that fall within the category are not tried as unique cases with a variety of individual and structural factors that should be taken into account, but rather, as "aggravated felons"—serious criminals who must be detained and removed with as little chance for legal relief as is allowable by international law. Anchored by the racialized "criminal alien" folk devil that has held such influence throughout the history of this country, this binary rationalizes the funneling of Black and Latinx immigrants to deportation while further crystalizing the importance of criminal legal system markers that uphold broader social hierarchies. This reflects a central tenet of critical race theory which is interested in the way apparently race-neutral laws reproduce racial inequality.[103] In my research, the "good immigrant, bad immigrant" binary was evident in the criminalizing treatment of detained migrants fighting their aggravated felony cases, participants' descriptions of the development of the aggravated felony and related policies, and the erasure of structural considerations in aggravated felony cases.

In contrast to the larger NYC immigration court at Federal Plaza, where noncitizens attend their hearings in their own clothes and arrive—at least somewhat—of their own free will, the atmosphere at the Varick Street detained court clearly denotes the criminalized status of "respondents" facing deportation. While ICE was still physically bringing detained immigrants to the court for their hearings—a practice since eschewed for "tele-video" appearances[104]—they were transported by ICE directly from detention early in the morning of their hearings. While at Varick Street, detained migrants were confined in unseen holding cells throughout the day, except for during their hearings, when they were brought into the courtrooms in their orange prison jumpsuits, shackled at the wrists, waist, and sometimes ankles, and accompanied by privately contracted security. In my interviews, lawyers referred to this environment as criminalizing and harmful to the cases of their clients. May described how on the nondetained docket at Federal Plaza, respondents "have the chance to show that [they're] a normal person." She went on to say, "It's very hard at the detained court for judges to look at you and see you in your orange jumpsuit and your shackles to your waist and to your hands, and see you as someone who is fully human, as sad and fucked up as that is." This problem was intensified by the switch to tele-video appearances in June 2018—which resulted in respondents being forced to testify from the jails themselves, their humanity reduced to the grainy image of a prisoner wearing a jumpsuit on a television screen.

The criminalization of detained respondents at Varick Street is also seen in the racialized "othering" of immigrants and their families. In the courtroom, the difference between respondents and other actors is denoted not only by their orange jumpsuits, but also by the language barriers described in the previous chapter. Individuals facing deportation are prohibited from talking to each other or anyone else while in the courtroom—except when questions are directed at them through their translator—and they often appear isolated and uncomprehending, due to incomplete translation throughout most of the proceedings. On one occasion, when two detained migrants from Latin America were seated on the side bench of the courtroom, one whispered to the other— apparently asking a question about translation—only to be immediately silenced and separated by security. In another hearing, when the two young daughters of a shackled respondent from Guatemala attempted to approach him during a break in proceedings, guards acted just as swiftly, shutting down the interaction before it could even begin.

This was not the only time I observed the dehumanizing treatment directed at migrants facing deportation extend to their families. As a white woman and a graduate student, I was mostly treated with respect by court staffers. While family members—almost exclusively Latinx—were rushed into and out of the court and scolded for knocking on the door separating the waiting rooms and the courtrooms, I was often asked if I was a lawyer and was ushered in to observe court with very few questions. One morning, while going through security in the lobby of the government building that the Varick Street court is housed in, the guard made a point of having me pass through as an "employee," while a line of Latinx families—also there for immigration court—were of course afforded no special treatment. In the courtroom, I was likely to be moved to the front row when family was placed behind, and one judge who had previously ejected the young child of a respondent for playing with a phone, excused me with a friendly smile when a DHS attorney accused me of having looked at my phone myself—an act that was forbidden of visitors but routine among lawyers, clerks, and security.

The criminalizing environment at Varick Street was underscored by the treatment of respondents and their cases by DHS lawyers and immigration court judges. DHS trial attorneys would regularly inject references to, and questions about, respondents' criminal records throughout proceedings—even when not relevant—despite these records already being well-documented in case materials. While defense attorneys usually object to this practice, they are often overruled. In one case, after asking about the respondent's criminal history during questioning related to a fear-based Convention against Torture (CAT) claim, the DHS attorney posited that the man's testimony was not credible and that his documents may be fabricated—because of his criminal history as well as political corruption in the Dominican Republic, his home country.

The view that respondents with aggravated felony convictions were innately criminal—"bad immigrants" who could not be trusted—was made explicit in bond hearings, when judges had to determine whether detained migrants were "flight risks" or "dangers to the community," or both. Criminal history is often the most important factor in this determination—with the aggravated felony designation lending an instant seriousness to one's crimes. Jon explained that this was especially the case "if the crime involved violence of any kind, or actual drug sales." In these instances, he said, "You're going to have a tough time convincing a judge to let you out." Despite it being the government's burden to prove that a detained individual is a danger to the community, Jon explained, "A lot of judges sort of say, 'Well, I consider drug dealing to be a dangerous offense.'" In my own observations, I saw decade-old low-level drug crimes cited as "serious criminal records" that made respondents too likely to flee or cause danger to be offered bail—despite obvious rehabilitation since. Raina found these cases particularly incongruous, saying, "If you've already released them into the community, and there's been nothing happening, then you can't actually prove risk of flight or danger."

Although relief hearings in cases with aggravated felony convictions were most likely concerned with fear-based relief under CAT—which is not a discretionary form of relief—lawyers felt that judges' personal feelings about respondents still came into play in their decisions. Seth described how immigrants with aggravated felony convictions often face a double bias in these situations. He explained how, due to the limited nature of CAT relief (described in the previous chapter), creative claims that do not neatly fit are met with "skeptical" judges, who "think that you're just trying to bootstrap yourself into a form of relief." In addition, he explained that noncitizens with aggravated felony convictions were less likely to be "sympathetic characters," a view expressed by a few other participants as well. Seth said, "Judges don't generally like people with aggravated felonies, and particularly if they're very unpleasant violent crimes, or serious drug crimes, the judge is—many judges are probably not going to want to have you around in the country." This view is backed up by research demonstrating the pivotal role of criminal history in guiding immigration judge decisions.[105] Although not the only factor that comes into play, the aggravated felony category works as a marker clearly delineating "bad immigrants" who are dangerous and deserving of deportation.

Beyond the increased stigma placed on noncitizens facing aggravated-felony-based deportation, participants also confirmed the importance of the "good immigrant, bad immigrant" binary in the politics surrounding the category's development (detailed in chapter 1), as well as those regarding related local policies. Lisa explained how advocates who had been part of the negotiation process for the IIRIRA of 1996—the law that expanded and harshened the aggravated felony category more than any other—had since admitted "giving away certain things to get other things," meaning throwing immigrants with criminal records under the bus to negotiate benefits for "good immigrants." George, a lawyer and advocate with thirty years of experience in immigration law, characterized the "good immigrant, bad immigrant" binary as "that false dichotomy which ignores the role of racial bias in the criminal justice system" and described the harsh consequences it has had for noncitizen criminal offenders—a group who, "from an advocacy point of view," has "historically always [been] sold out." The resultant system maintains a face of neutrality while relying on criminal legal markers known to be unequal.

Lawyers found the indiscriminate grouping of immigrants based on criminal convictions especially problematic in the context of growing acknowledgment of injustice in the criminal legal system. Pia said that while there has been more recognition in recent years of "racial disparities in policing," she does not see that recognition extended to immigration law, despite the fact that, "Most immigrants I'm representing who are indigent are immigrants of color, and they're in these same communities, or being policed in a way, that we sort of acknowledge, from the criminal side, how disproportionately it affects people of color." Pia went on to say,

> I don't think the immigration system has come to as sophisticated of a conversation around understanding that policing in the immigration context. You know I think very often the rhetoric goes to . . . "good versus bad immigrant," and there's a real lack of significant understanding of the policing that goes on, the communities that people are embarking from, that people may in fact have criminal convictions, but what is that about? And where is it coming from? Versus "good versus bad."

Marco agreed, saying that "the US has in many ways understood the flaws that our criminal justice systems have, but it's interesting how the public opinion is still not able to translate that understanding of the criminal justice system as not fair to the immigration arena." He explained how the same politicians who say that we need criminal system reform go on to talk about immigrants and say "We're only going to take the ones who haven't committed a crime" even though the crimes arose in that same flawed system.

Immigration court is largely unconcerned with the structural disadvantages that contextualize migrants' criminal convictions—especially in aggravated felony cases, where limits on relief make home country conditions more relevant than individual-level factors related to someone's history in the United States, as detailed in the previous chapter. Cori explained that there is room for such structural considerations in immigration court "if you're not dealing with an aggravated felony," but because of the lack of discretion in aggravated felony cases, "It's so black and white that, like, it doesn't really matter what the circumstances were surrounding that individual's conviction." Cori described a recent case, which was not an aggravated felony, of a client whose deportable conviction stemmed from him having been "caught up in the crack epidemic" decades ago. As part of his legal team, Cori "presented his story in the context of what was happening to communities of color in Brooklyn in that time period in the late '80s and the early '90s, and how it wasn't just his life, but his entire community was being destroyed by this. And I think we were able to put together a compelling narrative and we ultimately won in that case, but that's because he didn't have an aggravated felony." Emily said that immigration judges, at Varick Street in particular, "are super resistant to having, maybe you could call it sociological context to our clients' criminal history." She said that while judges are willing to consider certain individual-level factors, "If you try to put evidence like, 'Oh, they live in this community in the Bronx, this precinct that has incredibly high levels of police brutality and overpolicing'—that, no one will even look at or consider as valid evidence."

Structural inequities impacting deportation are additionally obfuscated by systemic decisions on what data is worth keeping. Statistical portraits of groups most affected by deportation—like those described in the previous section—are largely pieced together through the work of scholars and advocates, often after securing data through Freedom of Information Act (FOIA) requests to ICE. Even once data is apprehended, there is the fact that immigration authorities simply do not record information on demographic variables like race and socioeconomic status, leaving researchers to make their own estimations of these inequalities based on the data provided. The racial diversity of Latin America and the Caribbean, where the majority of those detained and deported originate, makes this particularly complicated—contributing to the erasure of Black immigrants from these regions. Systematically recorded in the criminal justice context, race and socioeconomic status are key measures of inequality used by researchers, advocates, and policymakers to better understand the effects of various policies and processes. By counting immigrants by nationality, but not race or socioeconomic status, in statistics on the detention and deportation of noncitizens, the immigration system further disguises its role in the reproduction of these pervasive inequities.

Although immigration judges are sometimes more willing to consider mental health—an individual-level characteristic—than structural dynamics around race and class, immigration law processes offer even fewer protections to mentally ill respondents than the criminal legal system offers. As mentioned, it has been estimated that 15 percent of migrants in ICE detention are mentally ill[106]—similar to the rates seen in the criminally incarcerated population. Yet evaluations of "competency to stand trial," which have been called "the most significant mental health inquiry pursued in the system of criminal law," have not been the norm in immigration court, despite their institutionalization in the criminal system.[107] A precedential decision issued by the Board of Immigration Appeals (BIA) in the 2011 *Matter of M-A-M* created guidelines to be used by immigration judges when hearing cases with mental competency issues and made it so judges could administratively close cases "where no procedural safeguards would ensure a fair hearing."[108] Former Trump administration attorney general Jeff Sessions's barring of administrative closure in the 2018 *Matter of Castro-Tum* (described in the previous chapter) halted this practice and reopened the deportation cases of many mentally ill noncitizens. Though Biden administration attorney general Merrick Garland reversed *Castro-Tum* in 2021, reinstating administrative closure, the administration's stated focus on deporting immigrants with aggravated felonies makes it unclear how many cases in this category will be affected.

In my interviews, several participants spoke to the difficulties of mentally ill immigrants facing deportation for aggravated felonies. Marco described how noncitizens affected by mental illness who "slip through cracks in the criminal justice system" are met with laws that are "incredibly harsh towards people in that condition" and "offer very little protection for people who are mentally ill in immigration court." He explained, "The amount of things an immigration judge can do when they have somebody who is mentally incompetent are so few, so little, that people who are mentally ill end up being deported for the same aggravated felony convictions, even though they may not be competent to proceed in immigration court." Laura expressed disappointment at Sessions having "taken aim at" *M-A-M* hearings, which she described as "competency hearings so you can get safeguards for your clients." She lamented, "But that's like gone, and I don't think those people should be—it's just such a huge waste of resources that we're detaining them or having deportation proceedings for them." Seth explained the difficulty of arguing for CAT relief (the only form of relief available for many with aggravated felonies) based on mental illness, despite the difficulties faced by mentally ill people deported to countries that often lack adequate mental health services, where deportees are already stigmatized.[109] Yet, as explained in the previous chapter, to win a CAT claim one must prove that a deportee would be subjected to torture, either at the instigation of, or with the acquiescence of, government authorities acting within their official capacity. Seth explained,

> So you have to show that somehow either . . . mobs of enraged people are going to know that they have state protection if they attack mentally ill people, or that state-sponsored doctors or nurses in state-run facilities are going to subject your client to treatment or lack of treatment that meets the definition of torture, and so you're kind of out at the far edges of what's likely to be defined as torture with the acquiescence or at the instigation of the government.

Marco elaborated on his previously mentioned case in which a mentally ill client was detained by immigration enforcement for an old aggravated felony after he was caught stealing cheddar cheese and salami from a bodega. Marco explained how he had applied for CAT relief, while also arguing that his client was incompetent to proceed "because he couldn't even completely make any sort of assistance for us, his immigration attorneys." Marco went on, "We were not able to find out anything about his past . . . because he was incompetent." Still, "The immigration judge ended up finding that he was ineligible for CAT because he did not meet the really, really high burden of proof, and he's in the Dominican Republic now." Once again, the aggravated felony worked as a master status demarcating the line between "good immigrant" and "bad immigrant" while erasing the complex inequalities that affect criminal convictions.

Conclusion

Previous chapters have illustrated the role of a racialized moral panic linking immigrants with drugs and crime in the enactment, development, and sustenance of the aggravated felony category despite its expansive reach, severe outcomes, and limits on due process under immigration law. Yet to understand the continued function of the aggravated felony in perpetuating existing inequality and funneling already criminalized populations toward deportation, an examination of the part played by the criminal legal system is vital. While previous research has examined a variety of "crimmigration" connections,[110] there has been limited study of criminal-conviction-based deportation in particular. Further, while crimmigration enforcement has primarily been examined in the context of official agreements between immigration and local law enforcement,[111] this chapter examines the role of criminal justice enforcement in a "sanctuary" city where such agreements are prohibited. Even when countered by sanctuary policies like those of NYC, findings show criminal legal system practices and policies—especially those rooted in the War on Drugs—to be vital in the apprehension and detention of immigrants with aggravated felony convictions. The United States has long been an epicenter of "tough-on-crime" criminal justice enforcement, and the extreme inequities that plague the broader US system of mass incarceration—disparities around race, class, gender, immigration status, and mental health—are mirrored in the targeted "broken windows" policing of poor communities of color in NYC and its suburbs. In this context, the aggravated felony designation serves to further stigmatize and punish marginalized groups while inducing the enhanced sanctions of mandatory detention and likely deportation.

A key example of the crimmigration nexus—a contemporary intertwining that increases state potential to punish and exclude[112]—the aggravated felony is an important mechanism through which the immigration system enforces a "good immigrant, bad immigrant" binary while ignoring the structural realities of the criminal justice system and amplifying inequality. Findings show how immigration court processes surrounding the aggravated felony serve to "other," dehumanize, and re-criminalize affected noncitizens, reinforcing a racialized image of the undeserving "bad immigrant," and rationalizing the severe and unequal outcomes of the category. By taking the aggravated felony designation at face value and disallowing further interrogation of the unequal circumstances that produce criminal convictions, immigration courts maintain a face of neutrality while upholding existing inequities and intensifying punishment by adding mandatory detention and lifetime banishment onto criminal sentences already served. Therefore, just as inequality in the criminal justice system works to uphold white supremacy, class hierarchies, and a demonized image of Black and Latino young men,[113] the aggravated felony targets already criminalized populations and further excludes them through forced removal from the country. Thus, a criminal legal system long shown to be a mainstay of institutionalized racism is given further authority by guiding immigration outcomes, even in "sanctuary cities" where criminal law enforcement is officially forbidden from engaging in immigration enforcement.

4

The "Wild West of Law"

Tactics of Legal Resistance

You know, I don't know if it's completely correct to say that aggravated felony cases are less likely to have relief. It kind of depends on a more holistic look at the case, because there are still quite a lot of aggravated felony cases that do have relief, and have strong cases for relief.
—Nicole, immigration lawyer

I always look for any ability to contest the aggravated felony ground, just because it's so devastating. . . . That's really at the heart of what I'm doing the most with in terms of aggravated felonies . . . arguing, "No, you're wrong ICE, this is actually not an aggravated felony." And then the question is, how do we make those arguments? What are those arguments?
—Jon, immigration lawyer

This is a time, post-*Mathis*, *Moncrieffe*, and *Mellouli* when only your creativity can limit you in challenging deportability.
—Legal expert and panelist at immigration law conference

Beginning this research after reviewing the foreboding legal scholarship on the aggravated felony—in the context of a presidential administration committed to the further harshening of immigration policy—I did not expect to hear much optimism from interview participants with regard to immigration court outcomes for noncitizens convicted of aggravated felonies. Despite the extreme examples of aggravated felony cases relayed to me throughout this research, the severity and breadth of the category's results were not altogether shocking. The unequal outcomes of the law—while pronounced—were also not wholly unexpected considering the racial hierarchies and stereotypes that supported the category's historical evolution, as well as the intense disparities inherent to systems of policing and mass incarceration in the United States. Yet, in addition to accounts of the law's harsh and unequal use, this research also quickly revealed creative legal responses that have emerged since the aggravated felony's extreme expansion in the immigration reforms of 1996. This chapter draws from interviews with lawyers and legal workers; ethnographic observation of immigration court proceedings, legal conferences, and workshops; and archival analysis of existing court decisions to describe strategies of "legal resistance" that have developed in response to the aggravated felony.

I begin by defining my concept of "legal resistance" and demonstrating its applicability to observed responses. Next, I describe resistance to the aggravated felony that works within immigration law, through the injection of sociological considerations into claims for relief from deportation under the Convention against Torture (CAT) and the use of the "categorical approach" to contest deportability. This is followed by a discussion of strategies that work within criminal law, such as preconviction advisement on immigration-safe pleas and postconviction appeals to expunge existing aggravated felonies. Findings contribute to law and society debates on the role of law as a tool for social change and expand the concept of "crimmigration"—which has mostly been used to describe the punitive results of the intertwining of criminal and immigration law—by demonstrating ways that this intertwining also creates opportunities for resistance.

Conceptualizing Legal Resistance

Scholars of law and society have long debated the potency of law as a tool of resistance. Drawing on Gramsci, the field has been mindful of the hegemonic power of law—its ability to shape our lives while simultaneously naturalizing its own effects.[1] While this distinct power often works to uphold social hierarchies, researchers have also documented the harnessing of law's hegemonic power by groups resisting oppression and stratification.[2] Furthermore, while some have argued that the legal focus on individuals and "rights talk" can distract from broader movements for social change,[3] others have refuted these criticisms and contended that law and the invoking of legal rights are tools that—in the right context—can be successfully used toward social justice.[4] One way that movements harness the power of rights and the law is through partnerships with lawyers who are motivated to use their skills toward specific ends. Scholarship on "cause lawyering" describes the motives and ethical quandaries for lawyers turned advocates, as well as the difficulties and strategies of using law toward social justice.[5] The related concept of "legal activism" has been used to describe the work of movement-oriented practitioners specifically concerned with changing the law by winning precedential judicial decisions.[6] Researchers have emphasized the role of cause lawyering and legal activism in the broader fight for immigrant rights.[7]

Still, while legal scholars have described strategies and arguments used to avoid removal based on an aggravated felony or other deportable conviction,[8] social scientific research on "crimmigration" has largely focused on the punitive and oppressive outcomes of intersections between the criminal and immigration systems. Less attention has been paid to the tools and processes—also specific to these intersections— that function to ameliorate punishment or enhance due process.[9] In this research, interviews and observation emphasized a variety of legal strategies that draw on the interwoven intricacies of the immigration and criminal systems and are employed by noncitizens and their lawyers when facing aggravated-felony-based deportation. To describe these strategies—which work through the everyday practice of law to address its perceived limitations—I use the concept of "legal resistance," which overlaps with, yet is different from, cause lawyering, which largely refers to cases of "movement lawyers," activists in their own right, who use their legal skills to forward the goals of specific social movements.[10] Such strategies upset the breadth and definitiveness of the aggravated felony category in ways that are distinctly legal and are executed in the cases of individual immigrants through processes of both the immigration and criminal systems. While at times undertaken with an aim of amending the law or restricting its application, these strategies are not the exclusive work of activist lawyers with an eye toward social change, but rather, are professionally accepted best practices for lawyers representing immigrants with criminal records. Furthermore, though critical of the aggravated felony and the criminalization-to-deportation pipeline of which it is a part, participants largely framed the use of these tactics in terms of their professional duty to represent individual clients, protect established legal rights, and advance the law in ways beneficial to society.

The American Immigration Lawyers Association (AILA), a national organization of over fifteen thousand immigration lawyers and professors, cites the American Bar Association in their in-depth practice manual to describe the multilayered role of every lawyer as a "representative of clients, a public citizen having special responsibility for the quality of justice, and a member of a learned profession."[11] Attorneys are expected to be capable and conscientious in their representation and advisement of individual clients, as exemplified in the legal ideal of "zealous client-centered advocacy"—which scholars have deemed particularly urgent in the practice of immigration law.[12] At the same time, they must also seek to improve law and justice and work to advance legal knowledge and the legal profession in the public interest. As explained by J.C. Salyer, immigration lawyer turned anthropologist, "While most lawyers in their day-to-day practice do not reflect on their jurisprudential philosophy, their experiences and stories reflect a belief that a legal system should provide sufficient flexibility to consider context, to recognize the myriad factors that differentiate one case from the other, and to allow an adjudicator to apply a modicum of 'common sense.'"[13] All these concerns were evident in my participants description of the legal strategies employed in cases of aggravated-felony-based deportability.

Though these legal responses to the aggravated felony may lead to outcomes with important implications for future cases, lawyers were clear in their responsibility to individual clients. Speaking of one recent precedential case she had worked on, Raina, a public defender and immigration lawyer with six years of experience, maintained that the goal was to make sure the client got relief, with future implications a secondary benefit. She said, "I mean, often there is a convergence of interests, right? Where it's like, if we can get [this person] relief, then we can get so many people who are convicted of the same offense relief as well. But most of the time it's just making sure that the client can get access to relief that they want to get." Other lawyers confirmed the prioritization of representing individual clients over broader considerations. Seth, a public immigration lawyer with almost twenty-five years of experience, explained the emergence of innovative legal arguments in aggravated felony proceedings as necessity entailed by "the job of lawyers" to fit the facts of a particular case to legal options for relief. He explained, "Lawyers have had to become very creative in pushing the law in directions that perhaps it wasn't initially intended for, but it's the only relief you have left for your clients." With relation to aggravated felony cases in particular, Jon, a private criminal and immigration lawyer for six years, described a feeling of responsibility to provide quality representation to individual clients, even those who are otherwise maligned for their criminal convictions. Referencing a client who was convicted of "attempted possession of child pornography," he explained how upon hearing about the case, his wife responded, "I understand you have to do what you have to do, but who cares about this guy?" Jon said, "Well, I care. I care about his daughter. I care about his wife. I care about his niece and his nephew. I care about the people who fall on the ground when we leave the court, because the person they know is a loving, beautiful father and uncle. They haven't been able to see him, and he's gonna get deported."

Participants also described innovative legal responses to the aggravated felony category as contextualized by a responsibility to improve the law and ensure the proper administration of justice. Naomi, a public immigration lawyer for ten years, explained that while legal responses to the aggravated felony may be seen as resistance against deportation more broadly, they should also be understood in the context of lawyers' commitment to justice, saying, "Even if you're kind of like, 'We don't want to get involved in what those decisions are, those are for immigration judges,' it's also just sort of a statement about basic due process rights and basic fairness. Even if you're not actively trying to stop the deportation machine, you're just trying to make sure things are fair for people." Lisa, an immigration lawyer and educator with over twenty years of experience, exemplified this perspective, explaining, "I'm not making a judgment call about the folks or the offenses. I think more my interest in this area is more so on the due process . . . what's fair." She said, "for me, it's not about who gets deported or not. That's not my decision. It's about due process." Jackie, a public immigration lawyer and advocate for eight years, explained how a case early in her career, where a client would have been eligible for discretionary relief from deportation if it wasn't for the aggravated felony bar, inspired her further work in crimmigration law. She said, "It was a very emotional and difficult case to do, but also I had a real sense of this is what's right and what's fair under any kind of approximation of what law means." Jane, a public immigration lawyer for eight years, expressed concerns with the administration of laws related to aggravated felonies and argued they need to be changed, saying, "We need legislative reform. I don't believe that the way that the law is being applied by the current administration and by the prosecutors carrying out the administration's policies on a daily basis is consistent with what Congress intended."

In terms of advancing the law and regulating their profession in the public interest, some lawyers framed the emergence of creative legal strategies as part of a broader responsibility to the communities they represent. Such concern for serving the public was particularly poignant for NYIFUP lawyers working in public defense offices.[14] Sheria, a public immigration lawyer for four years, said,

> One of the reasons I love it here is because I guarantee if it's an issue affecting poor immigrant New Yorkers, someone at [this organization] knows how to do it. So we're not scared of the law not being on someone's side, because we figure something out. . . . When you're a public defender at your core, then you're like, "No, I'm not going to accept that this is the law and then therefore, we have to lay down and let this person be deported back to a place that they don't even know, or where it is dangerous for them to be there."

Yet, it is important to note that not all lawyers who engage in strategies of legal resistance do so with such lofty aims. Greg, a private immigration lawyer for eight years, explained his focus on crimmigration law as it being the most "interesting" area in the field. He said, "I find the cases where people have been convicted of serious crimes the most challenging, the most complex, and so that's what I've chosen to focus on." Still, most participants spoke to the value of building legal knowledge through individual cases or expressed a need to evolve legal interpretations. George, a lawyer, educator, and advocate with thirty years of immigration law experience, explained the importance of "developing theories for people, both individual and in terms of larger litigation to defeat or narrow the interpretation [of the aggravated felony]."

Thus, while largely focused on professional aims of representing their clients, protecting justice, and advancing their field in the public interest, legal resistance was also framed in response to what immigration lawyers deem to be the overreach or overapplication of the law. Though many of the strategies described evolved throughout the past two decades or beyond, several participants spoke of an invigorated mission to protect their clients and broader conceptions of justice under the Trump administration. Oren, a public defender and immigration lawyer for fifteen years, said,

> And you know, to see Jeff Sessions talk about return to the rule of law, what is he talking about? With this administration, like what rule of law are they following? . . . It's shocking. Everyday. And the federal courts have been really good recently, and they have been for a while, you know, in the sense that they're applying the law, and as much as the Trump administration doesn't like it, because the law is whatever Donald Trump says it is. But we believe in a fair administration of laws with dutiful rules that are applied equally, you know?[15]

The importance of quality representation in individual removal cases under the Trump administration was underscored in the legal scholarship as well; Nina Rabin, for example, wrote, "Tenacious, collaborative, individual representation on a massive scale may be the most effective tool we have to fight against the current enforcement onslaught that seems to bulldoze through humanitarian concerns."[16] Even the 2018 version of the AILA practice manual referred to the Trump administration directly in its preface, asserting that "It is more important than ever that immigration attorneys remain up to date on developments in the law and stay on top of their game to best support their clients in this challenging climate."[17] Still, while overlapping with larger movements (as will be discussed in more detail in chapter 5), the strategies of resistance described here are not limited in use to lawyers working for nonprofits or those who deem themselves activists. Instead, they have evolved as best practices for attorneys professionally tasked with—diligently and zealously—representing individual immigrants with criminal records who face deportation. I deem these tactics of legal "resistance" not because the term was often used in interviews by lawyers themselves, but because these strategies work to challenge and upset the expansive and definitive effects of the aggravated felony.

Resistance through Immigration Law: CAT Relief and the Categorical Approach

Severely limited by the punitive immigration reforms of 1996, the main forms of legal relief available for migrants facing aggravated-felony-based deportation are withholding of removal and deferral of removal under the Convention against Torture (CAT). In order to be granted CAT relief, a noncitizen must prove that there is a higher than 50 percent chance that they will be tortured or otherwise injured, by the government or at government acquiescence, upon return to their home country. This is a very difficult standard to prove, especially for those who are mandatorily detained and without a lawyer, like many immigrants fighting deportation are, and especially for those with aggravated felony convictions. Resultantly, less than 3 percent of applications for CAT relief from deportation are granted around the country.[18] While study participants emphasized the difficulty of obtaining this form of relief, they did not deem it impossible, and many lawyers reported having successfully argued for it. When I asked Greg, "What are the common outcomes of aggravated felony cases you see? Do you see it as something that is able to fought?" he responded, "Oh yeah. I win a lot of these cases. I just won one last week," before going on to explain these wins are always based on CAT relief. Nicole, a public immigration lawyer with fifteen years of experience, said, "You know, I don't know if it's completely correct to say that aggravated felony cases are less likely to have relief. It kind of depends on a more holistic look at the case, because there are still quite a lot of aggravated felony cases that do have relief, and have strong cases for relief, like CAT claims."

Despite the narrow standard of relief under CAT, lawyers have developed strategies to make CAT relief arguments fit onto cases that it has not traditionally been applied to—or, as explained by Seth, lawyers are "pushing the law in directions that perhaps it wasn't initially intended for" because "it's the only relief you have left for your clients."

Throughout my interviews and ethnographic observation, lawyers described arguing for CAT in cases of mental illness by showing that a lack of available treatment could amount to state-allowed torture and winning CAT claims based on credible fear of drug organizations that have become "quasi-state actors" in many places. Some described inserting discretionary factors—such as people's ties to the United States, demonstrated rehabilitation, or non-torture-related hardship they will face in the country of return—into CAT cases despite it not being a discretionary form of relief. Laura, a public immigration lawyer for three years, explained, "We will definitely put everything sympathetic in there. If the judge really likes your client, and wants to grant your client, hopefully they'll be able to do that." May, a public immigration lawyer for five years, agreed, saying, "Even in a CAT claim, you still want the judge to like your client. You're still going to try to get in as much information like that as you can."

One of the most effective ways lawyers work to bring context and evidence to the likelihood of torture into CAT cases is through the use of expert witnesses. Laura said, "You need an expert witness really to prove a CAT claim"; Greg concurred, "You always need an expert witness. You can't do a CAT case without an expert." Experts are most often brought in to speak to either country conditions or the mental or physical health, or both, of an immigrant arguing for fear-based relief from deportation. I observed hearings in several CAT cases that utilized country conditions experts, including two that successfully received relief during the period of study. Neither were traditional CAT cases but instead were based on the expert-supported assertion that respondents would be harmed or killed with impunity by narco-cartel actors upon return to their home country with the acquiescence of a corrupt "narco-state" government. The expert in both of these cases, a scholar who had studied the experiences of deportees in the respondents' home country, was able to speak to conditions such as criminal impunity and police corruption, as well as the specific treatment of other criminal deportees. When asked in court how he saw his role as an expert witness, he responded, "Probably to shed light on the country conditions in relation to the case. Basically, to educate the court." He spoke of "social conditions" and their specific relevance. Although experts' credentials and testimonies are often picked apart and fiercely fought in court by

Department of Homeland Security (DHS) attorneys—as reported in my interviews and observed firsthand—it was clear that expert credentials and well-cited testimonies were valued by judges in making their CAT decisions, despite a general reluctance to consider structural factors in immigration court. In both successful cases I observed, the judge used language directly from the country conditions expert testimony in delivering her decisions to grant deferral of removal under CAT.

While creative legal strategies around CAT relief challenge the severe limits to relief and discretion activated by aggravated felonies, they only have potential to help those with a credible fear of harm upon returning to their home country—and CAT relief does not confer actual legal status, just the "withholding" or "deferral" of deportation. Another observed form of legal resistance is the contestation of aggravated-felony-based deportability by arguing that the underlying conviction is, in fact, not an aggravated felony. As a ground of deportability, the burden is on the government to prove that an immigrant has been convicted of an aggravated felony and is therefore removable. Yet aggravated-felony-based deportability usually goes uncontested, in a large part because 86 percent of detained immigrants in removal proceedings go without legal representation.[19] Although legally complex to contest deportability based on an aggravated felony, if successful, this strategy has the benefit of opening up forms of relief less restricted than withholding of removal and CAT, like cancellation of removal and asylum, which also allow for eventual legal status. Lawyers described their use of this strategy as a response to the severity of the aggravated felony's outcomes and its perceived overuse by ICE. Jess, a public immigration lawyer for eleven years, explained,

> The first line of defense, and really the strongest line of defense, is trying to defeat the government allegation that the person committed an aggravated felony, which is absolutely a ripe area for litigation. The government frequently misconstrues things as aggravated felonies, and if you don't have someone who is poised to articulate why this crime is not an aggravated felony, everything is going to fall apart after, because once you're thought to have committed an aggravated felony almost every door is shut to you.

Jane explained how ICE "will allege that a large amount of crimes are aggravated felonies," while she and other lawyers hold the position "that those crimes actually don't meet the basic requirements for an aggravated felony. And so those are cases that have to be litigated in immigration court." Jon said, "I always look for any ability to contest the aggravated felony ground, just because it's so devastating." He elaborated, "That's really at the heart of what I'm doing the most with in terms of aggravated felonies . . . arguing, 'No, you're wrong ICE, this is actually not an aggravated felony.' And then the question is, how do we make those arguments? What are those arguments?"

As an administrative body that has ordered the removal of noncitizens based on criminal convictions since the late 1800s, US immigration law has long grappled with the question of how to determine whether a given state conviction should trigger federal immigration consequences. This determination has most commonly been made through the "categorical approach," a method of legal analysis—also used in federal court decisions regarding sentencing enhancements based on previous criminal convictions—that compares the elements of a given state offense to the elements of the offense type listed in federal law.[20] To use this approach, adjudicators must consider only the legal elements of a given state conviction—not the title of the conviction or the facts of the specific case—to establish whether it triggers the federal consequence written into federal immigration (or sentencing) law. The use of this approach in immigration law is based on the view that administrative immigration courts should only have the power to adjudicate a conviction's immigration law consequences and cannot decide factual questions concerning the underlying circumstances of a conviction.[21] Under a categorical analysis of aggravated-felony-based deportability, if the minimum conduct punishable under a state conviction does not fit the "generic elements" of a federal offense type listed in the Immigration and Nationality Act (INA) definition of an aggravated felony (see appendix), that state conviction is not an aggravated felony—no matter the specifics of the individual case at hand.

While the tenets of the categorical approach have been applied in US immigration and sentencing decisions for over a century, there has been some confusion over its proper application in the period since the 1990s[22]—a time of increasingly punitive policies around criminal sentencing and criminal deportation. In the decades since, courts have employed the categorical approach to varying degrees, often considering some circumstantial evidence. However, two key Supreme Court decisions related to sentencing enhancements under the Armed Career Criminal Act (ACCA)—*Descamps v. United States* (2013) and *Mathis v. United States* (2016)—"cemented the categorical approach as a true elements test" and set precedent for a stricter interpretation in both sentencing and immigration court decisions (although still with some exceptions).[23] The Supreme Court's commitment to the categorical approach was reinforced in immigration decisions made by the court during the same period, demonstrated in decisions such as *Moncrieffe v. Holder* (2013) and *Mellouli v. Lynch* (2015). The changed composition of the Supreme Court in recent years has led to several less than friendly decisions for immigrants. These include *Johnson v. Arteaga-Martinez* and *Garland v. Aleman*—June 2022 decisions confirming the legality of indefinite detention without bail and restricting immigrants' rights to file class-action lawsuits, respectively—as well as the July 2022 refusal to reinstate Biden administration enforcement priorities that reverse Trump-era net widening with a focus on the arrest and deportation of immigrants who pose a risk to "national security, public safety and border security."[24] Yet, to this point, the Supreme Court has continued to affirm the categorical approach, including in the June 2022 *United States v. Taylor* decision, a criminal sentencing decision where the court ruled 7–2 in favor of the defendant based on a categorical elements test.

Although categorical analysis could feasibly have positive or negative effects on an immigrant's case against deportation, legal scholars argue that by mandating a strict elements test under the categorical approach, courts address key due process concerns regarding the uniformity and predictability of immigration consequences of criminal convictions,[25] and they create a "bulwark against government overreach in . . . deportation proceedings."[26] In my interviews, lawyers attested to the justice inherent in the categorical approach, and emphasized the strategy's importance as a response the harsh and expansive effects of the aggravated felony. Oren said the categorical approach is "really about fairness," explaining that the fairest way of applying immigration law to state law is "to look at the state law and see what was required for conviction, and see whether that matches up with the immigration offense. . . . Because you can't go back and redetermine the criminal case." While admitting the approach had been helpful for NYIFUP clients, Oren emphasized, "I believe very strongly in the categorical approach . . . it's just the fairest way to do something like this." Nicole spoke of the "logic" inherent in the categorical approach, that "Even if it's a small overbreadth [in the state offense], the fact that the overbreadth exists means that we're not going to relitigate the case to figure out what that client actually did." Zara, a criminal defender, immigration lawyer, and advocate with five years of experience, said that increased use of the categorical approach has "probably been the best development for people who are charged with aggravated felonies," and Pia, a public immigration lawyer and educator with six years of experience, attested that "keeping the categorical approach intact . . . is extremely important."

At an observed immigration law conference panel on "crimmigration," panelists discussed the categorical approach in detail and urged attendees to be inventive in contesting clients' aggravated felonies—described as the "immigration law death penalty." One panelist explained how the current era—"post-*Mathis*, *Moncrieffe*, and *Mellouli*"—is a time when "only your creativity can limit you in challenging deportability." The same speaker used the phrase the "Wild West of law" to describe a contemporary legal landscape where there is space to argue that "Theft is not theft, assault is not assault, burglary is not burglary." Interview participants also identified the past several years as particularly favorable for contesting aggravated-felony-based deportability. Zara said that the law on how to analyze "whether a specific offense comes within a specific immigration ground . . . has sort of gone up and down." However, with an increased emphasis on the categorical approach, Zara explained, "the Supreme Court has been really, really strong and has made it increasingly difficult for the government to . . . meet its burden . . . when they're arguing that someone is deportable. So that's been a very helpful development over the last five years." Pamela, a public immigration lawyer with three years of experience, relayed how the categorical approach has "evolved over time," and said, "Judges are more amenable to seeing legal arguments because they realize these are prevailing in circuit courts and stuff like that, and so I think it's maybe not as laughable to argue. Because before people would be like, 'Of course it's an aggravated felony, it's drug trafficking.' But now it's like, 'No, it's not drug trafficking. It has to be a match. It's more complicated than that.'" Amy, a public immigration lawyer for ten years described recent cases as a "reaction to the government overcharging people for years and years and years, and the same issues getting pushed up to the Supreme Court over and over again about, 'What is the categorical approach? What does it mean to analyze state convictions to see if they're aggravated felonies?'" Amy went on to say that despite "really awful and horrible" immigration enforcement in the Trump era, that it was also a time when, "once your client has an aggravated felony charge, you go, 'Ughh. Oh my god. But what arguments can I make against it?' And I feel like right now we have arguments against it."

Many lawyers described the categorical approach as their first line of defense when representing a noncitizen facing aggravated-felony-based deportation. Marco, a public immigration lawyer for five years, explained how most aggravated felony cases seen by NYIFUP providers are state-level offenses, "And that's why we have to make sure that we apply the categorical approach." Jane relayed how upon receiving an aggravated felony case at her organization, "The first thing we'll do is do some legal research and see is there a way that we can argue . . . that regardless of the specific facts of this crime, under the categorical approach, the statutory offense itself doesn't match the definition of aggravated felony in the INA." This contestation is usually argued early on in a removal case, in response to the aggravated felony ground of deportability listed on a noncitizen's Notice to Appear, the charging document issued by ICE to initiate immigration court proceedings. Lisa explained how then, "The lawyer has to decide: are the factual allegations and charges correct? . . . So it's the same thing with the aggravated felony definition. You'd have to look at the underlying defense to determine, is the government correct in charging the allegation in the way they did?" If a lawyer finds reason to contest the aggravated felony, they then make an oral motion in immigration court, usually followed by a detailed written briefing as to why a client's conviction is not categorically an aggravated felony. While there may be a short argument made in court, as May explained, "The judge is going [to say], 'Well, I want to see a briefing on this,' you know, because it's really complicated." In the written briefing, a lawyer can then use the categorical approach to argue that the elements of the state conviction that their client was convicted of do not match the elements of the conviction listed in the INA definition of the aggravated felony with the goal of proving that their client is not removable or, if still removable, is eligible for additional forms of legal relief from deportation.

While participants described increasing success with the categorical approach, they also emphasized a reticence by immigration courts and the Board of Immigration Appeals (BIA) to apply the approach as dictated by circuit and supreme courts. In fact, misapplication of the categorical approach is one of most common reasons BIA decisions are appealed to higher courts.[27] Nicole said that while categorically contesting an aggravated felony can often be successful, "It can take many levels of appeal to reach success . . . you might not get the results you should get until you're at, sometimes the BIA, more likely at the second circuit. So the cases can go on for a long time." Laura agreed, saying, "A lot of the immigration judges will not grant your categorical approach arguments, so even if you might eventually win at the second circuit, the BIA sucks, so you know." Jon reported,

> One big frustration that we have is that we don't really see immigration judges . . . understanding and being receptive to even these Supreme Court cases that say, "This is how you're supposed to classify. This is how you're supposed to do your analysis." . . . Practitioners like myself don't feel like the immigration judges are really understanding or implementing the law, which forces us to appeal these decisions, right? But it's really frustrating, because why can't the immigration judge understand the Supreme Court case. Why can't they apply it?

With more likelihood of success upon appeal, participants emphasized the importance of presenting strong categorical arguments early on in order to "preserve the record" for appellate courts that may prove more amenable. Still, despite the potential of the approach, the fact that categorical cases are more often won on appeal makes it a difficult undertaking for migrants who are likely to be detained throughout proceedings—which may last several years. Laura said, "If the person is detained, [appeals are] going to take like three years. And they're going to be sitting in detention that entire time. And for a lot of people, that's not worth it necessarily. . . ." Jane concurred, "We're oftentimes success-ful, but it takes a lot of time to litigate those issues, and our clients are usually in jail the whole entire time."

Although lawyers were mostly concerned with the categorical ap-proach's potency as a tool for use in individual clients' cases, they also described its role in gradually narrowing interpretations of the aggra-vated felony. Participants referred to various Supreme Court, circuit court, and even BIA decisions (although to a lesser extent) that had precedentially restrained expansive application of the aggravated felony. Of these, precedential Supreme Court decisions have the broadest and most binding effects since they apply to the whole country and cannot be appealed to a higher court. Recent shifts in the Supreme Court's com-position are likely to make lawyers wary of pushing future categorical cases to this level, but decisions made by this court over the past two decades have played a key role in setting precedent around the aggra-vated felony. (A list of relevant Supreme Court decisions and descrip-tive details can be found in table 4.1.) An early Supreme Court decision related to the aggravated felony, *Leocal v. Ashcroft* (2004), used the cat-egorical approach to limit the inclusion of state DUI offenses as "crime of violence" aggravated felonies—a classification found partially void for vagueness in a later decision, *Sessions v. Garcia Dimaya* (2018). The *Dimaya* finding came down from the Supreme Court during the period of this research, much to my participants' approval. Before the decision, Celia, a public immigration lawyer with four years of experience said, "Particularly, I'm very anxious to see how *Dimaya* is going to come out. I think that will be a huge—that will do a lot for the crimimm [crimmi-gration] world more generally if we get a good ruling from the Supreme Court." After the *Dimaya* finding, Pia also called it "huge" and remarked how until then, "There were many people who were trapped under this really vague definition of crime of violence and ended up facing these consequences."

The Supreme Court has also used the categorical approach to limit the application of the drug trafficking aggravated felonies to preclude simple possession offenses or drug trafficking offenses that include the social sharing of a small amount of marijuana and to limit sexual abuse of a minor aggravated felonies to state statutory rape offenses with an age threshold of sixteen years or under. The approach has not been as

Table 4.1. Precedential Supreme Court Decisions Affecting Interpretation of Aggravated Felony

Year	Case	Findings
2004	*Leocal v. Ashcroft*	State DUI offenses that do not require intent, or require only a showing of negligence in the operation of a vehicle, are not aggravated felony crimes of violence.
2009	*Nijhawan v. Holder*	Immigration judges can inquire into underlying facts of prior fraud conviction for purposes of determining whether the loss to the victims exceeded $10,000. (Categorical approach does not apply.)
2010	*Carachuri-Rosendo v. Holder*	Second or subsequent simple drug possession offenses are not aggravated felonies when the state conviction is not based on the fact of a prior conviction.
2012	*Kawashima Et. Ux. v. Holder*	Falsified tax returns are categorically considered fraud for the purpose of determining an aggravated felony.
2013	*Moncrieffe v. Holder*	State marijuana offenses that do not require remuneration or or more than a small amount of marijuana are not considered aggravated felonies.
2017	*Esquivel-Quintana v. Sessions*	State statutory rape offenses with a threshold of older than sixteen years do not fit the the aggravated felony definition of "sexual abuse of a minor."
2018	*Sessions v. Garcia Dimaya*	The aggravated felony definition of "crime of violence" is void for vagueness.

successful in fraud cases, where the Supreme Court has held that the categorical approach does not apply, and therefore, immigration judges can inquire into the underlying facts of a fraud conviction for purposes of determining whether the loss to the victims exceeded $10,000. The Supreme Court has also held that falsified tax returns are categorically considered fraud for the purpose of determining an aggravated felony. Still, interviewees spoke to the importance of categorical decisions in the Supreme Court and referred to the "lopsided" split of many of them as an indicator of the distance between the higher court and immigration court or BIA interpretations. Barb, an immigration lawyer, educator, and advocate with almost thirty years of experience in the field, referred to unanimous Supreme Court decisions limiting previous interpretations of the aggravated felony, and she said that such imbalance demonstrates "that the government has been ridiculously overbroad in the way that they have applied this." She continued, "And the sad thing is that a lot of people who would have won under those cases were deported beforehand."

In addition to the Supreme Court cases listed in table 4.1, interview participants also referred to important precedential decisions in the United States Court of Appeals for the Second Circuit—the federal appellate court for New York, Connecticut, and Vermont—especially *Harbin v. Sessions* (2017) and *Hylton v. Sessions* (2018), both of which are drug related. In *Harbin*, the court applied the categorical approach to find that a major New York State "sale of a controlled substance" offense is not a drug trafficking aggravated felony for immigration purposes, because the state definition includes one substance—chorionic gonadotropin (hCG)—that is not included in the federal schedule of controlled substances. Mr. Harbin, a fifty-four-year-old man from Grenada, had been a lawful permanent resident (LPR) of the United States for thirty years when he was put into deportation proceedings in 2012 based on a 1991 controlled substance conviction. After he was denied cancellation of removal due to this alleged aggravated felony and denied CAT relief despite a mental health claim based on diagnoses of schizophrenia and bipolar disorder, Mr. Harbin's case went through five years of appeals before the favorable decision in the circuit court. In *Hylton*, a case decided during the period of this research, the court drew on *Moncrieffe* (2013) to find that a common New York State marijuana sale offense is categorically not an aggravated felony, because the state offense "explicitly extends to the distribution of less than an ounce of marijuana without renumeration."[28] Mr. Hylton, a Jamaica native and US LPR since 1989, had been convicted for a marijuana sale offense in 2011 before being detained by ICE in 2013, when he was charged as removable based on this supposed drug trafficking aggravated felony. In this case, the original immigration court judge correctly applied the categorical approach, disqualified the aggravated felony, and granted cancellation of removal based on Mr. Hylton's strong ties to the United States before the government appealed the case to the BIA, who overturned the original decision. Finally, after five years in court, the categorical argument was again successful at the circuit level.

Such decisions are often seen as collective hard-won victories by advocates and lawyers. A case litigated from immigration court through appeal by The Legal Aid Society of New York (one of the three NYIFUP providers), Sheria explained that "with *Harbin*, the goal was to change the law," and she characterized the favorable decision as the result of lawyers and advocates doing "a lot of work to try and show that New York's definition of these offenses is broader than the federal definition." Celia agreed that "*Harbin* was particularly a win for the crimimm community." She elaborated, "It was an argument that had been being made for years, that the New York controlled substance register was overbroad and not categorically a controlled substance or drug trafficking ag fel [aggravated felony], and it was like the argument that we made and lost on, and then finally got a good decision." Still, participants were clear that while broader impacts are exciting, such cases are not always fought with a goal beyond the particular client fighting for relief. Raina explained that while appeals may be pushed with an eye toward changing the law, "sometimes it's just happenstance." With regard to *Hylton*, originally litigated by NYIFUP defenders before being fought on appeal by the New York University Immigrant Rights Clinic, Raina explained how the government appealed the original immigration court decision, which they don't always do, "But this one they had a very big stake in, because the defense . . . [was] something that could be then applied in many other cases." Even in the appeal stages though, Raina emphasized that Mr. Hylton's lawyers' primary objective was "to make sure that Mr. Hylton got a plea" just as the goal is always to get clients relief so "they can stay with their families and not have to worry about this"—with broader impacts a secondary benefit.

Still, categorical-approach-based circuit court findings in *Harbin* and *Hylton*, as well as the Supreme Court decisions discussed in this section, were frequently cited by lawyers and advocates as key precedential victories, beneficial to the cases of current and future clients, beneficial to the practice of immigration law, and beneficial in moving overbroad aggravated felony application toward more just interpretations. Celia spoke to the importance of *Harbin* in setting precedent for clients' cases, saying, "What was amazing was right after *Harbin*, we saw the DHS attorneys terminating by themselves." She also referred to key categorical wins in the Supreme Court, like *Mathis* (2013), as having "really reinforced the categorical approach, which allowed these better rulings to come down on the circuit level," and she explained how for lawyers, "Once we get those good decisions from the circuit and the Supreme court, then we obviously have much more power with judges to agree with arguments that we've been making all along." After *Hylton*, Cori explained how, "Before this, no judge was probably going to make that finding, but now there is a clear finding in the circuit . . . so now [lawyers] could potentially go back and reopen something . . . based upon this new decision." Amy said recent Supreme Court and circuit court decisions have been a part of the case law on the aggravated felony "getting better and better" and relayed that precedential cases "have allowed us to win a lot of aggravated felony arguments at the immigration judge level." Pia explained how categorical wins, like in *Dimaya* (2018), left her "inspired to bring more claims," and she emphasized the key role of lawyers in shaping the law, elaborating, "I think lawyers thinking through really creative arguments for trying to strike down some of these laws while they still exist is really important. . . . I think preserving and making all these challenges and litigating it, and if a client is willing, to try and push and make a law."

Interviewed on the day *Hylton* was decided, Cori referred to the specific importance of such legal resistance in the Trump era:

> And then I think it's people just—as has been happening across the board . . . against the Trump administration—just like ramping up federal litigation, because immigration judges are not hearing us, the Board of Immigration Appeals is not hearing us. Jeff Sessions certainly isn't going to be making any concessions or any better case law for us, so I feel like decisions like the one that came down today from the second circuit are where we can possibly get those victories that then become binding upon the Board of Immigration Appeals and immigration court.

Therefore, just as strategies related to CAT relief use immigration law to challenge limits on legal relief and judicial discretion in the removal cases of noncitizens with aggravated felony convictions, the categorical approach also works within the boundaries of immigration law—and within the specific considerations of the legal profession—to resist perceived injustices related to the aggravated felony, namely its extreme bars on relief, its overbroad application, and its related due process concerns.

Resistance through Criminal Law: Preventive Defense and Postconviction Relief

While social scientific research on "crimmigration" has been vital in bringing attention to the punitive outcomes of the increased intertwining of criminal and immigration law,[29] there has been less attention paid to opportunities for resistance also created by the "crimmigration" nexus.[30] Innovative legal responses observed in this research work through the criminal justice system to challenge the capacious, severe, and unequal effects of the aggravated felony. This section describes two key aspects of this resistance—preconviction "preventive" defense, and postconviction relief.

Though the categorical approach was identified as one of the most effective strategies of avoiding deportation once placed in aggravated-felony-based removal proceedings, a defense described by many as even more fruitful is one that occurs long before the case reaches immigration court, prior to a noncitizen's criminal conviction. This preventive strategy centers on immigration lawyers and other experts working with criminal lawyers, prosecutors, and judges to identify and avoid potential immigration implications of noncitizens' criminal convictions. This is primarily done by educating criminal lawyers and judges on criminal-immigration consequences, installing in-house immigration experts in criminal defense offices, and negotiating with judges and prosecutors to procure immigration-safe convictions. As shown throughout this book, there is very little room for negotiation in immigration court once a noncitizen has entered removal proceedings based on an aggravated felony conviction. The norm of bargaining in criminal law—evidenced by the astonishing 97 percent of federal criminal cases and 94 percent of state criminal cases that end in plea bargains[31]—makes this early stage the final chance for discretion in many potential aggravated felony cases and for avoiding a so-classified conviction. Although practitioners have employed versions of these tactics for many years, preventive strategies against the immigration consequences of criminal convictions moved closer to institutionalization with the 2010 Supreme Court decision *Padilla v. Kentucky.*

In *Padilla*, the Supreme Court held that criminal defenders must advise noncitizen clients if a plea carries a risk of deportation, in order to satisfy the Sixth Amendment guarantee of effective counsel. In doing so, the court recognized that rather than a mere "collateral consequence" of a conviction, "deportation is an integral part—indeed, sometimes the most important part—of the penalty that may be imposed on noncitizen defendants who plead guilty to specified crimes."[32] Due to the dominant norm of plea bargaining in criminal proceedings, study participants relayed how convictions are often more reflective of negotiations between defense lawyers and prosecutors than the actual crime committed. Raina remarked that, "In criminal court, it's not really about guilt and innocence. It's about bargaining power and negotiation." Marco explained how pre- and even post-*Padilla*, many of his immigration clients would report never having been told that "this guilty plea that they made was going to have any sort of consequence in their immigration case," and explained how, "If the person would have known that the plea . . . was going to mean automatic deportation and mandatory deportation, they would have possibly found [another] or they would have just gone to trial, especially when a lot of them . . . are innocent of the convictions."

Padilla led to the instatement of special units of immigration lawyers in public defense offices, and the institutionalization of programs to provide immigration advice to other criminal lawyers—although to inconsistent degrees around the country. Despite variations of such programs already existing among certain legal defense organizations and advocacy groups in New York City pre-2010, *Padilla* was widely recognized by participants as a key win for immigrants with potential aggravated felony convictions.[33] Raina referred to the decision as "really important" and explained how pre-*Padilla* immigration lawyers had been "routinely filing ineffective assistance of council claims and things like that with defenders . . . because of the importance of that advisal and those discussions and those negotiations." Lisa said *Padilla* was vital in its acknowledgment of deportation as a punishment, and its "requirement that attorneys advise their clients accordingly, just like they would advise regarding sentencing issues or other legal matters"—advice she saw as fundamental to due process. Barb referred to preventive advisement on immigration implications of criminal pleas as "extremely important" and said, "There have been specialists advising criminal defense lawyers for decades, but the awareness has certainly picked up tremendously since the *Padilla* case." Celia was also quick to mention the history of organizations using similar strategies pre-*Padilla*, yet she acknowledged that the decision "has led to a much bigger role upfront for immigration advocates, a much more formalized role." George identified *Padilla* as a "sea change," and Jess agreed that after *Padilla*, "There's just been a lot more attention to having an immigration expert in public defender's offices, and vice versa, having a criminal defender in immigration offices."

Elena, a public immigration lawyer with eight years of experience in this area, described "working directly with the defense attorneys in the same office to make sure that whatever plea they're negotiating with the DA, that doesn't have a negative impact on the person's immigration status." Sheria outlined a *Padilla*-based position where she "would work closely with defense attorneys in identifying ways for them to either come up with plea bargains . . . that will mitigate or lessen the immigration consequences that their client would face." Celia recounted moving from removal defense to *Padilla* work "to try to correct what I perceived to be some of the mistakes on the front end, rather than having to deal with them on the back end." In this preventive line of work, immigration lawyers participate in holistic teams focused on noncitizens' criminal cases, informally advising criminal lawyers on immigration-safe pleas to negotiate for in individual cases, contributing written details on immigration consequences to be presented to prosecutors and judges, negotiating with or testifying to judges and prosecutors directly, and running training or creating resources for criminal practitioners on criminal-immigration issues more generally.

Participants emphasized how criminal legal system norms of negotiation and bargaining are what make these preventive strategies powerful. Raina spoke to the key combination of "criminal defense attorneys who are so wonderful . . . [and] have such great skill in negotiation and trial practice," with *Padilla* attorneys who are experts in immigration implications of criminal convictions. She elaborated, "All of this is about negotiation, and if the assistant district attorney is willing to trade one thing for another . . . to preserve the ability of an individual to stay in the United States with their family, that's a really important process, which occurs way before deportation proceedings are even an issue." Jackie reported, "The overprosecution that happens in immigration court I think is partially because there is no bargaining. We are not seeing bargaining the way we see it in criminal court, so they can charge high, and have no consequences for that"; she said that in training for criminal defenders, she would explain, "This is so important because you really are the last line of defense. Not only are you possibly the last advocate that this person will have on their side since they aren't entitled to a lawyer, but you might be the last person that actually has the power to do something that would help or save this person from deportation." George also referred to the absence of negotiation in the immigration system, and said, "Where charge bargaining, plea bargaining, sentence bargaining is a regular part of the criminal legal system, then lawyers can mitigate and avoid getting an aggravated felony."

Nora, a public defender for eight years, described her organization's in-house criminal-immigration specialists as "a very necessary and vital part of our practice" who she and other criminal defenders "heavily rely on" to guide plea negotiations for noncitizen clients. She explained, "Sometimes there are creative pleas that we can take, based on the specific charges that our clients are facing." As an immigration adviser on a criminal defense team, Jackie described having "pled people to felonies instead of misdemeanors because the felony was safe and the misdemeanor wasn't," or trading "jail time for immigration-safe consequences." A defense often mentioned by participants was negotiating for 364-day sentences for misdemeanors that require a year-long sentence to become an aggravated felony; Jackie recounted, "The one common thing to do as kind of a *Padilla* trick is if my client is charged with a theft offense . . . and the prosecutor wants two years jail time . . . I would say, 'Well let's plead my client to two theft offenses, with 364 days on each. So you're getting everything but the two days you want, but that's not an aggravated felony.'" Raina similarly recounted arguing for 364-day plea deals when she was a public defender and said how, in that position, "The aggravated felony ground was really important in thinking about how to negotiate pleas." She explained how, in criminal court, "People get around things all the time," so "if a defender is aware . . . they may be able to work something out with the district attorney so as to avoid draconian immigration consequences that don't really consider the . . . equities and . . . dynamic character traits of an individual."

In order to persuade prosecutors to agree to immigration-safe pleas—or at least pleas not considered aggravated felonies—lawyers provide detailed information on immigration consequences as well as discretionary details about their client that would become irrelevant in deportation proceedings once a person is convicted of an aggravated felony. In her work as a criminal-immigration specialist, Sheria recounted arguing to prosecutors that noncitizen offenders were being singled out with a "whole added penalty because of their birth-origin." She would go on to describe, for example, "what the consequence is for someone for pleading guilty to you know, petty larceny, and having a year sentence, and the consequence is then this mentally ill person gets sent back to a country where mentally ill people are ostracized." Jackie relayed writing "pre-pleading investigations" (PPIs) with in-house social workers to be presented to prosecutors. In these documents, she could include discretionary information that would become irrelevant in deportation proceedings once a person is convicted of an aggravated felony "like what are the ties [to family and community], how this would devastate lots of people, what explains how we got to this point we're at today." Jackie would conclude with something like, "Even though you've heard all these things, this is a real person with real family members and a chance at rehabilitation . . . that's not going to matter in immigration court unless they get a plea that is like this." Nora also reported submitting PPIs to prosecutors—"sympathetic memos of mitigating factors about our clients"—especially in cases where "they have a really hard life story and they have a long history of addiction or abuse." She said it is also common to have less formal conversations with prosecutors off the record, particularly when a client is undocumented, for fear that ICE could potentially gain access to court proceedings.

While there is far more discretion in criminal plea negotiations than there is in aggravated-felony-related immigration court proceedings, this discretion is largely in the hands of district attorneys (DAs) and assistant district attorneys (ADAs), who vary in their willingness to use it to protect immigrants. As a criminal lawyer, Nora remarked that these prosecutors "have a ton of power," which can be "frustrating." She said, "Overall, I'm not a fan of DAs. . . . I don't think many people on our side are . . . but of course there are DAs that are much more sympathetic or that you can work with, or do listen, on a case by case basis, and will listen to more sympathetic factors." Other times, they are "just the coldest, harshest . . . And that's what you're up against." For Sheria, the fact that prosecutors "don't want to be known for being 'soft on crime'" forced her to "remove emotion" from her arguments by being "more thorough with her work." She said, "If I've presented you with something that is evidence based from a clinical perspective, . . . like partnering with one of the social workers, what are you going to say exactly? I'm not asking you for a favor. We're not being nice here. At this point, it's cruel and unusual for you to insist on keeping this sentence." Laura, also a criminal-immigration specialist, relayed, "We push really hard on ADAs if they're only offering things that are not safe for immigration" and explained that receptivity "totally depends borough to borough. It also depends ADA to ADA." While some prosecutors are particularly amenable to considering immigration implications, Laura recalled others who had said, "Frankly, I think your client should get deported." In these cases, she remarked, "it sort of cuts the other way." Jackie identified Brooklyn as an example of "a pretty generous jurisdiction for immigrants," elaborating, "They understood pretty early on that immigration consequences are real and should be taken into consideration, and if they could get most of what they wanted, that was something they would look at—mitigating circumstances." At the other end of the spectrum, Nora referred to the city's "special narcotics" prosecutor office, as "awful," saying, "It's always surprising, but they don't care that much." Still, despite variation among prosecutors, participants generally viewed these preventive negotiations as far more fruitful than later fighting an existing aggravated felony conviction in immigration court.

Among observed forms of legal resistance to the aggravated felony that work through criminal law, participants viewed preconviction strategies as by far the most efficacious. Yet many interviewees also referred to "postconviction relief" (PCR)—a method of reopening a criminal case that has already resulted in a conviction—as an option for migrants in aggravated-felony-based deportation proceedings. Known for its utilization in reversing serious wrongful convictions—murder or rape cases with new DNA evidence, for example[34]—PCR is won by petitioning criminal courts to vacate or renegotiate existing convictions or sentences. The Supreme Court's decision in *Padilla v. Kentucky* increased the viability of this option for use by immigrants facing deportation—especially those with a potential claim of ineffective assistance of counsel in their original criminal case.[35] In my interviews, participants spoke of PCR as a key possibility for immigrants convicted of aggravated felonies, often attempted in concurrence with immigration court responses like CAT relief or the categorical approach. Jane explained how, at her organization, PCR is "one of the first defenses we'll look into, if there is an argument as to why the conviction in the first place was illegal." If successful, "we end up getting that plea vacated so that the person doesn't have an aggravated felony anymore." Emily, a public immigration lawyer for four years, said that her organization does "a lot of postconviction relief," often using "*Padilla* to go back and reopen the case and get it re-pled to something else that's not an aggravated felony." Speaking of a recent successful claim for CAT relief, Emily proffered that her client was "also going to seek postconviction relief," to hopefully remove the aggravated felony conviction and open up more beneficial forms of immigration relief. Nicole described PCR as "really, really important," and referred to using it in cases when a client wrongfully took an aggravated felony plea because they were "mentally ill and incompetent" or were "not advised of the immigration consequence." She continued, "If they're successful and it's re-pled, then they would be eligible in the future for relief."

In New York, under Article 440 of the New York Criminal Procedure Law, which outlines the bases and processes for challenging the legality of a conviction or sentence, a motion for PCR must be filed with the criminal court where the original conviction occurred. Out of various possible grounds for making such a claim, *Padilla*-related PCR motions are usually based on a violation of either state or federal constitutional rights in attaining the original conviction—most often a violation of the Sixth Amendment right to effective counsel. Although immigration courts may extend deportation proceedings to allow time for an open postconviction claim to be decided in criminal court,[36] they will not recognize the vacatur of an aggravated felony plea if it is vacated only for immigration purposes—such as hardship upon deportation—so such claims must include strong evidence of procedural defects in the original plea.[37] Sky, a criminal attorney with a focus on postconviction work for noncitizens facing deportation, described examining court minutes to discover breaches of justice while also partnering with immigration lawyers in order to ensure any new plea is immigration safe. In a recent case, Sky had re-pled a client from "criminal possession of a controlled substance in the third degree, which is a drug trafficking aggravated felony because the subsection that he pled to was intent to sell" to "criminal possession of a controlled substance in the second degree. Simple possession offense. No longer an aggravated felony." In another case, Sky was trying to re-plead a client's theft offense with a one-year sentence to the same offense with a one-day sentence reduction, based "on a theory that his plea was not knowing and voluntary because he wasn't advised of his Fifth and Sixth Amendment rights . . . which was something I realized when I got his plea minutes."

While several lawyers reported successful outcomes with postconviction re-pleaders of aggravated felonies, it is not an easy route, especially with no real guarantee of legal representation. In PCR cases, the burden of proof shifts to the convicted individual, and as Sky explained, "You have no right to anything on [Article] 440. So a judge can dismiss it outright without ever scheduling a hearing or anything." They also described the administrative difficulties of getting criminal courts to consider motions for PCR in a timely manner, especially with the ticking clock of concurrent removal proceedings, saying, "You have to find the legal error. You have to draft and file the motion. And then when you file the motion you have to babysit the shit out of it to actually make sure someone pays attention." In some cases, Sky recounted not being able to sleep at night, knowing that noncitizen clients are detained "while criminal court dicks around." They said this difficulty was exacerbated by the fact that immigration-related PCR claims are often based on misdemeanor convictions—including many of those related to aggravated felonies. Sky explained,

> People treat misdemeanors in criminal court as if it's nothing. . . . Clerks' offices don't know what to do with misdemeanor 440s. Because 440s are usually filed for murder convictions of people who are innocent . . . and clerks like to ignore those too. . . . And then we're coming in on these dinky misdemeanors, making like federal cases out of them, because they're grounds for deportability, and . . . clerks aren't calendaring our motions or docketing them until they've requested the court file, but the court file is like twenty years old and sitting in some warehouse in Rochester, and we're like, "No, but this guy has a check-in in two weeks. He needs access to the courts!"

When a judge does reopen a conviction based on a postconviction claim, there is no guarantee that the prosecutor will agree to an immigration-safe plea. For example, with regard to their theft case, Sky said, "The ADA's fighting like crazy, even though the only relief we've requested is a one-day sentence reduction." While Seth saw PCR as an important option, he described it as difficult "because the law likes things to be settled and they don't like people coming back." Still, for some immigrants, the reopening of aggravated felony cases in criminal court is a key, final opportunity to negotiate a conviction that will not ensure their deportation.

Just as creative strategies around CAT relief and the contestation of deportability through the categorical approach work through immigration law frameworks to resist the harsh and expansive effects of the aggravated felony, the tactics described in this section use criminal legal structures toward the same ends. Through preconviction preventive efforts and attempts at postconviction relief, immigration and criminal lawyers work with noncitizen clients to avoid and vacate aggravated felony convictions. In these strategies, lawyers challenge the aggravated felony's elimination of immigration court discretion through the criminal legal system norm of plea negotiation and resist its erosion of due process by ensuring noncitizens are notified of immigration consequences from potential criminal convictions. Furthermore, institutional changes achieved through these methods, like the Supreme Court's recognition of deportation as punishment in *Padilla v. Kentucky*, as well as fruitful outcomes in individual cases have been vital in helping immigrants avoid aggravated-felony-based deportation.

Conclusion

Drawing from interviews with legal practitioners; observation of immigration court proceedings, legal conferences, and workshops; and analysis of relevant court decisions, this chapter has described tactics of "legal resistance" that work to challenge and defend against the aggravated felony's harsh, expansive, and unequal effects. Distinctly legal in their substance, these strategies are undertaken by lawyers as a part of their professional commitments to their clients as well as for broader ideals of justice, and lawyers employ existing processes of immigration and criminal law in such tactics' implementation. Practitioners also frame these strategies as responses to the aggravated felony's severity, its limits on due process, and its overuse by ICE, as well as wider concerns about unjust immigration law (heightened under the Trump administration). Expanding previous research on "cause lawyers" and "legal activism,"[38] findings demonstrate how even lawyers who do not see themselves as activists or "movement lawyers" work to contest and ameliorate the harsh and expansive effects of the aggravated felony through strategies of "legal resistance" which occur within the course of professional commitments to their clients and the just administration of the law.

Long-standing debates in the study of law and society depict the duality of law as a key force of inequality that can, at times, become a potent tool for resistance. The unique power of law to shape our lives while simultaneous naturalizing its own effects has often been used to uphold unequal social hierarchies. Yet at times, the distinctive power of law is also successfully harnessed by those resisting persecution and injustice. As editors Mindie Lazarus-Black and Susan Hirsch write in the introduction to *Contested States*, a volume containing several case-studies of oppressed groups that successfully gain rights through laws that otherwise subjugate them, "Law is at once hegemonic and oppositional."[39] While previous chapters explicated the aggravated felony as a key example of a punitive "crimmigration nexus," this chapter has demonstrated how the increased intertwining of criminal and immigration law can also create opportunities for resistance. Observed strategies of legal resistance that work through immigration law—like the categorical approach—utilize differences in state criminal justice policy and enforcement to challenge and evolve interpretations of the aggravated felony, while those strategies that work through criminal law draw on norms of negotiation and local control to prevent and avoid indiscriminate and unyielding immigration system outcomes. Thus the same intertwining bodies of laws that create the punitive and unequal effects of the aggravated felony are also used by lawyers and advocates working to defend the rights of immigrants with criminal records. Though these legal strategies do not upend the aggravated felony or broader systems of criminalization and deportation, they are a tool within a broader web of resistance, working to change the law while also working to address its everyday effects.

5

"These Are People from Our Community"

Networks of Activism and Advocacy

Before NYIFUP you did have nonprofits that would do some cases, but they wouldn't do those aggravated felony cases, right? That's still true in other places. . . . It's a practical consideration for the nonprofits who are trying to do work, where they put their resources, where they think it would make the most impact."
—Jackie, immigration lawyer and advocate

We see communities in struggle as the motive force of social change, not lawyers winning things in court rooms.
—George, immigration lawyer and advocate

We work with folks like that. It's very rare that we have somebody roll in here . . . who is maybe a DACA [Deferred Action for Childhood Arrivals] recipient or trying to figure out where to go. We deal specifically people with criminal convictions.
—Community organizer, Families for Freedom

Strategies of legal resistance to the aggravated felony are not limited in use to lawyers who view themselves as activists. While at times employed with an eye toward broader change, such tactics operate within the existing boundaries of immigration and criminal law, exemplifying best practices for criminal and immigration attorneys working to meet professional mandates of due process and "zealous advocacy" for individual clients. Still, their development and ongoing use is enabled and supported by a broad and complex network of advocacy made up of progressive lawyers, nonprofit organizations, and community-based activists in New York City (NYC)—a center of the immigrant rights movement—as well as by overlapping movements for criminal legal reform and racial justice. This context has facilitated the early development of protective policies and programs, such as the installation of immigration advisers in public defender offices and the provision of universal representation for detained immigrants. Such initiatives are instrumental to the evolution and enactment of legal strategies that resist the aggravated felony's severe and expansive effects. Established networks of advocacy groups and organizations concerned with immigrant rights, legal due process, and criminal justice system inequality have pushed local policymakers to not only support these protective policies, but also to provide resources and collaboration that enable legal resistance. Yet vital to the construction and maintenance of any institutionalized support for immigrants with aggravated felonies is grassroots and intersectional community-based activism that fights for the recognition of the humanity and rights of noncitizens with criminal records.

Informed by interviews with legal practitioners and advocates, analysis of organizational resources, and observation of relevant events and workshops, this chapter demonstrates how legal responses to the aggravated felony are shaped and supported by a broader field of advocacy and social movement activism. It begins by describing how progressive lawyers, legal rights organizations, and immigrant rights organizations in NYC collaboratively create a context facilitative of legal resistance to the aggravated felony. I demonstrate the impact of these networks by describing NYC's pioneering program of universal legal representation for detained immigrants facing deportation; early institutionalization of "crimmigration" advisal in public defense offices; existing systems of public interest law; and practical organizational support. Yet underlying the robust and multifaceted advocacy that supports innovative legal responses to the aggravated felony are the voices and stories of impacted migrants and their loved ones. Thus follows a discussion of the central role of "communities in struggle" who continually fight to disrupt the essentializing "good immigrant, bad immigrant" binary that has been so long used to devalue and dismiss immigrants with criminal records. I argue that legal resistance to the aggravated felony—and the advocacy context that supports this resistance—is ultimately enabled by community-based activism that challenges this destructive binary and broader conceptions of who is "criminal."

Universal Representation

Beginning in 2013, New York City has guaranteed legal representation to detained noncitizens in deportation proceedings through the New York Immigrant Family Unity Project (NYIFUP)—the first universal representation program of its kind. Largely funded by the New York City Council, NYIFUP provides free legal representation for all immigrants whose deportation proceedings begin at Varick Street (NYC's detained immigration court) and whose household income does not exceed 200 percent of the federal poverty guidelines. The NYIFUP program— which funds immigration removal defense units within existing public defender offices, primarily The Legal Aid Society of New York, Brooklyn Defenders, and Bronx Defenders—plays an important role in facilitating observed strategies of legal resistance to the aggravated felony.[1] Since this pioneering project's induction, 43 percent of NYIFUP clients have successfully won relief from removal, as compared to 3 percent of detained cases without representation nationwide.[2] Universal representation in immigration court is particularly impactful for noncitizens with aggravated felonies or other criminal convictions as they are more likely to be detained and less likely to be represented by existing legal service providers.

Yet without a legal guarantee of representation, noncitizens facing deportation around the country largely do so without counsel. Only 37 percent of immigrants nationally—and just 14 percent of those who are detained—secure lawyers for their removal proceedings, with wide variance in access to council based on socioeconomic status, detention status, nationality, and location.[3] Interviewees saw such uneven representation as an affront to the legal rights of noncitizens and as an almost insurmountable obstacle to avoiding deportation. Sheria, a public immigration lawyer for four years, said she was "amazed when anyone without a lawyer is actually able to avoid removal." Pia, a public immigration lawyer and educator for six years, described representation in immigration court as "critical" due to the extreme legal complexities of the field, explaining how "there are immigration lawyers specializing in specialties of specialties because it's so complicated." She went on to say, "It's so unbelievable to me that there's an idea that someone who may not speak the language, who is pro se [without an attorney], could be expected to face a trained attorney on the other side." Participants also spoke to the specific disadvantages presented in aggravated felony cases. Jane, a public immigration lawyer with eight years of experience, said, "Legal representation is critical to any one of our defenses against aggravated felonies. Whether it's pursuing postconviction relief, using the categorical approach, or finding an application for CAT deferral . . . those are some of the toughest to accomplish in the legal system, and it's not realistic to expect any pro se person, even a native English speaker, to succeed on any of those defenses." Underscoring this point, May, a public immigration lawyer for five years, referred to facing deportation with an aggravated felony and without an attorney as "a death sentence in terms of your chance of success."

Whether attempting to claim the limited relief not barred to non-citizens with such convictions or contesting the conviction's designation altogether, the immigration court avenues available to those facing deportation for aggravated felonies are rife with legal complexities and lengthy appeals. Interview participants emphasized that to present strong and innovative legal challenges, mere representation is not enough; rather, noncitizens need knowledgeable and well-trained representation. Marco, a public immigration lawyer for five years, demonstrated this with regard to the "incredibly complicated" categorical approach, the primary method of contesting an aggravated felony.

> If you're not represented by, not just any immigration attorney, but an immigration attorney that has a lot of experience dealing with the immigration consequences of criminal convictions, it's almost impossible that the person will be able to actually apply the categorical approach correctly. So the government ends up deporting tons and tons of people who didn't even have aggravated felonies . . . and the government just gets away with it. Because they are fighting against people who are unrepresented or people who are not being represented by attorneys who have experience in the field.

The diverse range of experience, knowledge, and credibility among immigration lawyers was a theme that came up throughout the research, with wide acknowledgment among participants that not all representation is created equal, especially for noncitizens facing deportation based on aggravated felonies. Though some interviewees referred to the problem of notario fraud—where vulnerable noncitizens are taken advantage of by unscrupulous attorneys or impostors who offer faulty or harmful advice—more spoke to the lack of crimmigration knowledge among even well-intentioned and skilled practitioners. Elena, a public immigration lawyer with eight years of experience, explained how when representing someone with an aggravated felony or other criminal conviction "You can't just be an immigration lawyer because immigration law is very vast"; instead you need to be someone who has studied or worked specifically at the intersection between criminal and immigration law "because a lot of people don't know the consequences a certain plea can have."

Yet, the immigrants that do secure lawyers around the country receive a wide spectrum of services. While it has been found that small and solo private law firms have the lowest level of success getting removal cases closed or securing legal relief from deportation, the vast majority of immigration court representation is done by such firms.[4] The varying quality (and hefty expense) of private immigration lawyers is magnified in lengthy and complex crimmigration cases, where "zealous advocacy" is difficult yet essential for obtaining relief.[5] Nonprofits and law school clinics, on the other hand, have the highest level of success,[6] yet are only able to take on a small portion of all cases. Furthermore, organizations that work to fill the immense need for affordable immigration legal services largely operate on a "triage" model, where cases are selected with the aim of winning as many as possible. In this context, aggravated felony cases—time consuming with low rates of relief—are not top contenders for the inadequate support available. Jackie, a public immigration lawyer and advocate for eight years, recounted, "Before NYIFUP you did have nonprofits that would do some cases, but they wouldn't do those aggravated felony cases." She elaborated, "That's still true in other places. . . . It's a practical consideration for the nonprofits who are trying to do work, where they put their resources, where they think it would make the most impact."

Under the triage model, legal providers use intake interviews to select the "most compelling cases" and to weed out those deemed "less deserving."[7] Also common are "carve-outs" that explicitly exclude immigrants with criminal records or certain criminal convictions—with aggravated felonies or offenses so classified often at the top of the list.[8] Such policies reflect deservingness politics and the need to pander to funders—evidence of the "good immigrant, bad immigrant" binary that continues to hold so much power. Pamela, a public immigration lawyer for three years, described aggravated felony cases as the "hardest" to find representation for since "they're not as sympathetic." She explained how organizations create carve-outs for legal assistance, because "they don't want to say someone has a violent felony or something like that." Yet the lack of support for aggravated felony cases also relates to, again, a simple lack of knowledge of the law around immigrants with criminal records. Jess, a public immigration lawyer for eleven years, spoke of her time at an organization serving noncitizen survivors of domestic violence, where none of the lawyers on staff had experience with crimmigration law, as an example of a case where "there may be people who want to serve that population but don't feel like they have the expertise to do so."

The universal representation provided through NYIFUP in New York relieves providers of such decisions, allowing for the provision of quality legal assistance to a wider and more inclusive swath of noncitizens. Nicole, a public immigration lawyer for fifteen years, spoke of the difference in the diversity of cases at her organization after receiving NYIFUP funding compared to previously, under a triage model, when "the vast majority of cases would not get a lawyer." Now, as stated by Elena, "at NYIFUP, we basically take cases that pretty much nobody else can or is willing to take." Barb, an immigration lawyer, educator, and advocate for close to thirty years, relayed that for complex cases, like many of those related to the aggravated felony, "the funding through NYIFUP here in New York has made all the difference in the world." Jackie referred to NYIFUP as a "revolutionary gamechanger." Such sentiments are underscored by scholarly analyses, institutional evaluations of the program and, perhaps most dramatically, rates of relief increasing more than tenfold.[9] Yet these rates are not only the result of increased individual representation but also of NYIFUP's creation of a large-scale forum for the development of legal knowledge and innovative strategies of defense, particularly in the cases of immigrants with criminal records.

Key to the program's success is the development of institutional knowledge around cases—like those involving aggravated felonies—that are rarely litigated in other contexts. This collaborative approach to individual cases is reminiscent of an emergent "big immigration law" model described by Stephen Manning and Juliet Stumpf as an innovative response to "big immigration enforcement."[10] Such large-scale individual representation allows for the development of creative legal strategies, helps bring migrant stories and enforcement trends to light, and can even have lasting impact on the systems in which lawyers do their work.[11] For example, judges are educated as attorneys push innovative arguments, and due process violations are lessened as fewer migrants appear with no advocate. Distinguishing this universal representation model from previous forms of legal activism, J.C. Salyer explains how, with NYIFUP, "the advent of a public-defender-like system provides an institutional base from which to evaluate and challenge aspects of immigration law in an unprecedented manner."[12]

In my research, lawyers and advocates spoke to the many qualities of universal representation under NYIFUP. Jess explained how the program's universal model, "where you're required to represent the person, so you're going to find an argument to make," has contributed to the development of creative legal responses. For example, May reported that contesting removability through the categorical approach "is not something that occurs to the majority of immigration lawyers" and described the development of this strategy in New York, as well as in other "cities where there is a concentration of immigrants, a concentration of legal service providers." Pamela concurred that the aggravated felony is being contested more often under programs like NYIFUP, saying, "This knowledge has been developing over time, but I think it's being more implemented on the field now with these defender programs." Naomi, a public immigration lawyer for ten years, said that at NYIFUP providers, "People are building off each other" as "they're identifying more issues, they're sharing arguments, they're preserving arguments that weren't preserved before." May recounted that when NYIFUP began, "Noncitizens actually started challenging ground zero, [saying] 'I'm not removable,' so that you actually have to apply the categorical approach, like the

Supreme Court said." She saw this as spurring "a huge change in how Varick Street [New York's detained immigration court] operated"—a shift also evident in institutional evaluations and scholarly accounts of the program.[13]

Yet the impacts of NYIFUP cannot be considered outside of the local networks of advocacy that brought the program into existence. Bolstered by a history of "legal activism" by immigration lawyers in NYC,[14] a coalition of progressive practitioners and immigration rights advocacy organizations were crucial in gleaning support for the project and seeing its instatement through. For Salyer, NYIFUP was a response to a lack of representation and faulty representation by those working in the field, combined with lawyers' broader responsibility to justice.[15] Increasing attention to the difficulties experienced by unrepresented, detained noncitizens facing deportation got a boost from a speech by Judge Robert Katzmann of the United States Court of Appeals for the Second Circuit (of which New York is a part) at the Association of the Bar of New York City in 2007. In his speech, Judge Katzmann decried the lack of representation among noncitizens facing deportation, pointing to whether an immigrant has an attorney as key in whether the case would have a "just outcome." He spoke of exploitative private attorneys that "hover around the immigrant community, taking dollars from vulnerable people with meager resources"—while often offering little in return—and urged the New York Bar to confront these problems.[16] The momentum created by this passionate and high-profile lecture led to the creation of the Study Group on Immigrant Representation, where Katzman was joined by fifty or so attorneys from a variety of nonprofits, private firms, bar associations, legal service providers, and law school immigration clinics. The group produced two research reports, one in 2011 and one in 2012, outlining the "scope and consequences of the problem of migrants having to face immigration proceedings without representation" as well as "a blueprint for addressing the problem on a local level."[17]

The findings of these studies were harnessed by local advocates to draw political support and funding for a program of universal representation for detained immigrants facing deportation—the first of its kind in the United States. Spearheaded collaboratively by organizations including the Northern Manhattan Coalition for Immigrant Rights, the Center for Popular Democracy, Make the Road New York, the

Immigration Justice Clinic at the Benjamin N. Cardozo School of Law, and the Vera Institute of Justice, NYIFUP began as a pilot program in 2013 before it was funded more extensively by the New York City Council the following year.[18] While funding for the program would only go to three legal providers already tasked with public defense for the city's criminal courts (The Legal Aid Society of New York , Brooklyn Defender Services, and the Bronx Defenders), the city's network of legal rights and immigration rights advocacy came together in support of the program. Peter Markowitz, the director of the Cardozo Law School Clinic and an early member of the Study Group on Immigrant Representation, explained, "We had virtually every immigrant rights organization, every immigrant legal services organization in the city, sign on and say [NYIFUP] should be a funding priority."[19] Following NYIFUP's success, publicly funded immigrant representation programs have begun to proliferate throughout the country, many of them supported by the Advancing Universal Representation Initiative led by Vera Institute—an organization central to the founding and administration of NYIFUP. Working with "government leaders, legal service providers, and community partners," this initiative aims to achieve "a public defender system for all immigrants facing deportation," implemented at the local and state level nationwide.[20]

Institutionalized Crimmigration Advisal

In addition to its provision of legal representation for detained immigrants, NYC is distinct in its institutionalization of crimmigration advice for criminal defenders. In the 2010 seminal decision of *Padilla v. Kentucky*, the Supreme Court held that criminal defense lawyers must advise noncitizen clients if a plea may make them deportable. Yet almost a decade later, participants referred to inadequate levels of formalized immigration advisement for criminal cases in other places around the country, while speaking positively about local implementation. Interviewees described designated *Padilla* teams in the NYC public defender organizations and the institutionalization of "regional assistance centers" to provide immigration-related advice to criminal law practitioners around New York State. Many of the immigration lawyers I spoke to had worked with NYC public defenders as "*Padilla* attorneys" or "criminal-immigration specialists" even before the NYIFUP program added immigration defense to these organizations' officially funded mission in 2014. Elena, a public immigration lawyer with eight years of experience, recounted being hired by one of the city public defender organizations post-*Padilla* and pre-NYIFUP "when a lot of organizations started to create small immigration units or practices."

Today, units of immigration lawyers are embedded in each of the city's public defense organizations in addition to designated providers throughout the state who aid other criminal defenders in providing notice of immigration consequences.[21] Zara, a criminal defender, immigration lawyer, and advocate with five years of experience, remarked, "New York City is one extreme where not only is there systematic *Padilla* advisal, but you have immigration representation. And in many cities, many states, you still don't have the first piece. You still don't have the *Padilla* advising." Jackie referred to NYC as "One of the pioneers in . . . the aftermath of *Padilla* and what you do once this right has been established." Pia said, "In New York we have a really good system in place at this point, in terms of the public defender offices having pretty robust immigration teams. But I think throughout the country it's pretty abysmal." Victor, a criminal defender, immigration lawyer, and advocate on crimmigration issues for almost thirty years, explained, "California and New York, I would say, are where the most has been done, but there are other parts of the country, including some high-immigrant states where very little has been done. A prominent example is Texas."

While NYC and New York State institutionalized criminal-immigration advisal in response to *Padilla*, they drew on the existing work of progressive legal organizations in doing so. For example, interviewees explained how Bronx Defenders and other defender offices had begun using a team-based model of holistic defense—including immigration advisement—in their criminal defense practices long before *Padilla*. Sheria said the provider she worked at had been using "in-house criminal-immigration attorneys" since the passage of the punitive federal immigration reforms of 1996. Similarly, the Immigrant Defense Project (IDP)—selected to become a state-funded *Padilla* legal assistance center in 2015[22]—was founded in 1997 by Manny Vargas, a former Legal Aid criminal defender. Jackie explained how Vargas quickly realized the impact the 1996 laws would have for his noncitizen clients, and the importance of public defenders as a "last line of defense." Thus, IDP had already been engaging in multileveled advocacy for immigrants with criminal records for almost two decades by the time they were tapped to contribute institutionalized legal support.[23]

Participants agreed that in addition to the expansion of legal representation in immigration court, the expansion of preventive criminal legal system work is an important way cities and states can resist harsh and expansive outcomes related to the aggravated felony. As Amy, a public immigration lawyer for ten years, explained, "Even before you have universal representation in immigration court, you need public defender offices advising people of their immigration consequences. That's the first step. That's how we grew. We were able to use those people, the Padilla attorneys, as our first deportation defense lawyers, so the expertise kind of grows from there." Celia, a public immigration lawyer for four years, spoke of a need for "more formalized immigration roles in public defender offices across the country." Victor said that that even after *Padilla*, "there's still a lot of work to be done," and Pia concurred, "I think there's absolutely so much more to do on the criminal side." As urged by Amy, "Every state that doesn't have people advising on how to avoid aggravated felonies and other bad pleas needs to comply with *Padilla* and hire people to do that."

Established Systems of Holistic Public Interest Law

In addition to universal representation and formalized *Padilla* advice teams in public defense offices, legal resistance to the aggravated felony is supported by New York's long history of public interest law and progressive legal services. In 1963, when the landmark *Gideon v. Wainwright* decision by the Supreme Court ruled legal representation in criminal court was a constitutional right to be provided at government expense, The Legal Aid Society of New York had already been providing legal services in one form or another to the city's most economically marginalized communities for close to one hundred years. In 1965, Legal Aid became the primary defender for New York City defendants facing charges in state criminal courts.[24] Leila Kawar describes progressive legal activism of the 1970s as an emergent field of leftist lawyers aligned with grassroots organizations who "sought to use their legal skills to promote the causes of a wide array of oppressed or excluded groups."[25] The public interest orientation of Legal Aid was further cemented over the next few decades, as the organization continued to not only serve indigent New Yorkers with legal defense but also to fight for a variety of impact legislation, case law, and local reforms affecting the populations they serve. In the 1990s, a labor dispute between mayor Rudolph Giuliani and the public defenders at Legal Aid led to the expansion of city contracts to newly formed organizations including the Bronx Defenders and Brooklyn Defense Services. These organizations expanded attention to "holistic defense," which aims to address not just clients' criminal charges, but also the multilayered consequences and circumstances surrounding them.

Today, The Legal Aid Society's website describes their organization as "The largest and most influential social justice law firm in New York City" and includes a variety of campaigns and action areas in addition to information for those seeking legal services.[26] Brooklyn Defense Services' site declares the organization's mission to work "in and out of court, to protect and uphold the rights of individuals and change laws and systems that perpetuate injustice and inequality," and includes a section on the organization's Policy, Advocacy, and Reform Team.[27] The Bronx Defenders' site includes a section on holistic defense, describing the organization's work toward "radically transforming how low-income people in the Bronx are represented in the justice system, and in doing so . . . transforming the system itself."[28] Thus while the legal resistance observed in this study was not limited to lawyers who considered themselves to be progressively oriented or working with an aim of social change, there were others who proudly identified as such. Sheria said of the public defense provider where she had worked for several years, "One of the reasons I love it here is because I guarantee if it's an issue affecting poor immigrant New Yorkers, someone at [this organization] knows how to do it. We're not scared of the law not being on someone's side, because we figure something out." This commitment to "zealous advocacy" in the public interest—along with the resources and skills developed at these well-established criminal defense organizations—creates the conditions for legal resistance against the aggravated felony.

Though deferral and withdrawal of removal based on the Convention against Torture (CAT) are the only forms of legal relief from deportation available to most noncitizens convicted of aggravated felonies, the grant rates of these forms of relief are incredibly low, and such cases are most successful with not only a lawyer, but also an expert witness. NYIFUP providers' holistic approach to legal services means that their attorney pools are augmented by in-house social workers and mental health professionals, in addition to other support staff.[29] Kayla, a social worker with three years of experience at a NYIFUP provider, said that she worked on CAT cases "typically when there are mental health or substance abuse worries." She explained,

> So for example, I could talk about the history of their symptoms, how they manifest, what that looks like, what that looks like as far as criminal court contact, what would most likely happen in the future, like a prognosis kind of, if they did have medications, what would happen, you know, if they were—let's say that they were mentally deteriorating in detention, we could talk about what that looks like and the extent of that and what that would probably look like when they get out.

Lawyers also spoke of hiring outside experts, enabled at the NYIFUP providers through funding specifically for this purpose. Cori, a NYIFUP lawyer with twelve years of experience in the field, explained, "We're fortunate that we have pretty good funding sources and we're able to often hire expert witnesses." Although lawyers and investigative support staff work hard to put together packets of published research on country conditions and other relevant factors, expert witnesses were seen as providing superior evidence with more impact in court. Cori said that hiring experts "is often the key in these cases because there's just not the documentary evidence that you'd gather. Like it's not strong enough what you can find in print or through your own research." At a workshop panel on the topic, another NYIFUP attorney explained that while lawyers often file country conditions reports of four hundred to five hundred pages, judges won't usually look at them, nor will they give much validity to descriptions by defense lawyers or the respondents themselves, but they will listen to the accounts of expert witnesses. Along with other panelists, the attorney spoke of increasing success in CAT cases as judges at Varick Street progressively grew familiar with creative arguments and absorbed country conditions described by hired experts.

The strategy of arguing claims for postconviction relief (PCR)—with the aim of overturning or amending a conviction deemed an aggravated felony—is also bolstered by the city's robust and holistic systems of public defense, which include various forums for no-cost postconviction legal representation. The city's Office of the Appellate Defender (OAD) has a program specifically intended to provide assigned counsel for PCR claims. Established in 2007 with a mission of identifying and remedying cases of wrongful conviction, the OAD Reinvestigation Project chooses cases based on elements such as "possible false confessions, the use of informants, unreliable or improperly presented forensic science, police, and/or prosecutorial misconduct, and ineffective assistance of counsel."[30] Zara spoke to the uniqueness of this program and said while most places "do have public defender systems," many "don't have assigned council for the purpose of a postconviction claim." She explained that while the Reinvestigation Project does not take every case, "they have a screening system and there is funding for *Padilla* postconviction." Other lawyers referred to the in-house Criminal Appeals Bureau at The Legal Aid Society of New York—the largest of the three NYIFUP providers—which also works to vacate convictions based on misadvisement, especially post-*Padilla*. Participants also referred to support for PCR afforded by the city's network of progressive attorneys and legal rights organizations. Working at a smaller legal services organization, Jane described "pursuing postconviction relief in partnership with other New York City nonprofits" based on the argument that a noncitizen "wasn't properly or adequately advised of the immigration consequences of the plea that they took." Another attorney described their experience at a private NYC law firm that has traditionally specialized in pro bono PCR work on cases related to serious wrongful convictions (like those addressed by The Innocence Project[31]) but now has "one category of our docket . . . reserved for immigrants facing removal and/or who are being considered statutorily ineligible to seek relief in immigration court because of their convictions."

Organizational Networks and Practical Support

Beyond the nonprofits tapped to provide universal representation through NYIFUP, responses to the aggravated felony are bolstered by the city's long-standing and active climate of immigration and legal rights advocacy. Crucial in the initial push for universal representation, organizational networks also provide ongoing practical support for legal resistance through training, resources, impact litigation, network build-ing, community support for individual cases, and campaigns for broader legislative change. As a leader in the field of crimmigration, IDP's foun-dational and ongoing efforts continually came up as central to observed strategies of legal resistance to aggravated-felony-based deportation. Alongside other groups—such as the American Immigration Coun-cil, the Immigrant Legal Resource Center, the Immigrant Rights Clinic at New York University (NYU) School of Law, the National Immigra-tion Project of the National Lawyers Guild, and the Vera Institute of Justice—IDP provides legal training for lawyers and the community and generates in-depth materials on criminal and immigration law which are aimed at lawyers and are made readily available on the internet. IDP is well-known among practitioners for maintaining a detailed reference that outlines the immigration consequences of every New York State criminal offense, and they and other organizations regularly post "prac-tice advisories" about new Supreme Court and circuit court caselaw, as well as other relevant issues. Lawyers saw such resources as vital in the ever-changing field of crimmigration law. In challenging the aggravated felony, Pamela saw "spreading knowledge of this body of caselaw that has been emerging" as equally important to expanding legal representa-tion, and Jess emphasized how important it is for lawyers to "keep up with the caselaw on this issue," as it is "continuing to develop." In refer-ence to the categorical approach, Pia said it was key that practitioners are "really taking the time to deeply understand it, go to trainings, speak with people in the field who are really expert, and make sure they're making those arguments."

In addition to generating and distributing information that supports cutting-edge legal strategies, advocates also work with lawyers to pro-duce "friend of the court" or "amicus" briefs on key issues, which are often signed on to by a number of organizations—sometimes to be sub-mitted in one specific case but more likely relevant to several. Raina, a public defender and immigration lawyer for six years, explained how, "As an organization that is interested in the issue, they file a friend of the court brief saying, 'This is why you should rule on the issue this way,'" and she provided the example of a recent IDP amicus brief drafted by the NYU Immigration Clinic "about why immigration judges should suppress the evidence or terminate cases in which a respondent was arrested at a courthouse." Organizations also engage in "impact litigation" around legal issues affecting immigrants with aggravated felonies—such as the NYIFUP providers' joint lawsuit on the use of tele-video at Varick Street immigration court[32]—and work to identify cases that could have important precedential implications. Naomi explained how organizations like IDP are creative in facilitating impact litigation "because they look at where there are going to be decisions in individual cases that are going to a circuit, and if you win at the circuit level, then you get good precedent, and that's an impact strategy, even if it's an individual case." Advocacy organizations also nurture networks between community members and legal providers and draw community support for sympathetic individual cases—especially the high-profile deportation cases of movement activists, often targeted for their resistance.

Finally, and perhaps most importantly, advocates continue to push for legislative reform—both in criminal and immigration law—that has impacts directly relevant to the aggravated felony. For example, the One Day to Protect New Yorkers Act—drafted and campaigned for by the IDP and the Cardozo Immigration Justice Clinic—was signed into New York State law in 2019, changing the maximum sentence for class A and unclassified misdemeanors from 365 to 364 days and ensuring that such crimes are not deportable as aggravated felonies. Advocacy by the ICE Out of Courts Coalition—"comprised of over 100 organizations and entities across New York State"—led to the 2020 passing of the Protect Our Courts Act, banning immigration enforcement from New York State criminal courts. Both of these laws were included in the Justice Roadmap, which was created by IDP and other organizations in 2018 to serve as "a legislative agenda designed to address the deeply interconnected harms caused by the criminal legal and immigration systems" in New York. Including a wide variety of state and local measures aiming to "choose community safety over police power," "stop criminalizing mental illness, drug use, and workers," "decarcerate jails and prisons and end perpetual punishment," "secure the dignity and opportunity of New Yorkers behind bars," and "end wealth extraction and invest in our communities," the 2022 Justice Roadmap is endorsed by almost two hundred local and national organizations.[33]

One endorser is the Drug Policy Alliance (DPA), a leading organization working to promote alternative drug policy and end the US War on Drugs.[34] Over the past several years, DPA worked directly with IDP to make sure cannabis legalization in New York State was shaped in a way mindful of the impacts on noncitizens.[35] At an observed 2017 panel on marijuana and deportation at a local law school, speakers from the two organizations emphasized the problems faced by noncitizens even in states where cannabis had been made legal, yet the laws had not been changed with this community in mind. Highlighting concerns also raised by interview participants, panelists spoke to the need to make sure policy around noncriminal "violations" and expunged old convictions would be crafted in a way that ensures they are not still counted as controlled substance offenses or aggravated felonies under immigration law. After years of campaigning from the Start SMART (Sensible Marijuana Access through Regulated Trade) New York coalition—led by DPA and including advocacy groups concerned with migrant rights, criminal legal reform, and racial justice—the state legalized cannabis in 2021, largely following the blueprint laid out by these organizations.[36] Marie Mark, IDP's director of legal support and resources at the time, spoke to the important part played by immigration advocates in the drafting of the law, and called state lawmakers "very committed to ensuring that immigrants were included in how we can correct the harm" caused by cannabis prohibition.[37]

Community-Based Activism

New York's established network of public interest lawyers and legal rights organizations has been central in constructing an environment conducive to creative and effective legal responses to the aggravated felony. Yet underlying the development of the protective policies and practical resources that support such legal resistance is a broader struggle led by immigrant communities impacted by the aggravated felony and the punitive deportation pipeline of which it is a part. Policies like universal representation for detained migrants and additional support for noncitizens in criminal court are not popular in a country that has demonized and scapegoated "criminal aliens" for almost as long as we have been a nation—even in the "sanctuary" city of NYC. Throughout the late modern "tough-on-crime" era in particular, politicians and advocates on both sides of the political spectrum have relied on this symbolically salient folk devil, either as a reason to exclude immigrants altogether, or as a foil to "good immigrants" deserving of support and relief. Thus, central to any form of resistance to the aggravated felony is the ongoing work of community-based activists who have fought to expose the false "good, bad" immigrant binary that privileges criminal legal system markers while dehumanizing and punishing in patently unequal ways. In doing so, impacted communities and supporters wage intersectional resistance at the crimmigration nexus against the aggravated felony, the criminalization-to-deportation pipeline, and the broader structures and beliefs that support their existence.

While insistent on the importance of quality and comprehensive legal representation for noncitizens facing deportation, study participants— most of them attorneys themselves—were clear on the secondary role of legal practitioners in resisting the aggravated felony. George, an immigration lawyer and advocate for thirty years, explained that while it is important that lawyers "try to be very good at technical things," there must also be a "community organizing aspect." He emphasized "communities in struggle as the motive force of social change, not lawyers winning things in court rooms." Raina described legal representation as "one key aspect" of resisting aggravated-felony-based deportation, but continued, "It's not always the most important. There are plenty of people with aggravated felonies that have no relief, or that their relief is really difficult to obtain, and in that case the lawyers are really not that necessary, are not that helpful, and really what's the most helpful is the community, community support and advocacy." Zara agreed, saying, "I don't like to be like, 'lawyers are the answer,' because [we're] not." Instead, "it's really important that the movement come from impacted people" since "communities are seeing what this is doing and have been seeing it unfortunately for a long time." For Zara, community organizing around crimmigration-related issues is central to increasing public understanding that "the 1996 laws that created a lot of these things . . . or enhanced them, need to be changed." Otherwise, "as much as we can make all these creative arguments, as long as these laws stay in place, there's only so much lawyers can do." In this punitive context, Raina referred to the role of lawyers as "harm reduction" and pointed to community support as "essential" for any real progress.

Participants with longer histories in the field spoke to the importance of the "good immigrant, bad immigrant" binary in the politics surrounding the development of the aggravated felony. In describing the category's evolution and expansion throughout the 1990s, George explained, "When legislation would come around, there were very few organizations that, as the bill went through its process, would advocate for this constituency." As wide-reaching and punitive criminal justice enforcement in the city's communities of color combined with the draconian treatment of "criminal aliens" under the immigration laws of 1996— and subsequent backlash post-9/11—impacted communities fought back. George explained how groups like NYC's Families for Freedom— founded in 2002 by immigrants directly impacted by intensified links between criminal justice and immigration enforcement—have "helped break down the good versus bad immigrant [binary]. You know, 'These are people from our community. Our fathers and sisters and mothers.'" Departing from mainstream immigration rights advocacy at the time— which often relied on harmful narratives framing certain immigrants as deserving based on their lack of criminal justice system involvement[38]— emergent organizations like Families for Freedom focused specifically on opposing the "good immigrant, bad immigrant" binary, and supporting migrants with criminal records. One longtime organizer with the group explained, with regard to noncitizens facing deportation for aggravated felonies, "Yes. We work with folks like that. . . . It's very rare that we have somebody roll in here who is just basically maybe a DACA [Deferred Action for Childhood Arrivals] recipient or trying to figure out where to go. We deal with specifically people with criminal convictions."

In their work to shift cultural narratives around noncitizens with criminal records, and to influence local and federal policy impacting this population, community-based groups like Families for Freedom were identified by participants as fundamental to legal resistance to the aggravated felony. Zara attributed creative legal strategies confronting aggravated felonies to "really good organizing and advocacy putting all the dots together and showing cause and effect, showing how specific families have been harmed." Pia recounted, "NYIFUP was created due to community groups being like, 'This is crazy. Our community members are being torn away.'" Sheria described the importance of activists "working to take the local precincts to task," offering the example of the immigrant enclave of Jackson Heights, Queens, where groups like TransLatinX and the Sex Workers Project have brought attention to police targeting of Latinx trans women and nonbinary people who often then end up in removal proceedings. Activist efforts at reframing the narrative around criminal deportation were also described as key in electing and placing pressure on progressive legislators and prosecutors, like City Council Speaker Melissa Mark-Viverito, who has continually fought for the NYIFUP program,[39] and Brooklyn district attorney Eric Gonzalez, who hired immigration attorneys to advise his office and instated an official policy to help noncitizens avoid deportation based on misdemeanors and nonviolent crimes.[40]

Still, while some support for immigrants with criminal records has emerged since the reforms of 1996, there remains a fight for services and advocacy to include all immigrants—not just those deemed deserving based on the convictions of a notoriously unequal criminal justice system. In the "sanctuary city" of NYC, controversy struck in May 2017, when mayor Bill DeBlasio—a Democrat who campaigned as a progressive—announced that city money would no longer pay for the legal representation of immigrants who had any conviction on an expansive list of 170 "serious" crimes.[41] This is the same list of 170 crimes for which ICE detainer requests may be honored by the city, and it is a list that includes many offenses also deemed aggravated felonies. Lawyers, advocates, and city council members strongly refuted the mayor's plan, which would have effectively ended NYIFUP's mission of providing universal representation to the city's detained immigrants. Eventually private money was sourced to pay for the representation of immigrants with convictions from the mayor's list of crimes,[42] yet advocates and lawyers still saw the incident as indicative of the continued salience of the "good immigrant/bad immigrant" binary.

Jackie called the mayor's actions "heartbreaking," and said, "I'm glad there was a compromise, but it just to me signaled that even the people who want to shout from the rooftops that they're the head of a progressive city, and they're doing sanctuary, still believe that some people should somehow be thrown away." Cecy, a NYIFUP lawyer for two years, called the list of crimes "a very unsophisticated list of offenses" and referenced former clients with convictions on the list who ended up winning relief from removal. She explained, "Like robbery in the second degree, two kids steal a bag, or they get in a fight and at the end of the fight one of them takes off with a cell phone, robbery in the second degree because two kids are involved. So you're telling me that a lawful permanent resident who has been in NYC for many years, and whose family is here shouldn't get a lawyer because that's what he was convicted of, you know?" Cecy went on to describe one particular case of a young man who was convicted of robbery in the second degree—an aggravated felony which is also on the mayor's list of crimes—who "pleaded guilty, got two years, was upstate, got ordered removed." Because she was assigned as his immigration lawyer, Cecy helped the young man get out of immigration detention, appeal his original robbery case with an appellate criminal lawyer, and eventually become not removable. She said that now, "The kid is doing really well, not in trouble, and is applying to become a United States citizen. He had an original conviction which is on the mayor's list, you know what I'm saying?"

As the work to move beyond the binary continues, many maintain that an intersectional approach—remaining mindful of the various inequalities within the immigrant community and how these inequalities overlap to impact interactions with the criminal justice system in particular—is central for ongoing resistance.[43] As Alina Das explains, "In particular, activists who work in intersectional spaces across race, ethnicity, religion, and gender lines have done much to redefine sanctuary to be more inclusive of those who are often targets for state violence, including Black, LatinX, Indigenous, LGBT, and Muslim people, to name a few, citizen and immigrant alike."[44] The Black Alliance for Just Immigration (BAJI) and the UndocuBlack Network are two organizations that have brought attention to the injustices faced by Black immigrants in particular, who are targeted by a racially unequal criminal justice system as well as long-standing societal stereotypes about criminality. Groups like these demonstrate the power of intersectional coalition building among impacted activists—"Black, immigrant, and undocumented in the era of #BlackLivesMatter"—who work to move beyond the perceived "silos" of broader movements for immigrant rights and police brutality.[45]

Like Families for Freedom and TransLatinX, these organizations have emerged due to the lived experience of their members—who represent groups both disproportionately criminalized and traditionally left out of broader narratives around immigrant rights.

As national attention to the issues of police brutality and racial injustice have amplified public discussion of criminal legal reform, police defunding, and prison abolition, immigrant rights organizations have increasingly drawn from such frameworks. From widespread calls to "Abolish ICE" in 2018, to more recent campaigns from mainstream organizations to abolish immigration detention, the language of abolition has become a key part of national movements for immigrant rights. In 2020—in response to global uprisings for racial justice in the wake of the murder of George Floyd—immigrant rights organizations without a previous focus on criminal justice began to emphasize the impacts of policing on noncitizens. Detention Watch Network (DWN) and United We Dream issued a call to "Defund Racist Law Enforcement: Police, ICE, and CBP,"[46] and DWN has continued to call for "the immigrant justice movement to embrace the broader calls for prison abolition and defunding the police."[47] "An Open Letter from Undocumented, DACAmented and formerly Undocumented Leaders to the Immigrants' Rights Movement"—signed by hundreds of individuals and organizations—pledged support for the "Black Lives Movement's demand to defund the police" and urged advocates to "stop using narratives that promote anti-Blackness and that pit us against the movement for Black Lives."[48]

Yet it has been community-based groups representing over-criminalized populations that have continually led the way in making linkages between criminal justice and immigration system struggles. Families for Freedom was founded in 2003 by impacted families responding to the "aftermath of 9/11 and the increased policing and surveillance of Arab and Muslim communities," as well as subsequent impacts on other criminalized noncitizens as the "new national security focus began to fuse with the country's thirty-year focus on immigrants with criminal convictions."[49] Founded in 2006, BAJI has consistently reasserted the goals of police defunding and abolition as central to addressing the "76% of Black immigrants [who] are deported because of contact with the police"—stating "we are constantly forced to contend with the truth that we cannot address systematic racism without

confronting the police in Black communities."[50] TransLatinx—a "trans-
led, immigrant-led organization"—was founded in 2007, to respond to
violence and discrimination experienced by trans immigrants, as well
as "policing and arrests of sex workers [which] put their immigration
statuses in peril."[51] While advocating against expansive systems of immigration enforcement, militarized policing, and mass incarceration more
generally, intersectional organizations like these also prioritize the specific needs of the communities they serve, engaging in a wide range of
service provision and practical assistance, as well as community organizing toward relevant policy aims. Intersectional activists fight to terminate federal programs like Secure Communities and 287(g)—which link
local policing to immigration enforcement throughout the country—
once and for all. They have also called for an end to broken windows
policing and the use of gang databases, as well as the decriminalization
of sex work and drugs—all common entry points into the deportation
pipeline, even in "sanctuary" cities like New York City.[52]

Though mainstream immigration rights advocacy has yet to eschew
the "good/bad" binary, the voices of radical activists in coalition with
broader social movements, such as those for racial justice and LGBTQ
rights, are a key emergent force shaping today's immigrant-led resistance.[53] Beyond reforms to immigration and criminal justice policy, intersectional activism stresses the need to address the societal hierarchies
such policies work to uphold. Interviewed as part of this research, one
longtime organizer with Families for Freedom spoke to the broader
structural context reflected by the aggravated felony: "Understand, all of
this is not necessarily based on criminalization or immigration per se.
It's based, from our point of view, on population control or the preserva-
tion of white supremacy. Any which way they could remove the other,
they were going for it." While framed as though "we're getting rid of
undesirables," the organizer said, "It's not. It's the same population [that
is consistently targeted for criminalization]. It's social control, [ethnic]
cleansing, and whitening of the other." In his view, while amending the
legislation around the aggravated felony would be helpful, without addressing broader racial hierarchies and systemic inequality, impacted
groups will continue to experience oppression. He said, "if it's not an
aggravated felony tomorrow because we fight and we win, it will be
something else." Thus, for immigrant groups disproportionately targeted

by the criminal justice system—immigration reform is not enough. As Annie Lai and Christopher Lasch explain, even "de-linking immigration [enforcement] from crime control, without more, risks entrenching problems with the broader system of crime control that affects noncitizens and citizens alike."[54] Therefore, in order to truly provide justice for immigrants with criminal records, we must grapple as a society with our broader constructions of what, and who, is criminal.

Conclusion

As a long-standing hub of immigration, with a distinctly engrained system of public interest law, New York City in some ways creates "best case scenario" conditions for legal resistance. Countering the city's powerful and unequal systems of criminal justice enforcement that encumber noncitizens with convictions deemed aggravated felonies in the first place, are protective "sanctuary" policies that enable the development and zealous enactment of innovative responses to the aggravated felony. Initiatives like universal representation for detained migrants facing deportation and institutionalized immigration advisal in public defense offices are facilitated by long-standing collaborations between public interest law and immigration rights advocacy in NYC, as well as the knowledge and resources developed among these networks. Yet legal advocacy and service provision for immigrants with aggravated felonies are only made possible by the activism of impacted communities who have continually spoken out about the destructive and unequal workings of the 1996 immigration laws, the criminalization-to-deportation pipeline, and the false "good immigrant, bad immigrant" binary that upholds them. Thus, while distinctly legal in their character, observed immigration court responses to the aggravated felony are contextualized, enabled, and pushed forward by an intricate landscape of advocacy and activism.

Like the legal strategies detailed in the previous chapter, the advocacy portrayed here happens at the crimmigration nexus, drawing tools and points of confrontation from both the immigration and criminal systems. As originally conceptualized, the destructive nature of crimmigration lies in its ability to draw on the most punitive aspects of the two bodies of law.[55] In the case of the aggravated felony, we see the expansive enforcement capabilities and permanent markers of the criminal system combined with (civil) immigration law's lack of due process and potential for permanent banishment. Networks of advocacy in NYC bolster legal resistance by drawing on protective and due process elements of the criminal system—largely established or expanded in response to the punitive turn of the late modern era. These include systems of public defense—required in criminal courts since the 1960s—which universal representation for detained immigrants emulates, and institutionalized crimmigration advisal uses as a venue to contain immigration law's most expansive effects. In New York, such resources also include long-standing networks of progressive lawyers and legal advocates, many of them housed at one of the largest and longest-standing public legal service organizations in the country, who have helped develop resources to assist defendants in the criminal context—with tools like expert witnesses and postconviction relief—also particularly helpful for deportation cases involving aggravated felonies. Representing the city's most marginalized and over-criminalized populations, public criminal system defenders like Manny Vargas of IDP quickly jumped into action to after the 1996 laws, knowing all too well which communities, individuals, and families would be most affected by the expanded crackdown on "criminal aliens." Drawing on tools of both the criminal and immigration systems, legal advocacy by Vargas and other progressive defenders has been central in achieving impactful systems of universal representation for detained immigrants and Padilla support for crimmigration cases, alongside other reforms beneficial to noncitizens facing deportation for aggravated felonies.

However, beyond the work of lawyers, these systems are only achieved through the advancement of nuanced and humanistic frameworks around criminal deportation, led by impacted communities themselves. Diverging from mainstream immigration rights advocacy—which has so often rejected immigrants with criminal records in favor of deservingness politics—groups like Families for Freedom, Black Alliance for Just Immigration, and TransLatinX resist the binary and shout the humanity of immigrants with criminal records. This intersectional resistance draws on the experiences of criminalized groups long overlooked in broader struggles for immigrant rights—such as Black and Afro-Latinx communities besieged by broken windows policing, gang raids, and the War on Drugs, or trans women of color routinely targeted as sex workers. Organizing and activism led by impacted populations emphasizes the need to delink criminal and immigration enforcement, alongside reforms that decrease police interactions with immigrant communities and the breadth of criminal justice systems more generally. Demands speak to the centrality of criminal justice reform as part of any real challenge to the crimmigration nexus, and the vital work of social movements working to connect the dots between—and simultaneously oppose—irrevocably entwined structures of social control. Further, in opposing the demonizing stereotypes and destructive outcomes met by immigrants convicted of deportable crimes, activists draw attention to broader systemic inequalities and the taken-for-granted nature of the criminal markers that uphold them.

Conclusion

Beyond the Binary

In spring of 2022, Republican governors from Texas, Florida, and Arizona began systematically busing and flying thousands of asylum seekers apprehended at the country's southern border to northern "sanctuary" jurisdictions. As I write this, in October of 2022, these transports continue, and more than ten thousand migrants have been sent from the three states to cities like New York; Chicago; Washington, DC; and even the resort island of Martha's Vineyard. Blaming a historic surge of refugee arrivals—fueled in part by political and economic crises in Venezuela, Nicaragua, and Cuba (countries long impacted by the violence of US imperialism)—on the Biden administration's discontinuation of Trump-era border policies, the Republican governors have continually framed their strategy as an attempt to pressure Democratic lawmakers into action.[1] Advocates have decried the inhumane and illegal nature of the transports, in which traumatized asylum seekers are misled and sent to unsuspecting locales that are not prepared for large-scale refugee reception and resettlement.[2] Critics have also pointed out the misguided nature of the stated political strategy as Republican congresspeople in Texas, Florida, and Arizona have far more power to change federal immigration policy than the Democratic mayors of so-called sanctuary cities. Instead, the governors of the three states—all of whom are up for reelection in November of 2022—appear to be exploiting transported refugees in a display of political theater aimed at their Republican constituents, who are particularly concerned with immigration and border control and also distinctly wary of "out of touch" northern liberals. The dramaturgical nature of the refugee relocation is made clear in the choice of destinations: Democratic-run cities previously called out by the Trump administration for being "soft" on immigration, as well as new targets, like Martha's Vineyard, a left-leaning elite vacation destination with limited space, services, and infrastructure to support arriving migrants. The Martha's Vineyard airlift, orchestrated by Florida governor Ron DeSantis in September 2022, was described in the *New York Times* as "The cherry on top of a monthslong campaign to essentially troll liberal cities and states by transferring many asylum seekers to those communities."[3]

While municipal agencies, immigration rights groups, and religious organizations have worked tirelessly to welcome the transported migrants in their new destinations,[4] the cracks in the "sanctuary" label have also been made clear. In Washington, DC, where more than seven thousand asylum seekers were delivered from Texas and Arizona between April and August of 2022, Democratic mayor Muriel Bowser has called on the Defense Department to send in the National Guard.[5] In New York, where close to ten thousand asylum seekers have joined the city's existing fifty thousand unhoused people in the first nine months of 2022,[6] some have been met with punitive treatment and inhumane conditions—such as the twenty-one-year-old Venezuelan man hit in the face, pinned down, and tased by a Department of Homeless Services officer at a Brooklyn shelter in September and the thirty-two-year-old Colombian mother who committed suicide at a Bronx shelter the same month.[7] Despite condemning the Republican governors' transporting of migrants against their will as "horrific" and "unimaginable,"[8] Democratic mayor Eric Adams has spoken of reexamining New York's unique "right to shelter" which obligates the city's provision of housing for all,[9] claiming "asylum seekers are a 'humanitarian crisis' that is separate from the city's requirement for the right to shelter."[10] The "humanitarian relief center" being built by the Adams administration as emergency housing for arriving migrants has been deemed a "tent city" or worse by immigration advocates such as South Bronx Mutual Aid, which tweeted, "SLSCO, the Texas-based contractor chosen by city for site is the same contractor used by Trump to build the border wall. Migrants say the site build is identical to the 'Icebox' TX detention center."[11] As "sanctuary" leaders like Bowser and Adams adopt the language and tools of crisis, they play into the trap of the Republican governors, tacitly providing support for a federal crackdown on immigration.[12] In response, Florida governor Ron DeSantis has boasted, "All those people in D.C. and New

York were beating their chest when Trump was president, saying they were so proud to be sanctuary jurisdictions. The minute even a small fraction of what those border towns deal with every day are brought to their door, they all go beserk."[13]

As panic about the refugee surge spreads throughout the country, the public's responses are reminiscent to those of the late 1970s and early 1980s, when—as detailed in chapter 1—an influx of asylum seekers from the Caribbean was met with racism, demonization, and punitive policy foundational to the systems of mass detention and deportation that are in place today.[14] Forty years ago, Haitian refugees and "Mariel" Cubans were met with sketchy accusations of criminality; in 2022, Republicans have similarly played up fears around "public safety" in the current migrant surge, like in an unsubstantiated viral tweet by a Texas congressperson, claiming that, "DHS [Department of Homeland Security] has confirmed that Venezuela empties prisons and sends violent criminals to our southern border."[15] In New York, where concerns about crime have been reenflamed in recent years, responses to the influx of migrants has also been tinged with fears of the "criminal alien." While immigrant rights advocates have protested the inadequate conditions and services being extended to refugees arriving in the city, demonstrations have also been attended by conservatives, including self-identified "ultra MAGA supporters and Proud Boys" who[16]—citing concerns about crime and safety—deny the place of the city in providing any aid at all.[17] Speaking to a local news network at a protest outside city hall, Republican New York state senate candidate Samantha Zherka accused Democratic officials of being "more interested in sympathizing with rapists, murderers, drug dealers, and thieves than they are protecting the lives of men, women, children and seniors."[18]

Such flagrant fearmongering about immigrant criminality harkens back to that which allowed for the creation and expansion of the aggravated felony—the most consequential and comprehensive category of deportable offenses under US immigration law. Demarcating a wide range of criminal convictions for which noncitizens are mandatorily detained and almost surely deported, the aggravated felony is one legal manifestation of the "criminal alien" folk devil that has played on racist stereotypes and unfounded claims linking immigration and crime since the early days of this nation. This entrenched mythology was made even more salient throughout the 1980s and 1990s as racialized moral panic linking immigration with drugs and crime contributed to a punitive turn in policy around drugs, crime, and immigration. Created as part of the Anti-Drug Abuse Act of 1988, and drastically expanded in the immigration reforms of 1996, the aggravated felony is a clear example of the increased connectedness of immigration and criminal law throughout this period—a "crimmigration" nexus that has continued to increase its hold in decades since.[19]

* * *

The way crimmigration intertwining enhances the punitive and exclusionary potential of both the criminal and immigration systems is evident in the harsh and unequal impacts of the aggravated felony—impacts that this book has demonstrated based on findings from my qualitative research in New York City's detained immigration court. The lessor due process requirements of civil law leave the vast majority of those who face deportation in immigration courts around the country to do so sans legal representation, while detained without bond in the same facilities and conditions used for criminal punishment. Beyond the noncitizens who face this rarely surmountable immigration court context there are the many undocumented individuals convicted of offenses deemed aggravated felonies by immigration authorities who are subject to shadowy processes of expedited removal (outside the scope of this study), which is decided by an immigration officer with no lawyer or judge present at all.[20] Groups that are disproportionately impacted by infamously unequal systems of criminal justice are, by way of the aggravated felony and other deportable convictions, doled additional incarceration and funneled toward expulsion. At the same time, the immigration system's capabilities for punishment are expanded by its links to the criminal system through the aggravated felony—namely the permanent markers of criminal convictions that follow even those who have long moved on with their lives and the enforcement and detainment capabilities of the most expansive and well-funded systems of policing and incarceration in the world.

By focusing on the punitive impacts of the aggravated felony, this book expands on crimmigration research on the "criminalization" of migrants to better understand the impacts for those already criminalized. Though conceptualized around the ways that the modern intertwining enhances the punitive and exclusionary potential of both systems,[21] scholarship on crimmigration has largely focused on the ways that migrants are increasingly constructed or treated as criminal, whether it be through the classification of immigration violations as criminal convictions;[22] the engagement of local police in immigration enforcement;[23] or the jails and prisons used for immigration detention.[24] Recently, some have expressed concern that widespread, uncritical use of the term "crimmigration" itself may even further societal perceptions of migrants as criminal.[25] Yet in identifying the problem with our treatment of migrants more generally as the rhetorical and tangible processes through which they are "criminalized," we run the risk of crystalizing existing conceptions of crime and criminality. By allowing criminal history—and non-immigration-related criminal history in particular—to dictate which migrants should be deported, advocated for, or studied, criminal legal system markers are portrayed as objective fact, rather than the subjective, socially constructed outcomes that they are. This cements the need to punish and remove actual "criminals"—an imperative that allows for more extensive and aggressive enforcement and removals affecting all migrants while also rationalizing the treatment of nonmigrants impacted by notoriously unequal systems of policing and mass incarceration.

This book has emphasized the way that fearful designations like "criminal alien" and "aggravated felon" are shaped by systemic forces manifest in human decisions with extremely impactful results. Yet just as our conceptions of these categories are socially constructed, as are our conceptions of criminality more broadly. These conceptions are rooted in racial hierarchies that go back to slavery and colonialism as well as overlapping economic inequities that serve the needs of global capitalism. They are also shaped by the unique context of the late modern era, when crime has been brought to the forefront of the societal imagination and punitive apparatuses of social control expanded like never before. By demonstrating the social construction of the aggravated felony and the expansive and unequal ways in which it is applied, this book brings light to this oft-vilified yet rarely understood immigration law distinction. In doing so, it expands on existing critiques of the category, leveled by legal scholars and advocates, with regard to its sprawling, decisive, and disparate results. Beyond this, in deconstructing the aggravated felony—framed even within "humanitarian" proposals for immigration reform as an indicator of noncitizen dangerousness and criminality—this book questions the more general bases for the punitive systems of criminalization and deportation.

Yet the punitive outcomes of the aggravated felony are only part of the story. As the later chapters of this book document, the positioning of the aggravated felony on the axis of immigration and criminal law also provides opportunities for legal resistance to the category. Observed legal responses combine the tools of immigration and criminal law developed directly in response to what are perceived to be expansive and severe impacts of the aggravated felony. While some of the lawyers who engage in these tactics see themselves as activists fighting for immigrants' rights, this is a not a necessary component. Innovative strategies of legal resistance are largely carried out as part of immigration and criminal lawyers' professional commitments—like the zealous representation of individual clients and the protection of established legal rights. Responses to aggravated-felony-based deportability—like creative Convention against Torture (CAT) cases and contestation using the categorical approach in immigration court or preventive negotiation and postconviction relief in the criminal context—are in a large part made possible through NYC's provision of universal and holistic legal representation for noncitizens in both criminal and immigration court. Institutionalized protections are upheld by established networks of public interest lawyers and legal rights advocates but also by the intersectional activism of impacted communities who contest the "good immigrant, bad immigrant" binary that has long shaped the treatment of immigrants with criminal records.

By highlighting policies and advocacy that have been beneficial to the legal rights of immigrants facing aggravated-felony-based deportation, this book provides some hope that even with stringent federal immigration laws targeting "criminal aliens" remain in place, localities can take steps to protect the rights of *all* immigrants and not just those deemed most deserving. Yet the severe and unequal consequences observed even in these conditions also demonstrate the power of the criminalization-to-deportation pipeline and the need for more than current sanctuary policies to stop up its flow. In New York, activists from impacted communities have been central in the ongoing fight to bring attention to the unequal impacts of this pipeline and to the humanity of the loved ones and neighbors siphoned into its spiraling pull. Alongside legal rights nonprofits like Immigrant Defense Project, community-based groups like Families for Freedom and Black Alliance for Just Immigration advocate for not just changes to immigration policy but for criminal system reforms impactful for noncitizens vulnerable to criminalization, like reduced charging and sentencing for misdemeanors, the decriminalization of drugs, and an end to broken windows policing—all of which contribute to the net of crimmigration law and enforcement in distinctly racialized ways. Community-based groups also align with modern social movements, like #BlackLivesMatter and struggles for LGBTQ rights, to highlight the diverse experiences of criminalization among immigrants and the need to identify and defeat broader systems of oppression upheld through punitive social control. In doing so, these activists expand the struggle for immigrant rights to include the rights of those previously excluded.

This book expands the use of crimmigration to understand how the intertwining of immigration and criminal law creates both punitive outcomes and tools for resistance. The same complex web of policies, processes, and social actors that make these overlapping systems powerful in pulling migrants toward deportation also afford diverse tools and entry points that can be seized by the impacted communities, advocates, and legal practitioners. In the case of the aggravated felony, this means injecting due process into immigration law through the provision of quality, well-resourced legal representation and the proper use of the categorical approach while working around the marking power of criminal law through preventive crimmigration negotiation and attempts for postconviction relief. It also means activism and advocacy, fighting for the rights of noncitizens with criminal records alongside the rights of all immigrants, and including the specific struggles of immigrants into broader movements against unjust systems of criminal justice. In combining the needs of these overlapping populations, impactful resistance at the crimmigration nexus is distinctly intersectional.[26] By rejecting the pretense that criminalized means disposable, crimmigration resistance questions societal conceptions of criminality more generally, disrupting the solidity of the injustice and inequality these ideas serve to rationalize and uphold.

* * *

Broadly speaking, punitive and disparate outcomes of the aggravated felony are rooted in inequalities inherent in neoliberal capitalism, exclusionary border enforcement in an increasingly transnational world, and the continued salience of white supremacist racial hierarchies—complex problems not easily solved through individual policy recommendations. While opposing these larger structures, this book also indicates several more immediate implications for advocates and legislators concerned with protecting the rights of criminalized noncitizens nationwide. The ramped-up immigration enforcement and immigration court breaches of due process documented in this research underscore an intensely punitive focus on immigration under the Trump administration. Yet the development and entrenchment of the aggravated felony and the broader deportation regime under both conservative and liberal governments over the past thirty years, as well as the continued insistence of the Biden administration to single out immigrants with criminal records, demonstrate the ongoing need for diverse and multileveled resistance to the deportation regime. My findings critically emphasize the importance of movement support for issues of criminal deportation, an important source of racial inequality that is often swept aside for more sympathetic narratives, as well as an urgent need to eschew the "good immigrant, bad immigrant" binary. This support and change can come through intersectional movements that include the stories of migrants with criminal records, demonstrate the links between criminal justice system inequality and unjust deportation, and oppose criminalizing enforcement methods of both the criminal and immigration systems.

This research demonstrates the need to eliminate the aggravated felony category and end mandatory detention. Both enhance punishment and erode due process for immigrants targeted by the criminal justice system, and do far more to tear communities apart than to keep anyone safe. Findings further indicate a need to eradicate Secure Communities and other crimmigration structures that serve to funnel noncitizens of color through a pipeline from racialized criminalization to deportation. These are steps toward broader goals of replacing immigration detention and the punitive enforcement of national borders with humane systems privileging the dignity and safety of migrants and refugees. Findings also support ongoing campaigns to end mass incarceration, drug prohibition, and the militarized policing of Black and Brown neighborhoods, and they support calls for improved services for mental health and substance abuse issues beyond the criminal justice system. There is a nationwide need at the local level for programs like those that have been established with great success in New York City to provide universal, quality immigration court representation for detained immigrants (at least) and institutionalized immigration experts in public defender offices. The effectiveness of such programs can be increased through local funding for expert witnesses and postconviction attorneys; technical support including resources, training, and network building; and the election and pressuring of progressive district attorneys. Furthermore, advocates and policymakers can work to interrupt the criminalization-to-deportation pipeline by refusing to honor ICE detainer requests and by banning ICE officers from local jails and courts. Finally, local and statewide criminal justice reform can play an important role in limiting the expansive use of the aggravated felony, by decriminalizing drugs and "broken windows" offenses, deprioritizing misdemeanor arrests, and capping the maximum sentence for misdemeanors at 364 days. These immediate goals are congruent with wider calls to defund the police, abolish prisons, and invest instead in care and communities.

There remains a need for critical research focused on criminal deportation and the mechanisms that support it. The literature on the aggravated felony in particular would benefit from a descriptive investigation, based on Freedom of Information Act (FOIA) requests, into the numbers and characteristics of deportations based on aggravated felonies and other criminal grounds; in-depth interview research that speaks directly to the stories of immigrants convicted of aggravated felonies; and comparative study of aggravated-felony-related outcomes in other locales around the country. This study underscores the necessity of grounding critical understandings of law and social control in the structural and cultural contexts from which they emerge, while interrogating categories and binaries presented as fixed. Rather than accepting such distinctions as a given, we must question what it means to be an "aggravated felon," a "bad immigrant," a "criminal alien," or even a "criminal" at all. It is through this deconstruction that we move beyond oversimplified binaries, to expose the socially constructed nature of laws and categories that invariably serve to exclude and punish.

ACKNOWLEDGMENTS

I began writing this book as a graduate student at the Graduate Center of the City University of New York (CUNY). I finished writing it as an assistant professor at Rutgers University–Camden. The final product is a tribute to the inspiration and support of those who are too many to name. I try my best to list some of them here.

First and foremost, I am indebted to my participants and all those who fight for the rights and humanity of criminalized people—in courtrooms, in the streets, and beyond. Organizations including the Immigrant Defense Project, Families for Freedom, and Black Alliance for Just Immigration, as well as the lawyers at New York Family Unity Project, have provided particular inspiration for this work through their tireless commitment to fighting for immigrants with criminal records.

My interest in criminology, the sociology of law, and critical perspectives in each was sparked and nurtured by Peter Yeager at Boston University. His confidence in my ideas and writing as an undergraduate played a large part in my later decision to pursue doctoral studies in sociology. I am thankful to the Department of Sociology at the Graduate Center, where I found myself as a scholar. I am particularly indebted to the late great Jock Young for his generous spirit and critical mind. His commitment to the field of critical criminology was only surpassed by his support for his students. He is truly missed. I am also ever grateful to my mentor, dissertation adviser, and collaborator David Brotherton, who has encouraged and facilitated this research since my early years of graduate school. I am inspired by his dedication to students, public scholarship, and social justice, as well as his focus on the stories of those all too often deemed disposable.

Monica Varsanyi and Leslie Paik provided a great deal of support for this project, nurturing its early roots and providing thoughtful feedback and advice as I moved from research to writing and publication. I am grateful to them for their guidance, as well as their modeling of incisive and rigorous qualitative research. Thank you to Jayne Mooney for her mentorship, support, and friendship in graduate school and beyond. Thank you to Lynn Chancer for her dedication to her students. Graduate Center faculty and staff—including Sujatha Fernandes, Mehdi Bozorg-mehr, Rati Kashyap, Alex Vitale, and the late Stanley Aronowitz—guided and encouraged my scholarship in ways for which I will always be thankful.

I am continually uplifted by the members of the Social Anatomy of a Deportation Regime working group at John Jay College, in particular Edwin Grimsley, Nick Rodrigo, Felicia Arriaga, Darializa Avila Cheva-lier, Brian Mercado, Marriane Madoré, and Lidia Vázquez—treasured comrades and researchers who inspire me with their dedication to critical scholarship and social change. Graduate school would have been a lot more difficult without the friendship of this group or that of David Frank, Vadricka Etienne, Jennifer Ortiz, Drea Martinez, and Erin Michaels.

Thank you to the Department of Sociology, Anthropology, and Criminal Justice at Rutgers–Camden, where I have found a home as an assistant professor for the past three years, as this book has come to fruition. Special thanks to Laura Napolitano, Nathan Link, Dan Semenza, Richard Stansfield, Jane Siegel, Joanie Mazelis, and Kayla Prieto-Hodge, whose levity, kindness, and advice helped me finish writing this book amid the early years of the tenure track and the chaos of teaching during the COVID-19 pandemic. At Rutgers, I am also grateful to Ulla Berg and Lorena Avila Jaimes, special humans and scholars I have been lucky to know and work with. Additionally, I would like to thank my students at Rutgers and at Brooklyn College, where I taught during graduate school. Their questions help me clarify and refine complex concepts, and their perspectives give me hope for the future.

Thank you to Nancy Hiemstra for supporting my book dreams and providing feedback on my prospectus and to Carolina Sanchez Boe for always encouraging my work. Their research, alongside that of people like Nicholas DeGenova, Amada Armenta, Patrisia Macías-Rojas, Philip Kretsedemas, Sofya Apteker, Tamara Nopper, Diedre Conlon, Tanya Golash-Boza, Cecilia Menjívar, Alina Das, César Cuauhtémoc García Hernández, and mentors David Brotherton and Monica Varsanyi, has been instrumental in creating a field of critical migration studies, without which this book would not be possible. I'd also like to collectively thank the members of the Common Sessions in Critical Criminology; the Crime, Law, and Deviance workshop at the Graduate Center; and the divisions of Convict Criminology and Critical Criminology & Social Justice of the American Society of Criminology. The feedback and inspiration provided in these forums has guided the development of this book in countless ways.

At New York University Press, I am particularly appreciative of Ilene Kalish, who took an early interest in this project and worked with me to develop it into a book, as well as Martin Coleman, Ann Boisvert, and the rest of the talented editorial, design, and production teams who have made this volume a reality. I am also thankful for the anonymous reviewers who gave thoughtful and generous feedback, which improved the quality of this final product.

The research that this book is based on was enabled by the Behavioral Science Training in Drug Abuse Research Fellowship at New York University and the National Development and Research Institute; the Pollis Dissertation Fellowship and David Garth Dissertation Award in Public Policy at the Graduate Center; and the Vera Institute and CUNY Graduate Center Research Fellowship at the Vera Institute of Justice. These fellowships provided financial support and essential feedback in the early stages of this project while also helping me hone the research and organizational skills needed to complete it.

Thank you to my family and friends for surrounding me with love and laughter throughout the long and intensive process of research and writing. My siblings, Katy and Nick Tosh, have made me who I am and are my continual support and inspiration. My aunt, Donna Herman, has always been there with the best hugs, most delicious meals, and sweetest kvelling. My mother-in-law, Mary Ellen Smolar, has welcomed me to New Jersey with so much kindness. Friends like Amy Pinder, Meg Marzo, Kayla Mahler, Irena Eaves, Keith Allen, Dioganhdih Hall, Laura Wood, Shelby Pirtle, Atoosa Esmaili, Stephanie Spock, Lindsay Hansen, Esmeralda Prado, and Cassidy Hogan fill my heart and give me life.

My husband, Catan Gray, has been a rock throughout this process, supporting me through the hard moments and celebrating with me through the good. Even on the longest writing days, he manages to fill my life with food, music, plants, cats, and love. I could not imagine a better partner, and for him I feel very lucky.

Finally, I owe everything to my parents, Diane and Stephen Tosh, who brought me up amid reading, writing, activism, and humor passed down by generations of radical New York Jews. Their support lifts me, and their enthusiasm for learning, commitment to justice, and revolutionary brand of kindness provide a guidepost for which I am eternally grateful.

APPENDIX

Alphabetized List of Aggravated Felonies

(As printed in the Immigration and Nationality Act [8 USC § 1101(a)(43)])

The term "aggravated felony" means-

(A) murder, rape, or sexual abuse of a minor;

(B) illicit trafficking in a controlled substance (as defined in section 802 of title 21), including a drug trafficking crime (as defined in section 924(c) of title 18);

(C) illicit trafficking in firearms or destructive devices (as defined in section 921 of title 18) or in explosive materials (as defined in section 841(c) of that title);

(D) an offense described in section 1956 of title 18 (relating to laundering of monetary instruments) or section 1957 of that title (relating to engaging in monetary transactions in property derived from specific unlawful activity) if the amount of the funds exceeded $10,000;

(E) an offense described in-

    (i)   section 842(h) or (i) of title 18, or section 844(d), (e), (f), (g), (h), or (i) of that title (relating to explosive materials offenses);

    (ii)   section 922(g)(1), (2), (3), (4), or (5), (j), (n), (o), (p), or (r) or 924(b) or (h) of title 18 (relating to firearms offenses); or

    (iii) section 5861 of title 26 (relating to firearms offenses);

(F) a crime of violence (as defined in section 16 of title 18, but not including a purely political offense) for which the term of imprisonment at least one year;

(G) a theft offense (including receipt of stolen property) or burglary offense for which the term of imprisonment at least one year;

(H) an offense described in section 875, 876, 877, or 1202 of title 18 (relating to the demand for or receipt of ransom);

(I) an offense described in section 2251, 2251A, or 2252 of title 18 (relating to child pornography);

(J) an offense described in section 1962 of title 18 (relating to racketeer influenced corrupt organizations), or an offense described in section 1084 (if it is a second or subsequent offense) or 1955 of that title (relating to gambling offenses), for which a sentence of one year imprisonment or more may be imposed;

(K) an offense that-

    (i) relates to the owning, controlling, managing, or supervising of a prostitution business;

    (ii) is described in section 2421, 2422, or 2423 of title 18 (relating to transportation for the purpose of prostitution) if committed for commercial advantage; or

    (iii) is described in any of sections 1581–1585 or 1588–1591 of title 18 (relating to peonage, slavery, involuntary servitude, and trafficking in persons);

(L) an offense described in-

    (i) section 793 (relating to gathering or transmitting national defense information), 798 (relating to disclosure of classified information), 2153 (relating to sabotage) or 2381 or 2382 (relating to treason) of title 18;

    (ii) section 3121 of title 50 (relating to protecting the identity of undercover intelligence agents); or

    (iii) section 3121 of title 50 (relating to protecting the identity of undercover agents);

(M) an offense that-

    (i) involves fraud or deceit in which the loss to the victim or victims exceeds $10,000; or

    (ii) is described in section 7201 of title 26 (relating to tax evasion) in which the revenue loss to the Government exceeds $10,000;

(N) an offense described in paragraph (1)(A) or (2) of section 1324(a) of this title (relating to alien smuggling), except in the case of a first offense for which the alien has affirmatively shown that the alien committed the offense for the purpose of assisting, abetting, or aiding only the alien's spouse, child, or parent (and no other individual) to violate a provision of this chapter 6

(O) an offense described in section 1325(a) or 1326 of this title committed by an alien who was previously deported on the basis of a conviction for an offense described in another subparagraph of this paragraph;

(P) an offense (i) which either is falsely making, forging, counterfeiting, mutilating, or altering a passport or instrument in violation of section 1543 of title 18 or is described in section 1546(a) of such title (relating to document fraud) and (ii) for which the term of imprisonment is at least 12 months, except in the case of a first offense for which the alien has affirmatively shown that the alien committed the offense for the purpose of assisting, abetting, or aiding only the alien's spouse, child, or parent (and no other individual) to violate a provision of this chapter;

(Q) an offense relating to a failure to appear by a defendant for service of sentence if the underlying offense is punishable by imprisonment for a term of 5 years or more;

(R) an offense relating to commercial bribery, counterfeiting, forgery, or trafficking in vehicles the identification numbers of which have been altered for which the term of imprisonment is at least one year;

(S) an offense relating to obstruction of justice, perjury or subornation of perjury, or bribery of a witness, for which the term of imprisonment is at least one year;

(T) an offense relating to a failure to appear before a court pursuant to a court order to answer to or dispose of a charge of a felony for which a sentence of 2 years' imprisonment or more may be imposed; and

(U) an attempt or conspiracy to commit an offense described in this paragraph.

NOTES

INTRODUCTION

1 William Walters, "Deportation, Expulsion, and the International Police of Aliens," *Citizenship Studies* 6, no. 3 (September 2002): 265–92, https://doi.org/10.1080 /1362102022000011612.

2 Daniel Kanstroom, "Reaping the Harvest: The Long, Complicated, Crucial Rhetorical Struggle Over Deportation," Connecticut Law Review 39, no. 5 (January 2007): 1911–1922.

3 Matthew Flynn and Michael Flynn, "Critiquing Zones of Exception: Actor-Oriented Approaches Explaining the Rise of Immigration Detention," in *Immigration Policy in the Age of Punishment: Detention, Deportation, and Border Control*, ed. David C. Brotherton and Philip Kretsedemas (New York: Columbia University Press, 2018), 118.

4 David C. Brotherton and Philip Kretsedemas, eds., *Immigration Policy in the Age of Punishment: Detention, Deportation, and Border Control* (New York: Columbia University Press, 2018); Katja Franko, *The Crimmigrant Other: Migration and Penal Power* (Abingdon, UK: Routledge, 2019); Mary Bosworth and Sarah Turnbull, "Immigration Detention, Punishment, and the Criminalization of Migration," in *The Routledge Handbook on Crime and International Migration*, ed. Sharon Pickering and Julie Ham (Abingdon, UK: Routledge, 2017), 91–106, https://doi.org/10 .4324/9780203385562-7; Robert Koulish and Maartje van der Woude, *Crimmigrant Nations: Resurgent Nationalism and the Closing of Borders* (New York: Fordham University Press, 2020).

5 Jonathan Simon, "Sanctioning Government: Explaining America's Severity Revolution," *University of Miami Law Review* 56, no. 1 (2001): 217–53; Malcolm M. Feeley and Jonathan Simon, "The New Penology: Notes on the Emerging Strategy of Corrections and Its Implications," *Criminology* 30, no. 4 (November 1992): 449–74, https://doi.org/10.1111/j.1745-9125.1992.tb01112.x; David Garland, *The Culture of Control: Crime and Social Order in Contemporary Society* (Oxford, UK: Oxford University Press, 2001).

6 Dan Kanstroom, *Aftermath: Deportation Law and the New American Diaspora* (New York: Oxford University Press, 2012); Sarah Tosh, "Drugs, Crime, and Aggravated Felony Deportations: Moral Panic Theory and the Legal Construction of the 'Criminal Alien,'" *Critical Criminology* 27, (March 2019): 329–345, https://doi .org/10.1007/s10612-019-09446-8; Patrisia Macías-Rojas, "Immigration and the

War on Crime: Law and Order Politics and the Illegal Immigration Reform and Immigrant Responsibility Act of 1996," *Journal on Migration and Human Security* 6, no. 1 (2018): 1–25.

7   Tanya Maria Golash-Boza, *Immigration Nation: Raids, Detentions, and Deportations in Post-9/11 America* (Abingdon, UK: Routledge, 2015).

8   US Immigration and Customs Enforcement, "Secure Communities," ice.gov, 2021, https://www.ice.gov/secure-communities.

9   Tanya Maria Golash-Boza, "President Obama's Legacy as 'Deporter in Chief,'" in *Immigration Policy in the Age of Punishment: Detention, Deportation, and Border Control* (New York: Columbia University Press, 2018), 37–56.

10 US Immigration and Customs Enforcement, "Priority Enforcement Program (PEP)," ice.gov, 2021, https://www.ice.gov/pep.

11 Nick Miroff, "Deportations Slow under Trump despite Increase in Arrests by ICE," *Washington Post*, September 28, 2017, https://www.washingtonpost.com /world/national-security/deportations-fall-under-trump-despite-increase-in -arrests-by-ice/2017/09/28/1648d4ee-a3ba-11e7-8c37-e1d99ad6aa22_story.html.

12 US Immigration and Customs Enforcement, "Secure Communities."

13 Randy Capps, Muzaffar Chishti, Julia Gelatt, Jessica Bolter, and Ariel G. Ruiz Soto, *Revving up the Deportation Machinery: Enforcement and Pushback Under Trump* (Washington, DC: Migration Policy Institute, 2018).

14 Jorge Loweree and Aaron Reichlin-Melnick, *Tracking the Biden Agenda on Immigration Enforcement* (Washington, D.C.: American Immigration Council, May 20, 2021), https://www.americanimmigrationcouncil.org/research/tracking-biden -agenda-immigration-enforcement.

15 Immigrant Defense Project, "IDP Statement: 170 Organizations Send Letter to DHS Secretary Defending Local Policies That Protect Immigrant Communities," March 29, 2022, https://www.immigrantdefenseproject.org/idp-statement-170 -organizations-send-letter-to-dhs-secretary-defending-local-policies-that-protect -immigrant-communities/; American Civil Liberties Union, *License to Abuse: How ICE's 287(g) Program Empowers Racist Sheriffs*, 2022, https://www.aclu.org /report/license-abuse-how-ices-287g-program-empowers-racist-sheriffs; National Immigration Justice Center, "DHS Secretary Mayorkas Comments to U.S. Mayors Betray Administration's Commitment to Disentangle Local Police from Immigration Enforcement," January 21, 2022, https://immigrantjustice.org/press -releases/dhs-secretary-mayorkas-comments-us-mayors-betray-administrations -commitment.

16 Nick Miroff and Maria Sacchetti, "New Biden Rules for ICE Point to Fewer Arrests and Deportations, and a More Restrained Agency," *Washington Post*, February 7, 2021, https://www.washingtonpost.com/national/new-biden-rules-for-ice -point-to-fewer-arrests-and-deportations-and-a-more-restrained-agency/2021/02 /07/faccb854-68c6-11eb-bf81-c618c88ed605_story.html.

17 Michelle Ye Hee Lee, "Donald Trump's False Comments Connecting Mexican Immigrants and Crime," *Washington Post*, July 8, 2015, https://www.washingtonpost

.com/news/fact-checker/wp/2015/07/08/donald-trumps-false-comments
-connecting-mexican-immigrants-and-crime/?utm_term=.d49951b8fc76.

18 Ginger Thompson and Sarah Cohen, "More Deportations Follow Minor Crimes,
    Records Show," *New York Times*, April 6, 2014, https://www.nytimes.com/2014/04
    /07/us/more-deportations-follow-minor-crimes-data-shows.html.

19 See, for example, Iris Bennett, "The Unconstitutionality of Nonuniform Immi-
    gration Consequences of 'Aggravated Felony' Convictions," *New York University
    Law Review* 74 (1999): 1696–1740; Melissa Cook, "Banished for Minor Crimes:
    The Aggravated Felony Provision of the Immigration and Nationality Act as a
    Human Rights Violation," *Third World Law Journal* 23, no. 2 (2003): 293–329; Bill
    Ong Hing, "Re-Examining the Zero-Tolerance Approach to Deporting Aggra-
    vated Felons: Restoring Discretionary Waivers and Developing New Tools," *Policy
    Review* 8 (2017): 141–76; Kevin R. Johnson, "Racial Profiling in the War on Drugs
    Meets the Immigration Removal Process: The Case of *Moncrieffe v. Holder*," *Uni-
    versity of Michigan Journal of Law Reform* 48, no. 4 (2015): 967–98; Aaron Lang,
    "An Opportunity for Change? Aggravated Felonies in Immigration Proceedings
    and the Effect of *Moncrieffe v. Holder*," *Boston University Law Journal* 33 (2015):
    102–37; Nancy Morawetz, "Understanding the Impact of the 1996 Deportation
    Laws and the Due Process Clause," *New York University Law Review* 73 (2000):
    107–14; Diana R. Podgorny, "Rethinking the Increased Focus on Penal Measures
    in Immigration Law as Reflected in the Expansion of the Aggravated Felony
    Concept," *Journal of Criminal Law and Criminology* 99, no. 1 (2008): 287–316;
    Jeff Yates, Todd A. Collins, and Gabriel J. Chin, "A War on Drugs or a War on
    Immigrants? Expanding the Definition of 'Drug Trafficking' in Determining
    Aggravated Felon Status for Noncitizens," *Maryland Law Review* 64, no. 3 (2005):
    875–909; Alina Das, "Inclusive Immigrant Justice: Racial Animus and the Origins
    of Crime-Based Deportation," *University of California Davis Law Review* 52
    (2018): 171–92; Sara Salem, "Should They Stay or Should They Go: Rethinking The
    Use of Crimes Involving Moral Turpitude in Immigration Law," *Florida Law Re-
    view* 70, no. 1 (2018): 225–50; Alina Das, *No Justice in the Shadows: How America
    Criminalizes Immigrants* (New York: Bold Type Books, 2020).

20 Examples include Leisy J. Abrego, *Sacrificing Families: Navigating Laws, Labor,
    and Love Across Borders* (Stanford, CA: Stanford University Press, 2014); Eliza-
    beth Aranda and Elizabeth Vaquera, "Racism, the Immigration Enforcement
    Regime, and the Implications for Racial Inequality in the Lives of Undocumented
    Young Adults," *Sociology of Race and Ethnicity* 1, no. 1 (January 2015): 88–104; Julie
    A. Dowling and Jonathan Xavier Inda, *Governing Immigration Through Crime: A
    Reader* (Stanford, CA: Stanford University Press, 2013); Tanya Maria Golash-Boza,
    Immigration Nation: Raids, Detentions, and Deportations in Post-9/11 America
    (Abingdon, UK: Routledge, 2015); Roberto G. Gonzales, "Learning to Be Illegal:
    Undocumented Youth and Shifting Legal Contexts in the Transition to Adult-
    hood," *American Sociological Review* 76, no. 4 (August 2011): 602–19; Cecilia
    Menjívar and Leisy J. Abrego, "Legal Violence: Immigration Law and the Lives of

Central American Immigrants," *American Journal of Sociology* 117, no. 5 (March 2012): 1380–1421; Michael Welch, *Detained: Immigration Laws and the Expanding I.N.S. Jail Complex* (Philadelphia: Temple University Press, 2002).

21 Examples include Katherine Beckett and Theodore Sasson, *The Politics of Injustice: Crime and Punishment in America* (Thousand Oaks, CA: SAGE, 2004); Lawrence D. Bobo and Victor Thompson, "Unfair by Design: The War on Drugs, Race, and the Legitimacy of the Criminal Justice System," *Social Research* 73, no. 2 (2006): 445–72; William Chambliss, "Drug War Politics: Racism, Corruption, and Alienation," in *Crime Control and Social Justice: The Delicate Balance*, ed. Darnell Hawkins, Samuel Myers, Jr., and Randolph Stone (Westport, CT: Greenwood Press, 2003), 295–317; Doris Marie Provine, *Unequal under Law: Race in the War on Drugs* (Chicago: University of Chicago Press, 2008); Craig Reinarman and Harry G. Levine, *Crack in America: Demon Drugs and Social Justice* (Berkeley: University of California Press, 1997); Michael Tonry, *Malign Neglect: Race, Crime, and Punishment in America* (New York: Oxford University Press, 1995).

22 Notable exceptions include David Brotherton and Luis Barrios, *Banished to the Homeland: Dominican Deportees and Their Stories of Exile* (New York: Columbia University Press, 2011); Tanya Maria Golash-Boza, *Deported: Immigrant Policing, Disposable Labor and Global Capitalism* (New York: NYU Press, 2015); and Patrisia Macías-Rojas, *From Deportation to Prison: The Politics of Immigration Enforcement in Post-Civil Rights America* (New York: NYU Press, 2016).

23 Cook, "Banished for Minor Crimes."

24 Ingrid V. Eagly and Steven Shafer, "A National Study of Access to Counsel in Immigration Court," *University of Pennsylvania Law Review* 164, no. 1 (2015): 1–91.

25 Bennett, "Unconstitutionality."

26 César Cuauhtémoc García Hernández, "Deconstructing Crimmigration," *SSRN Electronic Journal*, 2019, https://doi.org/10.2139/ssrn.3326202; Juliet Stumpf, "The Crimmigration Crisis: Immigrants, Crime, and Sovereign Power," *American University Law Review* 56, no. 2 (2006): 367–419.

27 Dario Melossi, *Crime, Punishment and Migration* (London: SAGE, 2015).

28 See Leisy Abrego, Mat Coleman, Daniel E. Martínez, Cecilia Menjívar, and Jeremy Slack, "Making Immigrants into Criminals: Legal Processes of Criminalization in the Post-IIRIRA Era," *Journal on Migration and Human Security* 5, no. 3 (September 2017): 694–715, https://doi.org/10.1177/233150241700500308.

29 See Aranda and Vaquera, "Undocumented Young Adults"; Amada Armenta, "Racializing Crimmigration: Structural Racism, Colorblindness, and the Institutional Production of Immigrant Criminality," *Sociology of Race and Ethnicity* 3, no. 1 (January 2017): 82–95, https://doi.org/10.1177/2332649216648714; Felicia Arriaga, "Understanding Crimmigration: Implications for Racial and Ethnic Minorities Within the United States," *Sociology Compass* 10, no. 9 (September 2016): 805–12, https://doi.org/10.1111/soc4.12401.

30 Angela J. Davis, *Policing the Black Man: Arrest, Prosecution, and Imprisonment* (New York: Knopf Doubleday Publishing Group, 2017); Michelle Alexander, *The*

New Jim Crow: Mass Incarceration in the Age of Colorblindness (New York: New Press, 2012); Valeria Vegh Weis, "Criminal Selectivity in the United States: A History Plagued by Class & Race Bias" 10 (2017): 32; Devon Johnson, Patricia Y. Warren, and Amy Farrell, *Deadly Injustice: Trayvon Martin, Race, and the Criminal Justice System* (New York: NYU Press, 2015).

31 Jeffrey H. Reiman, *Rich Get Richer and the Poor Get Prison: Ideology, Class and Criminal Justice* (New York: John Wiley & Sons, 1979); Steven Spitzer, "Toward a Marxian Theory of Deviance," *Social Problems* 22, no. 5 (1975): 638–51; Austin T. Turk, "Law as a Weapon in Social Conflict," *Social Problems* 23, no. 3 (1976): 276–91; David Greenberg, *Crime And Capitalism: Readings in Marxist Criminology* (Philadelphia: Temple University Press, 2010).

32 Examples include Michael Walzer, *Spheres of Justice: A Defense of Pluralism and Equality* (New York: Basic Books, 1983); Giorgio Agamben, *Homo Sacer: Sovereign Power and Bare Life* (Stanford, CA: Stanford University Press, 1998); Walters, "International Police of Aliens."

33 See Nicholas DeGenova, "The Deportation Regime: Sovereignty, Space, and the Freedom of Movement," in *The Deportation Regime: Sovereignty, Space, and the Freedom of Movement*, ed. Nicholas DeGenova and Natalie Peutz (Durham, NC: Duke University Press, 2010), 33–68; Golash-Boza, *Deported*; Nik Theodore, "Closed Borders, Open Markets: Immigrant Day Laborers' Struggle for Economic Rights," in *Contesting Neoliberalism: Urban Frontiers*, ed. Helga Leitner, Jamie Peck, and Eric S. Sheppard (New York: Guilford Press, 2007), 250–65.

34 Alejandro Portes, "Migration, Development, and Segmented Assimilation: A Conceptual Review of the Evidence," *Annals of the American Academy of Political and Social Science* 610 (2007): 73–97; Alejandro Portes and Rubén G. Rumbaut, *Immigrant America: A Portrait* (Oakland: University of California Press, 1996).

35 Jock Young, "To These Wet and Windy Shores: Recent Immigration Policy in the UK," *Punishment & Society* 5, no. 4 (October 2003): 395, https://doi.org/10.1177/1462474503005400 5.

36 See also Robert King Merton, "Social Structure and Anomie," *American Sociological Review* 3, no. 5 (1938): 672–82.

37 See also Brotherton and Barrios, *Banished to the Homeland*.

38 Richard Delgado and Jean Stefancic, *Critical Race Theory: An Introduction* (New York: NYU Press, 2001); Kimberle Crenshaw, Neil Gotanda, Garry Peller, and Kendall Thomas, eds., *Critical Race Theory: The Key Writings That Formed the Movement* (New York: New Press, 1996).

39 Ian Haney-López, *White by Law: The Legal Construction of Race* (New York: NYU Press, 2006).

40 Kimberle Crenshaw, "Demarginalizing the Intersection of Race and Sex: A Black Feminist Critique of Antidiscrimination Doctrine, Feminist Theory and Antiracist Politics," *University of Chicago Legal Forum* 1989, no. 1 (1989):139–67.

41 Alexander, *New Jim Crow*; Chambliss, "Drug War Politics"; Provine, *Unequal under Law*; Tonry, *Malign Neglect*; Loic Wacquant, "Deadly Symbiosis: When Ghetto and Prison Meet and Mesh," *Punishment & Society* 3, no. 1 (2001): 95–134.

42 Daniel Olmos, "Racialized Im/Migration and Autonomy of Migration Perspectives: New Directions and Opportunities," *Sociology Compass* 13, no. 9 (September 2019): 4, https://doi.org/10.1111/soc4.12729.

43 Examples include Andrew Gyory, *Closing the Gate: Race, Politics, and the Chinese Exclusion Act* (Chapel Hill, NC: University of North Carolina Press, 1998); Kitty Calavita, *Inside the State: The Bracero Program, Immigration, and the I.N.S.* (Abingdon, UK: Routledge, 1992).

44 See Leo Ralph Chavez, *The Latino Threat: Constructing Immigrants, Citizens, and the Nation* (Stanford, CA: Stanford University Press, 2008); Catherine Dauvergne, *Making People Illegal: What Globalization Means for Migration and Law* (Cambridge: Cambridge University Press, 2008); Nicholas DeGenova, "The Legal Production of Mexican/Migrant 'Illegality,'" *Latino Studies* 2 (2004): 160–85; Joseph Nevins, *Operation Gatekeeper and Beyond: The War On "Illegals" and the Remaking of the U.S.—Mexico Boundary* (Abingdon, UK: Routledge, 2010); Mae M. Ngai, *Impossible Subjects: Illegal Aliens and the Making of Modern America* (Princeton, NJ: Princeton University Press, 2004); Mary Romero, "Racial Profiling and Immigration Law Enforcement: Rounding Up of Usual Suspects in the Latino Community," *Critical Sociology* 32, no. 2–3 (March 2006): 447–73, https://doi.org/10.1163/156916306777835376; San Juanita García, "Racializing 'Illegality': An Intersectional Approach to Understanding How Mexican-Origin Women Navigate an Anti-Immigrant Climate," *Sociology of Race and Ethnicity* 3, no. 4 (October 2017): 474–90, https://doi.org/10.1177/2332649217713315.

45 Armenta, "Racializing Crimmigration"; See also Aranda and Vaquera, "Undocumented Young Adults."

46 Martha D. Escobar, *Captivity Beyond Prisons: Criminalization Experiences of Latina (Im)Migrants* (Austin, TX: University of Texas Press, 2016).

47 Doris Marie Provine and Roxanne Lynn Doty, "The Criminalization of Immigrants as a Racial Project," *Journal of Contemporary Criminal Justice* 27, no. 3 (August 2011): 261–77, https://doi.org/10.1177/1043986211412559.

48 Tanya Golash-Boza and Pierrette Hondagneu-Sotelo, "Latino Immigrant Men and the Deportation Crisis: A Gendered Racial Removal Program," *Latino Studies* 11, no. 3 (September 2013): 271–92, https://doi.org/10.1057/lst.2013.14.

49 Tanya Golash-Boza, Maria D. Duenas, and Chia Xiong, "White Supremacy, Patriarchy, and Global Capitalism in Migration Studies," *American Behavioral Scientist* 63, no. 13 (November 2019): 1741–59, https://doi.org/10.1177/0002764219842624.

50 Tod G. Hamilton, *Immigration and the Remaking of Black America* (New York: Russell Sage Foundation, 2019); Asha Layne, "It's Not Just Black and White: How Black Immigrants Continue to Influence the Fight against Police Violence," *Journal of Liberal Arts and Humanities* 2, no. 6 (2021): 1–7; Monica Anderson and Gustavo Lopez, "Key Facts about Black Immigrants in the U.S.," *Pew Research*

Center (blog), January 24, 2018, http://www.pewresearch.org/fact-tank/2018/01/24/key-facts-about-black-immigrants-in-the-u-s/.

51 Christine Tamir, "Key Findings about Black Immigrants in the U.S.," *Pew Research Center* (blog), January 27, 2022, https://www.pewresearch.org/fact-tank/2022/01/27/key-findings-about-black-immigrants-in-the-u-s/.

52 Juliana Morgan-Trostle, Kevin Zheng, and Carl Lipscombe, "The State of Black Immigrants" (New York: Black Alliance for Just Immigration, 2016), http://www.stateofblackimmigrants.com/assets/sobi-fullreport-jan22.pdf; Jeremy Raff, "The 'Double Punishment' for Black Undocumented Immigrants," *Atlantic*, December 30, 2017, https://www.theatlantic.com/.

53 Moon-Kie Jung, "The Racial Unconscious of Assimilation Theory," *Du Bois Review: Social Science Research on Race* 6, no. 2 (2009): 375–95, https://doi.org/10.1017/S1742058X09990245; Jemima Pierre, "Black Immigrants in the United States and the 'Cultural Narratives' of Ethnicity," *Identities* 11, no. 2 (April 2004): 141–70, https://doi.org/10.1080/10702890490451929; Vilna Bashi Treitler, "Social Agency and White Supremacy in Immigration Studies," *Sociology of Race and Ethnicity* 1, no. 1 (January 2015): 153–65, https://doi.org/10.1177/2332649214560796.

54 Philip Kretsedemas, *The Immigration Crucible: Transforming Race, Nation, and the Limits of the Law* (New York: Columbia University Press, 2012); Tanya Golash-Boza, "Structural Racism, Criminalization, and Pathways to Deportation for Dominican and Jamaican Men in the United States," *Social Justice* 44, no. 2/3 (2017): 137–61.

55 Derron Wallace, "Safe Routes to School? Black Caribbean Youth Navigating Police Surveillance in London and New York City," *Harvard Educational Review* 88, no. 3 (2018); B. Heidi Ellis, Alisa K. Lincoln, Saida M. Abdi, Elizabeth A. Nimmons, Osob Issa, and Scott H. Decker, "'We All Have Stories': Black Muslim Immigrants' Experience with the Police," *Race and Justice* 10, no. 3 (2018): 341–62.

56 Breanne J. Palmer, "The Crossroads: Being Black, Immigrant, and Undocumented in the Era of #BlackLivesMatter," *Georgetown Journal of Law and Modern Critical Race Perspectives* 9, no. 1 (2017): 99–121; Robin Pomerenke, "Intersectional Resistance: A Case Study on Crimmigration and Lessons for Organizing in the Trump Era," *Hastings Women's Law Journal* 29, no. 2 (2018): 241–60.

57 See Richard L. Abel, *Politics by Other Means: Law in the Struggle Against Apartheid, 1980–1994* (Abingdon, UK: Routledge, 1994); Mindie Lazarus-Black and Susan F. Hirsch, *Contested States: Law, Hegemony, and Resistance* (London: Psychology Press, 1994); Boaventura de Sousa Santos and César A. Rodríguez-Garavito, *Law and Globalization from Below: Towards a Cosmopolitan Legality* (Cambridge: Cambridge University Press, 2005).

58 US Department of Justice (DOJ), "EOIR Immigration Court Listing," justice.gov, 2021, https://www.justice.gov/eoir/eoir-immigration-court-listing.

59 Cook, "Banished for Minor Crimes"; Das, *No Justice in the Shadows*.

60 Jennifer Lee Koh, "Removal in the Shadows of Immigration Court," *Southern California Law Review* 90 (2017): 180–235.

61 TRAC Immigration, "Outcomes of Dpeortation Proceedings in Immigration Court," TRAC, Syracuse University, 2020, https://trac.syr.edu/phptools /immigration/court_backlog/deport_outcome_charge.php.

62 In June 2018, ICE announced that they would no longer be physically bringing detained noncitizens to Varick Street for their court appearances. Detained individuals would instead have to appear from the jails and detention centers where they were confined using videoconferencing technology.

63 See Kitty Calavita, *Invitation to Law and Society: An Introduction to the Study of Real Law* (Chicago: University of Chicago Press, 2010); Malcolm M. Feeley, *The Process Is the Punishment: Handling Cases in a Lower Criminal Court* (New York: Russell Sage Foundation, 1992); Aaron Kupchik, "Prosecuting Adolescents in Criminal Courts: Criminal or Juvenile Justice?," *Social Problems* 50, no. 3 (August 2003): 439–60, https://doi.org/10.1525/sp.2003.50.3.439; Leslie Paik, *Discretionary Justice: Looking Inside a Juvenile Drug Court* (New Brunswick, NJ: Rutgers University Press, 2011); David Sudnow, "Normal Crimes: Sociological Features of the Penal Code in a Public Defender Office," *Social Problems* 12, no. 3 (1965): 255–76.

64 Jennifer Stave, Peter Markowitz, Karen Berberich, Tammy Cho, Danny Dubbaneh, Laura Simich, Nina Siulc, and Noelle Smart, "Evaluation of the New York Immigrant Family Unity Project: Assessing the Impact of Legal Representation on Family and Community Unity" (New York: Vera Institute of Justice, 2017).

65 "Immigration Attorney Demographics and Statistics in the US," Zippia: The Career Site, January 29, 2021, https://www.zippia.com/immigration-attorney-jobs /demographics/.

66 Examples include Amada Armenta, *Protect, Serve, and Deport: The Rise of Policing as Immigration Enforcement* (Oakland: University of California Press, 2017); Felicia Arriaga, "Relationships between the Public and Crimmigration Entities in North Carolina: A 287(g) Program Focus," *Sociology of Race and Ethnicity* 3, no. 3 (2017): 417–31; Mathew Coleman, "The 'Local' Migration State: The Site-Specific Devolution of Immigration Enforcement in the U.S. South," *Law & Policy* 34, no. 2 (April 2012): 159–90, https://doi.org/10.1111/j.1467-9930.2011.00358.x; Doris Marie Provine, Monica W. Varsanyi, Paul G. Lewis, and Scott H. Decker, *Policing Immigrants: Local Law Enforcement on the Front Lines* (Chicago: University of Chicago Press, 2016).

67 Also see Annie Lai and Christopher N. Lasch, "Crimmigration Resistance and the Case of Sanctuary City Funding," *Santa Clara Law Review* 57 (2018): 539–610; and Jennifer Chacón, "Immigration Federalism in the Weeds," *University of California Los Angeles Law Review* 66 (2019): 1332–93.

68 The Marshall Project, "How Donald Trump's War on Immigrants Is Playing Out in NYC," The Marshall Project, July 23, 2018, https://www.themarshallproject.org /2018/07/23/new-york-on-ice; TRAC Immigration, "Latest Data: Immigration and Customs Enforcement Removals," TRAC, Syracuse University, 2020, https://trac .syr.edu/phptools/immigration/remove/.

69 Ryan Devereaux and John Knefel, "ICE Evades Sanctuary Rules by Using NYPD Fingerprints to Find Immigrants and Send Them Call-In Letters," *Intercept*

(blog), April 26, 2018, https://theintercept.com/2018/04/26/ice-sends-threatening
-letters-to-immigrants-increasing-climate-of-fear-in-new-york-city/; Abigail
Hauslohner, Maria Sacchetti, and Colby Itkowitz, "Trump Says ICE Raids to Start
Sunday, Emphasizing Purge of Criminal Immigrants," *Washington Post*, July 12,
2019, https://www.washingtonpost.com/immigration/trump-says-ice-raids-to
-start-sunday-emphasizing-purge-of-criminal-immigrants/2019/07/12/b063e87c
-a4b5-11e9-bd56-eac6bb02d01d_story.html; Scott M. Stringer, *The Demographics of Detention: Immigration Enforcement in NYC Under Trump* (New York City
Comptroller, Bureau of Policy and Research, February 2019).

70 Liz Robbins, "In a 'Sanctuary City,' Immigrants Are Still at Risk," *New York Times*,
April 11, 2018, https://www.nytimes.com/2018/02/27/nyregion/sanctuary-cities
-immigrants-ice.html.

71 Marcella Alsan and Crystal S. Yang, "Fear and the Safety Net: Evidence from Secure
Communities" (Cambridge, MA: National Bureau of Economic Research, 2019).

72 Randol Contreras, *The Stickup Kids: Race, Drugs, Violence, and the American
Dream* (Berkeley: University of California Press, 2013).

73 Julilly Kohler-Hausmann, "'The Atilla the Hun Law': New York's Rockefeller
Drug Laws and the Making of a Punitive State," *Journal of Social History*, 2010,
71–95; Brian Mann, "The Drug Laws That Changed How We Punish," *Morning
Edition* (National Public Radio, February 14, 2013), https://www.npr.org/2013/02
/14/171822608/the-drug-laws-that-changed-how-we-punish; Amanda Geller and
Jeffrey Fagan, "Pot as Pretext: Marijuana, Race and the New Disorder in New York
City Street Policing," *Journal of Empirical Legal Studies* 7, no. 4 (2010): 591–633;
Innocence Project, "Racial Disparities Evident in NYC Arrest Data for Marijuana
Possession," Innocence Project, May 14, 2018, https://www.innocenceproject.org
/racial-disparities-in-nyc-arrest-data-marijuana-possession/.

74 Monica Anderson, "A Rising Share of the U.S. Black Population Is Foreign Born,"
Pew Research Center's Social & Demographic Trends Project (blog), April 9, 2015,
https://www.pewsocialtrends.org/2015/04/09/a-rising-share-of-the-u-s-black
-population-is-foreign-born/; Monica Anderson and Gustavo Lopez, "Key Facts
about Black Immigrants in the U.S.," *Pew Research Center* (blog), January 24,
2018, http://www.pewresearch.org/fact-tank/2018/01/24/key-facts-about-black
-immigrants-in-the-u-s/; Layne, "It's Not Just Black and White"; Migration Policy
Institute, "State Immigration Data Profiles," migrationpolicy.org, 2019, https:
//www.migrationpolicy.org/programs/data-hub/state-immigration-data-profiles.

75 Eagly and Shafer, "National Study of Access," 7–8.

76 Stave et al., "Evaluation of the New York Immigrant Family Unity Project."

1. "SAVAGING OUR SOCIETY"

Epigraphs: Alina Das, *No Justice in the Shadows: How America Criminalizes Immigrants*
(PublicAffairs, 2020), 74. Jacquelyn Swearingen, *States News Service*, April 14, 1988.

1 Roxanne Dunbar-Ortiz, *Not "A Nation of Immigrants": Settler Colonialism, White
Supremacy, and a History of Erasure and Exclusion* (Beacon, MA: Beacon Press,

2021); Ethan Blue, *The Deportation Express: A History of America through Forced Removal* (Oakland: University of California Press, 2021); Reece Jones, *White Borders: The History of Race and Immigration in the United States from Chinese Exclusion to the Border Wall* (Beacon, MA: Beacon Press, 2021); Michelle Alexander, *The New Jim Crow: Mass Incarceration in the Age of Colorblindness* (New York: New Press, 2012).

2 Melissa Cook, "Banished for Minor Crimes: The Aggravated Felony Provision of the Immigration and Nationality Act as a Human Rights Violation," *Third World Law Journal* 23, no. 2 (2003): 293–329.

3 Mathew Coleman, "Immigration Geopolitics Beyond the Mexico–US Border," *Antipode* 39, no. 1 (February 2007): 61, https://doi.org/10.1111/j.1467-8330.2007.00506.x.

4 Cook, "Banished for Minor Crimes," 298.

5 Diana R. Podgorny, "Rethinking the Increased Focus on Penal Measures in Immigration Law as Reflected in the Expansion of the Aggravated Felony Concept," *Journal of Criminal Law and Criminology* 99, no. 1 (2008): 291.

6 Cook, "Banished for Minor Crimes"; Dan Kanstroom, *Aftermath: Deportation Law and the New American Diaspora* (New York: Oxford University Press, 2012).

7 Immigration and Nationality Act, H.R. 5678, 82nd Cong. §2 (1952).

8 Alina Das, "Inclusive Immigrant Justice: Racial Animus and the Origins of Crime-Based Deportation," *University of California Davis Law Review* 52 (2018): 171–92.

9 David Garland, *The Culture of Control: Crime and Social Order in Contemporary Society* (Chicago: University of Chicago Press, 2001).

10 Melissa Hickman Barlow, David E. Barlow, and Theodore G. Chiricos, "Economic Conditions and Ideologies of Crime in the Media: A Content Analysis of Crime News," *Crime & Delinquency* 41, no. 1 (1995): 3–19; Gray Cavender, "Media and Crime Policy: A Reconsideration of David Garland's The Culture of Control," *Punishment & Society* 6, no. 3 (July 1, 2004): 335–48, https://doi.org/10.1177/1462474504043636.

11 Steven R. Belenko, *Drugs and Drug Policy in America: A Documentary History* (Greenwood Press, 2000); Craig Reinarman and Harry G. Levine, *Crack in America: Demon Drugs and Social Justice* (Berkeley: University of California Press, 1997).

12 Katherine Beckett and Theodore Sasson, *The Politics of Injustice: Crime and Punishment in America* (Thousand Oaks, CA: SAGE, 2004); Steven Chermak, "The Presentation of Drugs in the News Media: The News Sources Involved in the Construction of Social Problems," *Justice Quarterly* 14, no. 4 (December 1997): 687–718, https://doi.org/10.1080/07418829700093551; James D. Orcutt and J. Blake Turner, "Shocking Numbers and Graphic Accounts: Quantified Images of Drug Problems in the Print Media," *Social Problems* 40, no. 2 (1993): 190–206.

13 Tracy L. Meares, "Simple Solutions? The Complexity of Public Attitudes Relevant to Drug Law Enforcement Policy," in *Crime Control and Social Justice: The Deli-

cate Balance, ed. Darnell Felix Hawkins, Samuel L. Myers, and Randolph N. Stone (Westport, CT: Greenwood Publishing Group, 2003), 269–94.

14 Richard L. Berke, "Poll Finds Most in U.S. Back Bush Strategy on Drugs," *New York Times*, September 12, 1989, https://www.nytimes.com/1989/09/12/us/poll -finds-most-in-us-back-bush-strategy-on-drugs.html.

15 Thomas C. Rowe, *Federal Narcotics Laws and the War on Drugs: Money Down a Rat Hole* (Abingdon, UK: Routledge, 2006).

16 Clarence Lusane and Dennis Desmond, *Pipe Dream Blues: Racism and the War on Drugs* (Boston, MA: South End Press, 1991).

17 Jeff Yates, Todd A. Collins, and Gabriel J. Chin, "A War on Drugs or a War on Immigrants? Expanding the Definition of 'Drug Trafficking' in Determining Aggravated Felon Status for Noncitizens," *Maryland Law Review* 64, no. 3 (2005): 875–909.

18 Anti-Drug Abuse Act, H.R. 5210, 100th Cong. §2 (1988).

19 Cook, "Banished for Minor Crimes"; Teresa Miller, "Citizenship and Severity: Recent Immigration Reforms and the New Penology," *Georgetown Immigration Law* 17, no. 4 (2003): 611–66; Podgorny, "Rethinking the Increased Focus."

20 Yates, Collins, and Chin, "War on Drugs or a War on Immigrants?," 886.

21 Cook, "Banished for Minor Crimes," 300.

22 Podgorny, "Rethinking the Increased Focus," 292.

23 Immigration Act, Stat. 4978, 101st Cong. §1 (1990).

24 Miscellaneous and Technical Immigration and Naturalization Amendments, H.R. 3049, 102nd Cong. §2 (1991).

25 William Chambliss, "Crime Control and Ethnic Minorities: Legitimizing Racial Oppression by Creating Moral Panics," in *Ethnicity, Race, and Crime*, ed. Darnell Hawkins (Albany: SUNY Press, 1995), 237.

26 William J. Chambliss, *Power, Politics, and Crime* (Abingdon, UK: Routledge, 2001), 135.

27 William Chambliss, "Drug War Politics: Racism, Corruption, and Alienation," in *Crime Control and Social Justice: The Delicate Balance*, ed. Darnell Hawkins, Samuel Myers, Jr., and Randolph Stone (Westport, CT: Greenwood Press, 2003), 295.

28 Violent Crime Control and Law Enforcement Act, H.R. 3355, 103rd Cong. §1 (1994).

29 Immigration and Nationality Technical Corrections Act, H.R. 783, 103rd Cong. §1 (1994).

30 Steven W. Bender, *Greasers and Gringos: Latinos, Law, and the American Imagination* (New York: NYU Press, 2005); Judith Ann Warner, "The Social Construction of the Criminal Alien in Immigration Law, Enforcement Practice and Statistical Enumeration: Consequences for Immigrant Stereotyping," *Journal of Social and Ecological Boundaries* 1, no. 2 (2005): 56–80.

31 Yolanda Vazquez, "Advising Noncitizen Defendants on the Immigration Consequences of Criminal Convictions: The Ethical Answer for the Criminal Defense

Lawyer, the Court, and the Sixth Amendment," *Berkeley La Raza Law Journal* 20 (2010): 37; Patrisia Macías-Rojas, "Immigration and the War on Crime: Law and Order Politics and the Illegal Immigration Reform and Immigrant Responsibility Act of 1996," *Journal on Migration and Human Security* 6, no. 1 (2018): 1–25; Jones, *White Borders*.

32 Miller, "Citizenship and Severity," 8.

33 John S. Lapinski, Pia Peltola, Greg Shaw, and Alan Yang, "Trends: Immigrants and Immigration," *Public Opinion Quarterly* 61, no. 2 (1997): 356, https://doi.org/10 .1086/297799; C. P. Muste, "The Dynamics of Immigration Opinion in the United States, 1992–2012," *Public Opinion Quarterly* 77, no. 1 (March 1, 2013): 398–416, https://doi.org/10.1093/poq/nft001; Adrian Pantoja, "Against the Tide? Core American Values and Attitudes Toward US Immigration Policy in the Mid-1990s," *Journal of Ethnic and Migration Studies* 32, no. 3 (April 1, 2006): 515–31, https://doi .org/10.1080/13691830600555111.

34 Antiterrorism and Effective Death Penalty Act, Stat. 1214, 110th Cong. §2 (1996); Illegal Immigration Reform and Immigration Responsibility Act, Stat. 110, 104th Cong. §2 (1996).

35 Nancy Morawetz, "Understanding the Impact of the 1996 Deportation Laws and the Due Process Clause," *New York University Law Review* 73 (2000): 107–14; Donald Kerwin, "From IIRIRA to Trump: Connecting the Dots to the Current US Immigration Policy Crisis," *Journal on Migration and Human Security* 6, no. 3 (September 2018): 192–204, https://doi.org/10.1177/2331502418786718.

36 Cook, "Banished for Minor Crimes," 305.

37 Coleman, "Immigration Geopolitics," 58.

38 Miller, "Citizenship and Severity," 13.

39 Podgorny, "Rethinking the Increased Focus," 297.

40 Cook, "Banished for Minor Crimes," 308–9.

41 Cook, "Banished for Minor Crimes," 309.

42 Miller, "Citizenship and Severity," 12.

43 Michael Tonry, *Malign Neglect: Race, Crime, and Punishment in America* (New York: Oxford University Press, 1995); Eva Bertram, Morris Blachman, Kenneth Sharpe, and Peter Andreas, *Drug War Politics: The Price of Denial* (Berkeley: University of California Press, 1996).

44 Examples include D. A. Andrews and James Bonta, "Rehabilitating Criminal Justice Policy and Practice," *Psychology, Public Policy, and Law* 16, no. 1 (2010): 39–55, https://doi.org/10.1037/a0018362; Bertram et al., *Drug War Politics*; Marc Mauer, *Race to Incarcerate* (New York: New Press, 1999); James Gray, *Why Our Drug Laws Have Failed: A Judicial Indictment of War on Drugs* (Philadelphia: Temple University Press, 2001).

45 See Dario Melossi, *Controlling Crime, Controlling Society: Thinking about Crime in Europe and America* (Polity, 2008); Robert Adelman, Lesley Williams Reid, Gail Markle, Saskia Weiss, and Charles Jaret, "Urban Crime Rates and the Changing Face of Immigration: Evidence across Four Decades," *Journal of Ethnicity in*

Criminal Justice 15, no. 1 (January 2, 2017): 52–77, https://doi.org/10.1080/15377938
.2016.1261057; John Hagan, Ron Levi, and Ronit Dinovitzer, "The Symbolic Violence of the Crime-Immigration Nexus: Migrant Mythologies in the Americas,"
Criminology & Public Policy 7, no. 1 (February 2008): 95–112, https://doi.org/10.1111
/j.1745-9133.2008.00493.x; Matthew T. Lee and Ramiro Martinez, Jr., "Immigration Reduces Crime: An Emerging Scholarly Consensus," in *Immigration, Crime,
and Justice*, ed. William McDonald (Bingley, UK: Emerald Publishing Group,
2009), 3–16; Michael T. Light and Ty Miller, "Does Undocumented Immigration
Increase Violent Crime?," *Criminology* 56, no. 2 (May 2018): 370–401, https://doi
.org/10.1111/1745-9125.12175; Graham C. Ousey and Charis E. Kubrin, "Immigration and Crime: Assessing a Contentious Issue," *Annual Review of Criminology* 1,
no. 1 (January 13, 2018): 63–84, https://doi.org/10.1146/annurev-criminol-032317
-092026; María B. Vélez and Christopher J. Lyons, "Situating the Immigration
and Neighborhood Crime Relationship across Multiple Cities," in *Punishing Immigrants: Policy, Politics, and Injustice* (New York: NYU Press, 2012), 159–77, http:
//nyu.universitypressscholarship.com/view/10.18574/nyu/9780814749029.001.0001
/upso-9780814749029-chapter-8; Tim Wadsworth, "Is Immigration Responsible
for the Crime Drop? An Assessment of the Influence of Immigration on Changes
in Violent Crime Between 1990 and 2000," *Social Science Quarterly* 91, no. 2 (June
2010): 531–53, https://doi.org/10.1111/j.1540-6237.2010.00706.x; Marjorie S. Zatz
and Hilary Smith, "Immigration, Crime, and Victimization: Rhetoric and Reality,"
Annual Review of Law and Social Science 8, no. 1 (December 2012): 141–59, https:
//doi.org/10.1146/annurev-lawsocsci-102811-173923.

46 Jock Young, *The Drugtakers: The Social Meaning of Drug Use* (London: McGib-
bon and Kee, 1971); Stanley Cohen, *Folk Devils and Moral Panics: The Creation of
Mods and Rockers* (London: Granada, 1972).

47 Cohen, *Folk Devils and Moral Panics*, 1.

48 Marshall McLuhan, *Understanding Media: The Extensions of Man* (London:
Sphere, 1967).

49 Young, *Drugtakers*; Eugene McLaughlin, "See Also Young, 1971: Marshall McLuhan, Moral Panics and Moral Indignation," *Theoretical Criminology* 18, no. 4
(November 1, 2014): 422–31, https://doi.org/10.1177/1362480614557207.

50 Jock Young, "Moral Panic: Its Origins in Resistance, Ressentiment and the Translation of Fantasy into Reality," *British Journal of Criminology* 49, no. 1 (January 1,
2009): 6, https://doi.org/10.1093/bjc/azn074.

51 Howard S. Becker, *Outsiders: Studies in the Sociology of Deviance* (New York: Free
Press, 1963).

52 Young, *Drugtakers*.

53 Cohen, *Folk Devils and Moral Panics*.

54 Cohen, *Folk Devils and Moral Panics*, 80.

55 Cohen, *Folk Devils and Moral Panics*, 81.

56 Cohen, *Folk Devils and Moral Panics*; See also Becker, *Outsiders*.

57 Cohen, *Folk Devils and Moral Panics*; Young, "Moral Panic."

58 David Garland, "On the Concept of Moral Panic," *Crime, Media, Culture* 4, no. 1 (April 1, 2008): 9–30, https://doi.org/10.1177/1741659007087270; Young, "Moral Panic"; McLaughlin, "See Also Young, 1971."

59 Young, "Moral Panic"; Jock Young, "Moral Panics and the Transgressive Other," *Crime Media Culture* 7, no. 3 (2011): 245–58.

60 See Katja Franko, *The Crimmigrant Other: Migration and Penal Power* (Abingdon, UK: Routledge, 2019).

61 Das, "Inclusive Immigrant Justice"; Andrew Gyory, *Closing the Gate: Race, Politics, and the Chinese Exclusion Act* (Chapel Hill: University of North Carolina Press, 1998); Daniel Kanstroom, "Reaping the Harvest: The Long, Complicated, Crucial Rhetorical Struggle Over Deportation," *Connecticut Law Review* 39 (2007): 1911–22; Warner, "Social Construction of the Criminal Alien."

62 Leo Ralph Chavez, *The Latino Threat: Constructing Immigrants, Citizens, and the Nation* (Stanford, CA: Stanford University Press, 2008); Vazquez, "Advising Noncitizen Defendants"; Dunbar-Ortiz, *Not "A Nation of Immigrants."*

63 Alexander, *New Jim Crow*; Das, "Inclusive Immigrant Justice"; Tanya Golash-Boza, "Structural Racism, Criminalization, and Pathways to Deportation for Dominican and Jamaican Men in the United States," *Social Justice* 44, no. 2/3 (2017): 137–61; Breanne J. Palmer, "The Crossroads: Being Black, Immigrant, and Undocumented in the Era of #BlackLivesMatter," *Georgetown Journal of Law and Modern Critical Race Perspectives* 9, no. 1 (2017): 99–121.

64 César Cuauhtémoc García Hernández, *Migrating to Prison: America's Obsession with Locking Up Immigrants* (New York: New Press, 2019), 21.

65 Das, *No Justice in the Shadows*, 52.

66 Jenna M. Loyd and Alison Mountz, *Boats, Borders, and Bases: Race, the Cold War, and the Rise of Migration Detention in the United States* (Oakland: University of California Press, 2018); Jeffrey S. Kahn, *Islands of Sovereignty: Haitian Migration and the Borders of Empire* (Chicago: University of Chicago Press, 2019); Carl Lindskoog, *Detain and Punish: Haitian Refugees and the Rise of the World's Largest Immigration Detention System* (Gainesville: University of Florida Press, 2018); Elliott Young, *Forever Prisoners: How the United States Made the World's Largest Immigrant Detention System* (New York: Oxford University Press, 2021).

67 Das, *No Justice in the Shadows*; García Hernández, *Migrating to Prison.*

68 Adam Goodman, *The Deportation Machine: America's Long History of Expelling Immigrants* (Princeton, NJ: Princeton University Press, 2021); Jenna Loyd and Alison Mountz, "The Caribbean Roots of U.S. Migration Policy: How Deterrence, Detention, and Deportation of Caribbean Migrants and Refugees in the '70s and '80s Laid the Groundwork for the Militarization of the U.S.–Mexico Border Today," *NACLA Report on the Americas* 51, no. 1 (March 29, 2019): 78–84, https://doi.org/10.1080/10714839.2019.1593695; Kristina Shull, "Reagan's Cold War on Immigrants: Resistance and the Rise of a Detention Regime, 1981–1985," *Journal of American Ethnic History* 40, no. 2 (January 1, 2021): 5–51, https://doi.org/10.5406/jamerethnhist.40.2.0005.

69 Kanstroom, "Reaping the Harvest"; Peter H. Schuck and John Williams, "Removing Criminal Aliens: The Pitfalls and Promises of Federalism," *Harvard Journal of Law and Public Policy* 22 (1999): 367–463.

70 Das, *No Justice in the Shadows.*

71 Clifford D. May, "Security Is Toughened at Alien Custody Center," *New York Times*, 1987, sec. Metropolitan News.

72 Swearingen, *States News Service.*

73 Schuck and Williams, "Removing Criminal Aliens."

74 Ira Kurzban, "Democracy and Immigration," in *Keeping Out the Other: A Critical Introduction to Immigration Enforcement Today*, ed. David Brotherton and Philip Kretsedemas (New York: Columbia University Press, 2008), 66.

75 Leo Chavez, "Spectacle in the Desert: The Minuteman Project on the U.S.-Mexico Border," in *Governing Immigration Through Crime: A Reader*, ed. Julie A. Dowling and Jonathan Xavier Inda (Stanford, CA: Stanford University Press, 2013), 115–28.

76 Charles R. Taylor and Hae-Kyong Bang, "Portrayals of Latinos in Magazine Advertising," *Journalism & Mass Communication Quarterly* 74, no. 2 (June 1997): 285–303, https://doi.org/10.1177/107769909707400204; Lucia Vargas and Bruce dePyssler, "Using Media Literacy to Explore Stereotypes of Mexican Immigrants," *Social Education* 62, no. 7 (1998): 407–12; Bender, *Greasers and Gringos*; Warner, "Social Construction of the Criminal Alien"; Jessica Autumn Brown, "Running on Fear: Immigration, Race and Crime Framings in Contemporary GOP Presidential Debate Discourse," *Critical Criminology* 24, no. 3 (September 1, 2016): 315–31, https://doi.org/10.1007/s10612-016-9317-8.

77 Alexander, *New Jim Crow*; Deborah Small, "The War on Drugs Is a War on Racial Justice," *Social Research* 68, no. 3 (2001): 896–903.

78 Peter Andreas, *Border Games: Policing the U.S.-Mexico Divide* (Ithaca, NY: Cornell University Press, 2012); Gary A. Mauser and June Francis, "Collateral Damage: The 'War on Drugs,' and the Latin America and Caribbean Region: Policy Recommendations for the Obama Administration," (Rochester, NY: Social Science Research Network, January 12, 2011), https://papers.ssrn.com/abstract=1739203; Tony Payan, *The Three U.S.-Mexico Border Wars: Drugs, Immigration, and Homeland Security* (Westport, CA: Greenwood Publishing Group, 2006).

79 John Hagan and Alberto Palloni, "Sociological Criminology and the Mythology of Hispanic Immigration and Crime," *Social Problems* 46, no. 4 (1999): 617–32; Joseph Nevins, *Operation Gatekeeper: The Rise of the "Illegal Alien" and the Making of the U.S.-Mexico Boundary* (London: Psychology Press, 2002); Mary Romero, "Racial Profiling and Immigration Law Enforcement: Rounding Up of Usual Suspects in the Latino Community," *Critical Sociology* 32, no. 2–3 (March 2006): 447–73, https://doi.org/10.1163/156916306777835376; Warner, "Social Construction of the Criminal Alien."

80 Lina Newton, *Illegal, Alien, or Immigrant: The Politics of Immigration Reform* (New York: NYU Press, 2008).

81 Newton, *Illegal, Alien, or Immigrant*, 118.

82 Newton, *Illegal, Alien, or Immigrant*, 218–19.

83 Southern Poverty Law Center, "Federation for American Immigration Reform," Southern Poverty Law Center, 2018, https://www.splcenter.org/fighting-hate /extremist-files/group/federation-american-immigration-reform; Das, *No Justice in the Shadows*.

84 H. Richard Friman, "Migration and Security: Crime, Terror, and the Politics of Order," in *Immigration, Integration, and Security: America and Europe in Comparative Perspective*, ed. Ariane Chebel d'Appollonia and Simon Reich (Pittsburgh, PA: University of Pittsburgh Press, 2008), 5; Jones, *White Borders*.

85 Daniel J. Tichenor, "The Politics of Immigration Reform in the United States, 1981–1990," *Polity* 26, no. 3 (March 1, 1994): 12, https://doi.org/10.2307/3235150.

86 Margarita Rodriguez, "Interview with Ira Kurzban," *International Migration Trends and Perspectives-Magazine on Migration Issues* (Spring 2013): 8, http: //trendsandperspectives.com/pdf/E-InteRod.pdf.

87 Friman, "Migration and Security," 140.

88 Dara Lind, "The Disastrous, Forgotten 1996 Law That Created Today's Immigration Problem," *Vox*, April 28, 2016, https://www.vox.com/2016/4/28/11515132/iirira -clinton-immigration; Patrisia Macías-Rojas, *From Deportation to Prison: The Politics of Immigration Enforcement in Post-Civil Rights America* (New York: NYU Press, 2016).

89 Young, *Drugtakers*; Cohen, *Folk Devils and Moral Panics*; See also Young, "Moral Panic."

90 Jock Young, *The Vertigo of Late Modernity* (London: SAGE, 2007), 141.

91 Friedrich Hayek, *The Road to Serfdom* (Chicago: University of Chicago Press, 1944).

92 Naomi Klein, *The Shock Doctrine: The Rise of Disaster Capitalism* (New York: Picador, 2007), 10.

93 David Harvey, *A Brief History of Neoliberalism* (Oxford: Oxford University Press, 2007); Klein, *The Shock Doctrine*.

94 Jamie Peck and Adam Tickell, "Neoliberalizing Space," *Antipode* 34, no. 3 (June 2002): 389, https://doi.org/10.1111/1467-8330.00247.

95 Kurzban, "Democracy and Immigration," 67; See also Dominic Corva, "Neoliberal Globalization and the War on Drugs: Transnationalizing Illiberal Governance in the Americas," *Political Geography* 27, no. 2 (February 2008): 176–93, https:// doi.org/10.1016/j.polgeo.2007.07.008.

96 Garland, *Culture of Control*.

97 Mauer, *Race to Incarcerate*; Garland, *Culture of Control*.

98 Douglas S. Massey, "The New Immigration and Ethnicity in the United States," *Population and Development Review* 21, no. 3 (September 1995): 633, https://doi .org/10.2307/2137753.

99 Ramiro Martinez, Jr., and Matthew T. Lee, "On Immigration and Crime," *Criminal Justice* 1, no. 1 (2000): 495.

100 Pew Research Center, "Immigrants Are a Growing Share Among Black Americans . . . As the Black Immigrant Population Has More than Quadrupled Since 1980," *Pew Research Center's Social & Demographic Trends Project* (blog), April 2015, https://www.pewresearch.org/social-trends/wp-content/uploads/sites /3/2015/04/ST_2015-04-09_black-immigrants-01.png.

101 Monica Anderson, "A Rising Share of the U.S. Black Population Is Foreign Born," *Pew Research Center's Social & Demographic Trends Project* (blog), April 9, 2015, https://www.pewsocialtrends.org/2015/04/09/a-rising-share-of-the-u-s-black -population-is-foreign-born/.

2. THE "IMMIGRATION LAW DEATH PENALTY"

1 Examples include Iris Bennett, "The Unconstitutionality of Nonuniform Immigration Consequences of 'Aggravated Felony' Convictions," *New York University Law Review* 74 (1999): 1696–1740; Melissa Cook, "Banished for Minor Crimes: The Aggravated Felony Provision of the Immigration and Nationality Act as a Human Rights Violation," *Third World Law Journal* 23, no. 2 (2003): 293–329; Jeff Yates, Todd A. Collins, and Gabriel J. Chin, "A War on Drugs or a War on Immigrants? Expanding the Definition of 'Drug Trafficking' in Determining Aggravated Felon Status for Noncitizens," *Maryland Law Review* 64, no. 3 (2005): 875–909; Diana R. Podgorny, "Rethinking the Increased Focus on Penal Measures in Immigration Law as Reflected in the Expansion of the Aggravated Felony Concept," *Journal of Criminal Law and Criminology* 99, no. 1 (2008): 287–316.

2 See Bennett, "Unconstitutionality"; Dawn Marie Johnson, "AEDPA and the IIRIRA: Treating Misdemeanors as Felonies for Immigration Purposes," *Journal of Legislation* 27, no. 2 (2001): 477–91; Yates, Collins, and Chin, "War on Drugs or a War on Immigrants?"; Aaron Lang, "An Opportunity for Change? Aggravated Felonies in Immigration Proceedings and the Effect of *Moncrieffe v. Holder*," *Boston University Law Journal* 33 (2015): 102–37; Podgorny, "Rethinking the Increased Focus."

3 See Appendix for the complete list, as included in the Immigration and National Act (INA).

4 Kathy Brady, *Aggravated Felonies*, Practice Advisory (San Francisco: Immigration Legal Research Center, April 2017).

5 See Johnson, "AEDPA and the IIRIRA"; Miller, "Citizenship and Severity"; Podgorny, "Rethinking the Increased Focus"; Lang, "An Opportunity for Change?"

6 Ira Kurzban, *Kurzban's Immigration Law Sourcebook: A Comprehensive Outline and Reference Tool* (Washington, DC: American Immigration Lawyers Association, 2016); Executive Office for Immigration Review, "Statistics Yearbook Fiscal Year 2017" (Department of Justice, 2018).

7 Non-LPRs facing removal for convictions in other categories of deportable crimes—like crimes of moral turpitude and controlled substance offenses—are also barred from this form of relief.

8 Cook, "Banished for Minor Crimes"; Bill Ong Hing, "Re-Examining the Zero-Tolerance Approach to Deporting Aggravated Felons: Restoring Discretionary Waivers and Developing New Tools," *Harvard Law & Policy Review* 8 (2017): 141–76.

9 Jennifer Lee Koh, "Removal in the Shadows of Immigration Court," *Southern California Law Review* 90 (2017): 180–235.

10 Executive Office for Immigration Review, "Statistics Yearbook Fiscal Year 2018."

11 Johnson, "AEDPA and the IIRIRA"; Cook, "Banished for Minor Crimes"; Jonathan Baum, Rosha Jones, and Catherine Barry, In the Child's Best Interest? The Consequences of Losing a Lawful Immigrant Parent to Deportation (Berkeley: International Human Rights Law Clinic, University of California, Berkeley School of Law, March 2010); Lang, "An Opportunity for Change?"

12 Koh, "Removal in the Shadows."

13 Baum, Jones, and Barry, "In the Child's Best Interest?"

14 While crimes that are not aggravated felonies but are deemed "violent or dangerous" also evoke bars on asylum and withholding of removal, the aggravated felony is the only deportable ground that is categorically barred.

15 Executive Office for Immigration Review, "Statistics Yearbook Fiscal Year 2018."

16 Kurzban, *Kurzban's Immigration Law Sourcebook*, 737.

17 Executive Office for Immigration Review, "Statistics Yearbook Fiscal Year 2018."

18 David Brotherton and Luis Barrios, *Banished to the Homeland: Dominican Deportees and Their Stories of Exile* (New York: Columbia University Press, 2011); Jeremy Slack, *Deported to Death: How Drug Violence Is Changing Migration on the US-Mexico Border* (Oakland: University of California Press, 2019).

19 US Citizenship and Immigration Services, "Victims of Human Trafficking & Other Crimes," USCIS.gov, 2017, https://www.uscis.gov/humanitarian/victims-human-trafficking-other-crimes.

20 US Citizenship and Immigration Services, "Form I-914, Application for T Nonimmigrant Status by Fiscal Year, Quarter, and Case Status (Fiscal Year 2018, 4th Quarter, July 1-Sept. 30, 2018) (CSV, 3.16 KB)," 2019, https://www.uscis.gov/sites/default/files/document/data/I914t_visastatistics_fy2018_qtr4.csv; US Citizenship and Immigration Services, "Number of Form I-918, Petition for U Nonimmigrant Status, by Fiscal Year, Quarter, and Case Status 2009–2018," 2019, https://www.uscis.gov/sites/default/files/document/data/I918u_visastatistics_fy2018_qtr4.pdf.

21 On liminal legality, see Jennifer M. Chacon, "Producing Liminal Legality," *Denver Law Review* 92, no. 4 (2015): 709–67.

22 Michael Kaufman, "Detention, Due Process, and the Right to Counsel in Removal Proceedings," *Stanford Journal of Civil Rights & Civil Liberties* 4 (2008): 113.

23 See Cook, "Banished for Minor Crimes"; Warner, "Social Construction of the Criminal"; and Ira Kurzban, "Democracy and Immigration," in *Keeping Out the Other: A Critical Introduction to Immigration Enforcement Today*, ed. David Brotherton and Philip Kretsedemas (New York: Columbia University Press, 2008), 63–78.

24 Ingrid V. Eagly and Steven Shafer, "A National Study of Access to Counsel in Immigration Court," *University of Pennsylvania Law Review* 164 (2015).

25 Nancy Morawetz, "Understanding the Impact of the 1996 Deportation Laws and the Due Process Clause," *New York University Law Review* 73 (2000): 107–14; Alina Das, "Immigration Detention: Information Gaps and Institutional Barriers to Reform," *University of Chicago Law Review* 80 (2013). See also Sarah Tosh, "Mandatory Detention for Criminal Convictions: The Reproduction of Racial Inequality through U.S. Immigration Law," *Law & Policy* 44, no. 1 (January 2022): 70–97, https://doi.org/10.1111/lapo.12179.

26 Eagly and Shafer, "Access to Counsel in Immigration Court"; Anil Kalhan, "Rethinking Immigration Detention," *Columbia Law Review Sidebar* 110 (2010): 42–58; Emily Ryo, "Fostering Legal Cynicism through Immigration Detention," *Southern California Law Review* 90, no. 5 (2017): 999–1054.

27 Examples include Tanya Maria Golash-Boza, "The Immigration Industrial Complex: Why We Enforce Immigration Policies Destined to Fail," *Sociology Compass* 3, no. 2 (2009): 295–309; Roxanne Lynne Doty and Elizabeth Shannon Wheatley, "Private Detention and the Immigration Industrial Complex," *International Political Sociology* 7, no. 4 (December 2013): 426–43, https://doi.org/10.1111/ips .12032; Dierdre Conlon and Nancy Hiemstra, "Examining the Everyday Micro-Economies of Migrant Detention in the United States," *Geographica Helvetica* 69, no. 5 (December 22, 2014): 335–44, https://doi.org/10.5194/gh-69-335-2014; Denise Gilman and Luis A. Romero, "Immigration Detention, Inc.," *Journal on Migration and Human Security*, May 3, 2018, https://doi.org/10.1177/2311502418765414; Nancy Hiemstra, *Detain and Deport: The Chaotic U.S. Immigration Enforcement Regime* (Athens: University of Georgia Press, 2019); Dierdre Conlon and Nancy Hiemstra, "'Unpleasant' but 'Helpful': Immigration Detention and Urban Entanglements in New Jersey, USA," *Urban Studies*, February 8, 2022, https://doi.org/10.1177 /00420980211072695.

28 See DHS-OIG (Department of Homeland Security, Office of Inspector General), "Concerns about ICE Detainee Treatment and Care at Four Facilities, June 18." (Washington, DC: DHS-OIG, 2019); DHS-OIG, "Issues Requiring Action at the Essex County Correctional Facility in Newark, New Jersey" (Washington, DC: DHS-OIG, 2019); DHS-OIG, "DHS Pandemic Planning Needs Better Oversight, Training, and Management" (Washington, DC: DHS-OIG, 2016).

29 Sarah R. Tosh, Ulla D. Berg, and Kenneth Sebastian León, "Migrant Detention and COVID-19: Pandemic Responses in Four New Jersey Detention Centers," *Journal on Migration and Human Security* 9, no. 1 (March 2021): 44–62, https://doi .org/10.1177/23315024211003855. Robert Koulish, "COVID-19 and the Creeping Necropolitics of Crimmigration Control," *Social Sciences* 10, no. 12 (December 6, 2021): 467, https://doi.org/10.3390/socsci10120467.

30 US Immigration and Customs Enforcement (ICE), "ICE Guidance on COVID-19" (US Department of Homeland Security, September 2020).

31 Nina Agrawal, "Interpreters Play a Vital Role in Immigration Courts—but Their Rights Are Being Violated, Labor Board Says," *Los Angeles Times*, June 1, 2017, https://www.latimes.com/business/la-fi-immigration-interpreters-20170601-story .html.

32 Laura Abel, *Language Access in Immigration Courts* (New York: Brennan Center for Justice at New York University School of Law, 2011).

33 Appleseed and Chicago Appleseed, *Assembly Line Injustice Blueprint to Reform Americas Immigration Courts*, 2009, https://www.appleseednetwork.org /wp-content/uploads/2012/05/Assembly-Line-Injustice-Blueprint-to-Reform -Americas-Immigration-Courts1.pdf; National Lawyers Guild, *Immigration Court Observation Project of the National Lawyers Guild, Fundamental Fairness: A Report on the Due Process Crisis in New York City Immigration Courts*, 2011, http://nycicop.files.wordpress.com/2011/05/icop-report-5-10-2011.pdf; Special to The New York Times, "Full Translation Is Required In Immigration Proceedings," *New York Times*, November 9, 1989, https://www.nytimes.com/1989/11/09/us/full -translation-is-required-in-immigration-proceedings.html.

34 Abel, *Language Access in Immigration Courts*.

35 Abel, *Language Access in Immigration Courts*.

36 Appleseed and Chicago Appleseed, *Assembly Line Injustice Blueprint*; National Lawyers Guild, *Immigration Court Observation Project*; Maya P. Barak, "Can You Hear Me Now? Attorney Perceptions of Interpretation, Technology, and Power in Immigration Court," *Journal on Migration and Human Security* 9, no. 4 (December 2021): 207–23, https://doi.org/10.1177/23315024211034740.

37 Liz Robbins, "New Yorkers Facing Deportation Lose Their (Physical) Day in Court," *New York Times*, June 28, 2018, https://www.nytimes.com/2018/06/27 /nyregion/new-york-immigrants-deportation-video-hearings.html.

38 See Aaron Haas, "Videoconferencing in Immigration Proceedings," *Pierce Law Review* 59 (2006); Emily Leung, "Technology's Encroachment on Justice: Video-conferencing in Immigration Court Proceedings," *Immigration Briefings* 1 (2014); Ingrid V. Eagly, "Remote Adjudication in Immigration," *Northwestern University Law Review*, 2015; Barak, "Can You Hear Me Now?"

39 Tosh, "Mandatory Detention for Criminal Convictions."

40 Barak, "Can You Hear Me Now?"

41 Christina Goldbaum, "Videoconferencing in Immigration Court: High-Tech Solution or Rights Violation?," *New York Times*, February 13, 2019, https://www .nytimes.com/2019/02/12/nyregion/immigration-court-video-teleconferencing .html.

42 Michelle Ye Hee Lee, "Donald Trump's False Comments Connecting Mexican Immigrants and Crime," *Washington Post*, July 8, 2015, https://www.washingtonpost .com/news/fact-checker/wp/2015/07/08/donald-trumps-false-comments -connecting-mexican-immigrants-and-crime/?utm_term=.d49951b8fc76; Jennifer Medina, "Trump's Immigration Order Expands the Definition of 'Criminal,'" *New York Times*, December 22, 2017, https://www.nytimes.com/2017/01/26/us/trump

-immigration-deportation.html; Jeremy Duda and Anne Gearan, "'This Country Doesn't Want Them': Trump Rails against Migrants Trying to Enter the U.S.," *Washington Post*, October 19, 2018, https://www.washingtonpost.com/politics /this-country-doesnt-want-them-trump-rails-against-migrants-trying-to-enter -the-us/2018/10/19/1cbdd8de-d3ab-11e8-83d6-291fcead2ab1_story.html?utm_term =.b3628ac53053; "Full Transcript of Trump's State of The Union Address," *New York Times*, February 5, 2020, https://www.nytimes.com/2020/02/05/us/politics /state-of-union-transcript.html; Gina Martinez and Abigail Abrams, "Trump Repeated Many of His Old Claims About the Border to Justify the State of Emergency. Here Are the Facts," *Time*, February 15, 2019, http://time.com/5530506 /donald-trump-emergency-border-fact-check/.

43 Nina Rabin, "Victims or Criminals—Discretion, Sorting, and Bureaucratic Culture in the U.S. Immigration System," *Southern California Review of Law and Social Justice* 195 (2013).

44 Immigrant Defense Project, "IDP Statement: 170 Organizations Send Letter to DHS Secretary Defending Local Policies That Protect Immigrant Communities," March 29, 2022, https://www.immigrantdefenseproject.org/idp-statement-170 -organizations-send-letter-to-dhs-secretary-defending-local-policies-that-protect -immigrant-communities/; Camilo Montoya-Galvez, "After 1 Year and Many Changes, Biden's Immigration Record Frustrates Opponents and Allies Alike," *CBS News* (blog), January 20, 2022, https://www.cbsnews.com/news/immigration -biden-first-year-title-42-ice-texas/; Muzaffar Chishti and Jessica Bolter, "Biden at the One-Year Mark: A Greater Change in Direction on Immigration Than Is Recognized," *Migration Policy Institute*, January 18, 2022, https://www.migrationpolicy .org/article/biden-one-year-mark; Owen Quinn, "Biden's 1st-Year Record on Immigration: Tough Challenges, Harsh Criticism," *ABC News*, January 22, 2022, https://abcnews.go.com/Politics/bidens-1st-year-record-immigration-touch -challenges-harsh/story?id=82404626.

45 See Bennett, "Unconstitutionality"; Johnson, "AEDPA and the IIRIRA"; Miller, "Citizenship and Severity"; Cook, "Banished for Minor Crimes"; Yates, Collins, and Chin, "A War on Drugs or a War on Immigrants?"; Podgorny, "Rethinking the Increased Focus"; Lang, "An Opportunity for Change?"

3. MARKING THE "BAD IMMIGRANT"

1 See Juliet Stumpf, "The Crimmigration Crisis: Immigrants, Crime, and Sovereign Power," *American University Law Review* 56, no. 2 (2006): 367–419.

2 Examples of this crimmigration scholarship include Katherine Beckett and Heather Evans, "Crimmigration at the Local Level: Criminal Justice Processes in the Shadow of Deportation," *Law & Society Review* 49, no. 1 (2015): 241–77; Jize Jiang and Edna Erez, "Immigrants as Symbolic Assailants: Crimmigration and Its Discontents," *International Criminal Justice Review* 28, no. 1 (March 2018): 5–24, https://doi.org/10.1177/1057567717721299; César Cuauhtémoc García Hernández, "Deconstructing Crimmigration," *University of California Davis Law Review* 52

(2018): 197–253, https://doi.org/10.2139/ssrn.3326202; Jennifer M. Chacón, "Managing Migration Through Crime," *SSRN Electronic Journal*, 2009, https://doi.org/10.2139/ssrn.2033931; Shirley P. Leyro and Daniel L. Stageman, "Crimmigration, Deportability and the Social Exclusion of Noncitizen Immigrants," *Migration Letters* 15, no. 2 (April 29, 2018): 255–65, https://doi.org/10.33182/ml.v15i2.372; Robert Koulish and Maartje van der Woude, *Crimmigrant Nations: Resurgent Nationalism and the Closing of Borders* (New York: Fordham University Press, 2020); Katja Franko, *The Crimmigrant Other: Migration and Penal Power* (Abingdon, UK: Routledge, 2019).

3 Katherine Beckett and Theodore Sasson, *The Politics of Injustice: Crime and Punishment in America* (Thousand Oaks, CA: SAGE, 2004); Lawrence D. Bobo and Victor Thompson, "Unfair by Design: The War on Drugs, Race, and the Legitimacy of the Criminal Justice System," *Social Research* 73, no. 2 (2006): 445–72; William Chambliss, "Drug War Politics: Racism, Corruption, and Alienation," in *Crime Control and Social Justice: The Delicate Balance*, ed. Darnell Hawkins, Samuel Myers, Jr., and Randolpjh Stone (Westport, CT: Greenwood Press, 2003), 295–317; Doris Marie Provine, *Unequal under Law: Race in the War on Drugs* (Chicago: University of Chicago Press, 2007); Michelle Alexander, *The New Jim Crow: Mass Incarceration in the Age of Colorblindness* (New York: New Press, 2012); Michael Tonry, *Malign Neglect: Race, Crime, and Punishment in America* (New York: Oxford University Press, 1995); Craig Reinarman and Harry G. Levine, *Crack in America: Demon Drugs and Social Justice* (Berkeley: University of California Press, 1997); Jeffrey H. Reiman, *Rich Get Richer and the Poor Get Prison: Ideology, Class and Criminal Justice* (New York: John Wiley & Sons Inc, 1979).

4 See Amada Armenta, *Protect, Serve, and Deport: The Rise of Policing as Immigration Enforcement* (Oakland: University of California Press, 2017); Doris Marie Provine, Monica W. Varsanyi, Paul G. Lewis, and Scott H. Decker, *Policing Immigrants: Local Law Enforcement on the Front Lines* (Chicago: University of Chicago Press, 2016).

5 Monica W. Varsanyi, "Rescaling the 'Alien,' Rescaling Personhood: Neoliberalism, Immigration, and the State," *Annals of the Association of American Geographers* 98, no. 4 (2008): 877–96.

6 Mathew Coleman, "The 'Local' Migration State: The Site-Specific Devolution of Immigration Enforcement in the U.S. South," *Law & Policy* 34, no. 2 (April 2012): 159–90, https://doi.org/10.1111/j.1467-9930.2011.00358.x; Felicia Arriaga, "Relationships between the Public and Crimmigration Entities in North Carolina: A 287(g) Program Focus," *Sociology of Race and Ethnicity* 3, no. 3 (2017): 417–31.

7 Joanne Lin, "End It: 287(g) Is Beyond Repair and Harms Local Communities Every Day," *American Civil Liberties Union* (blog), April 5, 2010, https://www.aclu.org/blog/end-it-287g-beyond-repair-and-harms-local-communities-every-day; Marcella Alsan and Crystal S. Yang, "Fear and the Safety Net: Evidence from Secure Communities" (National Bureau of Economic Research, 2019);

Coleman, "'Local' Migration State"; García Hernández, "Deconstructing Crimmigration."

8 David C. Brotherton and Philip Kretsedemas, eds., *Immigration Policy in the Age
of Punishment: Detention, Deportation, and Border Control* (New York: Columbia
University Press, 2018); Huyen Pham, "287(g) Agreements in the Trump Era,"
Washington & Lee Law Review 75, no. 3 (2018): 1253–86.

9 US Immigration and Customs Enforcement, "Delegation of Immigration Authority Section 287(g) Immigration and Nationality Act," ice.gov, 2018, https://www
.ice.gov/287g.

10 US Immigration and Customs Enforcement, "Secure Communities," ice.gov, 2021,
https://www.ice.gov/secure-communities.

11 Carrie Rosenbaum, "Priorities and the State of Implicit Bias in Crimmigration,"
Regulatory Review (blog), April 13, 2022, https://www.thegreview.org/2022/04/13
/rosenbaum-implicit-bias-in-crimmigration/; Immigrant Defense Project, "IDP
Statement: 170 Organizations Send Letter to DHS Secretary Defending Local
Policies That Protect Immigrant Communities," March 29, 2022, https://www
.immigrantdefenseproject.org/idp-statement-170-organizations-send-letter-to
-dhs-secretary-defending-local-policies-that-protect-immigrant-communities/;
American Civil Liberties Union, "License to Abuse: How ICE's 287(g) Program
Empowers Racist Sheriffs," 2022, https://www.aclu.org/report/license-abuse-how
-ices-287g-program-empowers-racist-sheriffs.

12 Examples include Armenta, *Protect, Serve, and Deport*; Arriaga, "Relationships
between the Public and Crimmigration Entities"; Coleman, "'Local' Migration
State"; Provine et al., *Policing Immigrants*.

13 Also see Jennifer Chacón, "Immigration Federalism in the Weeds," *University of
California Los Angeles Law Review* 66 (2019): 1332–93; Annie Lai and Christopher
N. Lasch, "Crimmigration Resistance and the Case of Sanctuary City Funding,"
Santa Clara Law Review 57 (2018): 539–610.

14 Michelle Chen, "Why Is ICE Arresting Immigrants in New York City's Courts?,"
Nation, December 4, 2017, https://www.thenation.com/article/archive/why-is
-ice-arresting-immigrants-in-new-york-citys-courts/; Ryan Devereaux and John
Knefel, "ICE Evades Sanctuary Rules by Using NYPD Fingerprints to Find Immigrants and Send Them Call-In Letters," *Intercept* (blog), April 26, 2018, https:
//theintercept.com/2018/04/26/ice-sends-threatening-letters-to-immigrants
-increasing-climate-of-fear-in-new-york-city/; Scott M. Stringer, "The Demographics of Detention: Immigration Enforcement in NYC Under Trump" (New
York City Comptroller, Bureau of Policy and Research, February 2019).

15 Liz Robbins, "In a 'Sanctuary City,' Immigrants Are Still at Risk," *New York Times*,
April 11, 2018, https://www.nytimes.com/2018/02/27/nyregion/sanctuary-cities
-immigrants-ice.html.

16 Beth Fertig, "Local Police Can't Detain Immigrants For ICE, NY Court Finds,"
NPR.org, November 15, 2018, https://www.npr.org/2018/11/15/668374307/local
-police-cant-detain-immigrants-for-ice-ny-court-finds.

17 Camille J. Mackler, "When Help Is Nowhere to Be Found: What Government Documents Reveal About MS-13 Operations in Long Island, New York City, and the Lower Hudson Valley" (New York Immigration Council, May 2020).

18 US Immigration and Customs Enforcement, "3-Month Review Shows How New York City's Failure to Honor Immigration Detainers Leads to Hundreds of Dangerous Criminals Released," ice.gov, June 1, 2018, https://www.ice.gov/news /releases/3-month-review-shows-how-new-york-citys-failure-honor-immigration -detainers-leads; Stringer, "Demographics of Detention."

19 Janon Fisher, "ICE Busts 225 People during Sweeping Six-Day Raid in New York," *New York Daily News*, April 24, 2018, https://www.nydailynews.com/new-york/ice -busts-225-people-sweeping-six-day-raid-new-york-article-1.3950760.

20 Stringer, "Demographics of Detention."

21 Immigrant Defense Project, "Denied, Dissapeared, and Deported: The Toll of ICE's Operations at New York's Courts in 2019" (New York: Immigrant Defense Project, January 2020), https://www.immigrantdefenseproject.org/ice-courts/.

22 Benjamin Weiser, "Judge to ICE: Don't Ambush Immigrants at New York Court-houses," *New York Times*, June 10, 2020, https://www.nytimes.com/2020/06/10 /nyregion/ice-courts-immigrants-new-york.html.

23 Christopher J. Coyne and Abigail Hall, "Four Decades and Counting: The Continued Failure of the War on Drugs," Policy Analysis (Washington, DC: Cato Insititute, April 12, 2017); Christopher Wildeman and Emily A. Wang, "Mass In-carceration, Public Health, and Widening Inequality in the USA," *Lancet* 389, no. 10077 (April 2017): 1464–74, https://doi.org/10.1016/S0140-6736(17)30259-3; Beth Schwartzapfel, "Biden Could Have Taken the War on Drugs Down a Notch. He Didn't.," *Marshall Project* (blog), June 16, 2021, https://www.themarshallproject.org /2021/06/16/biden-could-have-taken-the-war-on-drugs-down-a-notch-he-didn-t.

24 Drug Policy Alliance, "Marijuana Decriminalization and Legalization," 2022, https://drugpolicy.org/issues/marijuana-legalization-and-regulation.

25 "President Biden Calls for Increased Funding to Address Addiction and the Over-dose Epidemic," The White House, March 28, 2022, https://www.whitehouse.gov /ondcp/briefing-room/2022/03/28/president-biden-calls-for-increased-funding -to-address-addiction-and-the-overdose-epidemic/; News US Health and Human Services, "HHS Acting Secretary Declares Public Health Emergency to Address National Opioid Crisis," HHS.gov, October 26, 2017, https://www.hhs.gov/about /news/2017/10/26/hhs-acting-secretary-declares-public-health-emergency -address-national-opioid-crisis.html.

26 Michelle S. Phelps and Devah Pager, "Inequality and Punishment: A Turning Point for Mass Incarceration?," *ANNALS of the American Academy of Political and Social Science* 663, no. 1 (January 1, 2016): 185–203, https://doi.org/10.1177 /0002716215596972; Todd R. Clear and Natasha A. Frost, *The Punishment Impera-tive: The Rise and Failure of Mass Incarceration in America* (New York: NYU Press, 2015); John Gramlich, "America's Incarceration Rate Falls to Lowest Level since

1995," *Pew Research Center* (blog), August 16, 2021, https://www.pewresearch.org /fact-tank/2021/08/16/americas-incarceration-rate-lowest-since-1995/.

27 Grace Meng, *A Price Too High: US Families Torn Apart by Deportations for Drug Offenses* (New York: Human Rights Watch, 2015); Ojmarrh Mitchell and Michael S. Caudy, "Race Differences in Drug Offending and Drug Distribution Arrests," *Crime & Delinquency* 63, no. 2 (February 1, 2017): 91–112, https://doi.org/10.1177 /0011128714568427; Drug Policy Alliance, "The Drug War, Mass Incarceration and Race" (New York: Drug Policy Alliance, January 2018); John Hudak, "Biden Should End America's Longest War: The War on Drugs," *Brookings* (blog), September 24, 2021, https://www.brookings.edu/blog/how-we-rise/2021/09/24/biden -should-end-americas-longest-war-the-war-on-drugs/.

28 Michelle Ye Hee Lee, "Donald Trump's False Comments Connecting Mexican Immigrants and Crime," *Washington Post*, July 8, 2015, https://www.washingtonpost .com/news/fact-checker/wp/2015/07/08/donald-trumps-false-comments -connecting-mexican-immigrants-and-crime/?utm_term=.d49951b8fc76; Gina Martinez and Abigail Abrams, "Trump Repeated Many of His Old Claims About the Border to Justify the State of Emergency. Here Are the Facts," *Time*, February 15, 2019, http://time.com/5530506/donald-trump-emergency-border-fact-check/.

29 TRAC Immigration, "Removals under the Secure Communities Program," TRAC, Syracuse University, 2018, https://trac.syr.edu/phptools/immigration/secure/.

30 Ted Galen Carpenter, *Bad Neighbor Policy: Washington's Futile War on Drugs in Latin America* (New York: St. Martin's Press, 2003); Ron Nixon and Fernanda Santos, "U.S. Appetite for Mexico's Drugs Fuels Illegal Immigration," *New York Times*, January 20, 2018, https://www.nytimes.com/2017/04/04/us/politics/us-appetite-for -mexicos-drugs-fuels-illegal-immigration.html; Jeremy Slack, *Deported to Death: How Drug Violence Is Changing Migration on the US-Mexico Border* (Oakland: University of California Press, 2019); Winifred Tate, *Drugs, Thugs, and Diplomats: U.S. Policymaking in Colombia* (Stanford, CA: Stanford University Press, 2015); Dawn Paley, *Drug War Capitalism* (Chico, CA: AK Press, 2014).

31 "History," *Office of the Special Narcotics Prosecutor* (blog), accessed February 21, 2019, http://www.snpnyc.org/about-us/history/.

32 Kristen Anderson, "Addiction Should Not Be Punishable by Deportation," *Huffington Post*, June 27, 2018, https://www.huffingtonpost.com/entry/opinion -anderson-opioid-deportation_us_5b22c38fe4b0d4fc01fc9c35.

33 Aviva Chomsky, *Central America's Forgotten History: Revolution, Violence, and the Roots of Migration* (Beacon, MA: Beacon Press, 2021); Naomi Klein, *The Shock Doctrine: The Rise of Disaster Capitalism* (New York: Picador, 2007); Justin Akers Chacón, *The Border Crossed Us: The Case for Opening the US-Mexico Border* (Chicago: Haymarket Books, 2021); Harsha Walia, *Border and Rule: Global Migration, Capitalism, and the Rise of Racist Nationalism* (Chicago: Haymarket Books, 2021).

34 Deborah Small, "The War on Drugs Is a War on Racial Justice," *Social Research* 68, no. 3 (2001): 896–903; Tony Payan, *The Three U.S.-Mexico Border Wars: Drugs,*

Immigration, and Homeland Security (Westport, CT: Greenwood Publishing Group, 2006); Peter Andreas, *Border Games: Policing the U.S.-Mexico Divide* (Ithaca, NY: Cornell University Press, 2012); Gary A. Mauser and June Francis, "Collateral Damage: The 'War on Drugs,' and the Latin America and Caribbean Region: Policy Recommendations for the Obama Administration," SSRN Scholarly Paper (Rochester, NY: Social Science Research Network, January 12, 2011), https://papers.ssrn.com/abstract=1739203; Alexander, *New Jim Crow*.

35 See Coletta Youngers and Eileen Rosin, *Drugs and Democracy in Latin America: The Impact of U.S. Policy* (Boulder, CO: Lynne Rienner Publishers, 2005); Julien Mercille, "Violent Narco-Cartels or US Hegemony? The Political Economy of the 'War on Drugs' in Mexico," *Third World Quarterly* 32, no. 9 (October 1, 2011): 1637–53, https://doi.org/10.1080/01436597.2011.619881; Carpenter, *Bad Neighbor Policy*; Nixon and Santos, "U.S. Appetite for Mexico's Drugs"; Tate, *Drugs, Thugs, and Diplomats*; Paley, *Drug War Capitalism*.

36 Mona Lynch, "Backpacking the Border: The Intersection of Drug and Immigration Prosecutions in a High-Volume US Court," *British Journal of Criminology* 57, no. 1 (January 2017): 112–31, https://doi.org/10.1093/bjc/azv105; Bill De La Rosa, "Mules for Cartels: Survival and Clandestine Migration in the Sonoran Desert," *Journal for Undergraduate Ethnography*, June 29, 2018, 84–102, https://doi.org/10.15273/jue.v8i1.8619.

37 Lynch, "Backpacking the Border."

38 Jeremy Slack and Scott Whiteford, "Violence and Migration on the Arizona-Sonora Border," *Human Organization* 70, no. 1 (2011): 11; De La Rosa, "Mules for Cartels."

39 Lynch, "Backpacking the Border."

40 Angie Junck, "The Impact of Drug Trafficking on Unaccompanied Minor Immigration Cases," Practice Advisory (New York: Vera Institute of Justice, 2015), 2.

41 Seth Harp, "Globalization of the U.S. Black Market: Prohibition, the War on Drugs, and the Case of Mexico," *New York University Law Review* 85, no. 5 (2010): 1661; Brotherton and Barrios, *Banished to the Homeland*; Mercille, "Violent Narco-Cartels or US Hegemony?"; Peter Watt and Roberto Zepeda, *Drug War Mexico: Politics, Neoliberalism and Violence in the New Narcoeconomy* (London: Zed Books, 2012).

42 Examples include Marc Galanter, "Why the 'Haves' Come out Ahead: Speculations on the Limits of Legal Change," *Law & Society Review* 9, no. 1 (1974): 95–160; Steven Spitzer, "Toward a Marxian Theory of Deviance," *Social Problems* 22, no. 5 (1975): 638–51; Reiman, *Rich Get Richer and the Poor Get Prison*.

43 See Richard Delgado and Jean Stefancic, *Critical Race Theory: An Introduction* (New York: NYU Press, 2001); Loic Wacquant, "Deadly Symbiosis: When Ghetto and Prison Meet and Mesh," *Punishment & Society* 3, no. 1 (2001): 95–134; Nicholas DeGenova, "The Deportation Regime: Sovereignty, Space, and the Freedom of Movement," in *The Deportation Regime: Sovereignty, Space, and the Freedom of Movement*, ed. Nicholas DeGenova and Natalie Peutz (Durham, NC:

Duke University Press, 2010), 33–68; Ian Haney-López, *White by Law: The Legal Construction of Race* (New York: NYU Press, 2006).

44 Exceptions include Brotherton and Barrios, *Banished to the Homeland*; Tanya Maria Golash-Boza, *Deported: Immigrant Policing, Disposable Labor and Global Capitalism* (New York: NYU Press, 2015); Tanya Golash-Boza and Pierrette Hondagneu-Sotelo, "Latino Immigrant Men and the Deportation Crisis: A Gendered Racial Removal Program," *Latino Studies* 11, no. 3 (September 2013): 271–92, https://doi.org/10.1057/lst.2013.14; Amada Armenta, "Racializing Crimmigration: Structural Racism, Colorblindness, and the Institutional Production of Immigrant Criminality," *Sociology of Race and Ethnicity* 3, no. 1 (January 2017): 82–95, https://doi.org/10.1177/2332649216648714.

45 See Wacquant, "Deadly Symbiosis"; Marc Mauer, *Race to Incarcerate* (Washington, DC: The Sentencing Project, 1999); Alexander, *New Jim Crow*.

46 See Tonry, *Malign Neglect*; Reinarman and Levine, *Crack in America*; Chambliss, "Drug War Politics"; Bobo and Thompson, "Unfair by Design"; Provine, *Unequal under Law*.

47 Judith Greene and Marc Mauer, "Downscaling Prisons: Lessons from Four States" (Washington, DC: Sentencing Project, March 1, 2010), https://www.sentencingproject.org/publications/downscaling-prisons-lessons-from-four-states/; Drug Policy Alliance, "Marijuana Decriminalization and Legalization."

48 Wendy Sawyer and Peter Wagner, "Mass Incarceration: The Whole Pie 2022" (Easthampton, MA: Prison Policy Initiative, March 14, 2022), https://www.prisonpolicy.org/reports/pie2022.html.

49 The Sentencing Project, "Report to the United Nations on Racial Disparities in the U.S. Criminal Justice System" (Washington, DC: The Sentencing Project, April 19, 2018), https://www.sentencingproject.org/publications/un-report-on-racial-disparities/; Elizabeth Hinton and Cindy Reed, "An Unjust Burden: The Disparate Treatment of Black Americans in the Criminal Justice System" (New York: Vera Institute of Justice, 2018); Ashley Nellis, "The Color of Justice: Racial and Ethnic Disparity in State Prisons" (Washington, DC: The Sentencing Project, 2021), https://www.sentencingproject.org/publications/color-of-justice-racial-and-ethnic-disparity-in-state-prisons/.

50 Abby Budiman, "Key findings about U.S. immigrants," Pew Research Center, August 20, 2020, http://www.pewhispanic.org/fact-tank/2020/08/20/key-findings-about-u-s-immigrants/.

51 Jane Lorenzi and Jeanne Batalova, "Sub-Saharan African Immigrants in the United States," migrationpolicy.org, May 10, 2022, https://www.migrationpolicy.org/article/sub-saharan-african-immigrants-united-states-2019; Jie Zong and Jeanne Batalova, "Caribbean Immigrants in the United States," migrationpolicy.org, February 12, 2019, https://www.migrationpolicy.org/article/caribbean-immigrants-united-states-2017.

52 Monica Anderson and Gustavo Lopez, "Key Facts about Black Immigrants in the U.S.," *Pew Research Center* (blog), January 24, 2018, http://www.pewresearch.org

/fact-tank/2018/01/24/key-facts-about-black-immigrants-in-the-u-s/; Christine Tamir, "Key Findings about Black Immigrants in the U.S.," *Pew Research Center* (blog), January 27, 2022, https://www.pewresearch.org/fact-tank/2022/01/27/key -findings-about-black-immigrants-in-the-u-s/.

53 See Alex S. Vitale, *The End of Policing* (New York: Verso, 2017).

54 Kimberly Barsamian Kahn and Karin D. Martin, "Policing and Race: Disparate Treatment, Perceptions, and Policy Responses: Policing and Race," *Social Issues and Policy Review* 10, no. 1 (January 2016): 82–121, https://doi.org/10.1111/sipr .12019.

55 Stanford Open Policing Project, "The Stanford Open Policing Project," openpolic-ing.stanford.edu, 2019, https://openpolicing.stanford.edu/.

56 Sarah Eppler-Epstein, "We Don't Know How Many Latinos Are Affected by the Criminal Justice System," *Urban Wire: The Blog of the Urban Institute* (blog), October 17, 2016, https://www.urban.org/urban-wire/we-dont-know-how-many -latinos-are-affected-criminal-justice-system.

57 Kahn and Martin, "Policing and Race," 86.

58 The Sentencing Project, "Report to the United Nations," 5–6.

59 Drug Policy Alliance, "The Drug War, Mass Incarceration and Race."

60 Stanford Open Policing Project, "The Stanford Open Policing Project."

61 Bernadette Rabuy and Daniel Kopf, "Prisons of Poverty: Uncovering the Pre-Incarceration Incomes of the Imprisoned" (Northampton, MA: Prison Policy Initiative, 2015), https://www.prisonpolicy.org/reports/income.html.

62 Magnus Lofstrom and Steven Raphael, "Crime, the Criminal Justice System, and Socioeconomic Inequality," *Journal of Economic Perspectives* 30, no. 2 (May 2016): 103–26, https://doi.org/10.1257/jep.30.2.103; Victor M. Rios, *Punished: Policing the Lives of Black and Latino Boys* (New York: NYU Press, 2011); Abigail A. Sewell, Kevin A. Jefferson, and Hedwig Lee, "Living under Surveillance: Gender, Psychological Distress, and Stop-Question-and-Frisk Policing in New York City," *Social Science & Medicine* 159 (June 2016): 1–13, https://doi.org/10.1016/j.socscimed.2016.04.024.

63 . Alexi Jones, "Visualizing the Unequal Treatment of LGBTQ People in the Criminal Justice System," Prison Policy Initiative, March, 2, 2021, https://www .prisonpolicy.org/blog/2021/03/02/lgbtq/.

64 Mercedes Valadez and Xia Wang, "Citizenship, Legal Status, and Federal Sentenc-ing Outcomes: Examining the Moderating Effects of Age, Gender, and Race/Eth-nicity," *Sociological Quarterly* 58, no. 4 (October 2, 2017): 670–700, https://doi.org /10.1080/00380253.2017.1354736.

65 Lin, "End It."

66 New York Advisory New York Advisory Committee, "Civil Rights Implications of 'Broken Windows' Policing in NYC and General NYPD Accountability to the Public," Briefing Report (United States Commission on Civil Rights, March 2018); Stephen Lurie, "There's No Such Thing as a Dangerous Neighborhood," *Bloom-berg*, CityLab, February 25, 2019, https://www.citylab.com/perspective/2019/02 /broken-windows-theory-policing-urban-violence-crime-data/583030/.

67 George Kelling and James Wilson, "Broken Windows," *Atlantic*, 1982, https://www
.theatlantic.com/magazine/archive/1982/03/broken-windows/304465/.

68 Amanda Geller and Jeffrey Fagan, "Pot as Pretext: Marijuana, Race and the New
Disorder in New York City Street Policing," *Journal of Empirical Legal Studies 7*,
no. 4 (2010): 591–633; Vitale, *End of Policing*.

69 See David Garland, *The Culture of Control: Crime and Social Order in Contemporary Society* (Chicago: Chicago University Press, 2001); García Hernández, "Deconstructing Crimmigration"; Sarah Tosh, "Drugs, Crime, and Aggravated Felony
Deportations: Moral Panic Theory and the Legal Construction of the 'Criminal
Alien,'" *Critical Criminology*, March 30, 2019, https://doi.org/10.1007/s10612-019
-09446-8.

70 New York Advisory Committee, "Civil Rights Implications of 'Broken Windows,'" iv.

71 Geller and Fagan, "Pot as Pretext"; Christopher Dunn, Sara LaPlante, and Jennifer
Carnig, "Stop-and-Frisk 2012" (New York: New York City Liberties Union, 2013),
https://www.nyclu.org/sites/default/files/releases/2012_Report_NYCLU.pdf.

72 Garth Davies and Jeffrey Fagan, "Crime and Enforcement in Immigrant Neighborhoods: Evidence from New York City," *SSRN Electronic Journal*, 2012, https:
//doi.org/10.2139/ssrn.1987096.

73 Stewart Stout, "NYPD 'Stop and Frisk' Campaign Targets LGBTQ Residents,"
Make the Road New York, April 11, 2013, https://maketheroadny.org/nypd-stop
-and-frisk-campaign-targets-lgbtq-residents/.

74 Brentin Mock, "How Police Are Using Stop-and-Frisk Four Years after a Seminal
Court Ruling," CityLab, August 18, 2017, https://www.citylab.com/equity/2017/08
/stop-and-frisk-four-years-after-ruled-unconstitutional/537264/.

75 Innocence Project, "Racial Disparities Evident in NYC Arrest Data for Marijuana
Possession," Innocence Project, May 14, 2018, https://www.innocenceproject.org
/racial-disparities-in-nyc-arrest-data-marijuana-possession/; New York Advi-
sory Committee, "The Civil Rights Implications of 'Broken Windows,'"; Fred
Butcher, Michael Rempel, and Krystal Rodriguez, "Advancing Racial Equity:
Shrinking Misdemeanor Prosecution in New York" (New York: Center for Court
Innovation, February 2020), https://www.courtinnovation.org/publications
/misdemeanor-race-NYC.

76 Drug Policy Alliance, "NYC's Costly Drug Enforcement & Broken Windows
Policing," June 2020, https://www.drugpolicy.org/sites/default/files/dpa_drug
_policing_nypd_cost_0.pdf.

77 Aliza Chasan, "Advocates Slam NYPD Quality-of-Life Enforcement Initiative as
Return to Broken Windows Policing," *Pix11*, March 23, 2022, https://pix11.com
/news/local-news/nyc-return-to-broken-windows-policing-advocates-slam-nypd
-quality-of-life-enforcement-initiative/; Katie Glueck and Ashley Southall, "As
Adams Toughens on Crime, Some Fear a Return to '90s Era Policing," *New York
Times*, March 26, 2022, https://www.nytimes.com/2022/03/26/nyregion/broken
-windows-eric-adams.html.

78 NYCLU, "Stop-and-Frisk in the de Blasio Era" (New York: New York Civil Liberties Union, 2019).

79 Jacob Rosenberg and Dave Gilson, "Challenge Coins Are the Dirty Currency of American Law Enforcement," *Mother Jones* (January and February 2021) https://www.motherjones.com/crime-justice/2021/01/police-challenge-coins/.

80 Michael Cooper, "Officers in Bronx Fire 41 Shots, and an Unarmed Man Is Killed," *New York Times*, February 5, 1999, https://www.nytimes.com/1999/02/05/nyregion/officers-in-bronx-fire-41-shots-and-an-unarmed-man-is-killed.html; Asha Layne, "It's Not Just Black and White: How Black Immigrants Continue to Influence the Fight against Police Violence," *Journal of Liberal Arts and Humanities* 2, no. 6 (2021): 1–7.

81 Joseph Goldstein, "Grand Jury Decides Not to Charge Officer Who Fatally Shot Unarmed Youth in Bronx," *New York Times*, August 8, 2013, https://www.nytimes.com/2013/08/09/nyregion/grand-jury-declines-to-indict-officer-in-death-of-unarmed-youth.html; Samuel Maull, "Officer Cleared in Washington Heights Shooting," *AP News*, September 10, 1992, https://apnews.com/article/d8d75ff45eec58dfde57a344940b7a6d.

82 Thomas Maier and Ann Choi, "Unequal Justice: Racial Disparity in Arrests, Sentencings on LI," *Newsday*, October 19, 2017, https://projects.newsday.com/long-island/unequal-justice-part-1/.

83 Stefanie Coyle and Irma Solis, "Suffolk County Police Won't Disclose How It's Helping ICE Lock Up Innocent Students," *American Civil Liberties Union* (blog), April 12, 2018, https://www.aclu.org/blog/immigrants-rights/ice-and-border-patrol-abuses/suffolk-county-police-wont-disclose-how-its; Liz Robbins, "Latinos, in Class-Action Case, Accuse Suffolk County Police of Bias and Harassment," *New York Times*, December 21, 2017, https://www.nytimes.com/2015/04/30/nyregion/latinos-file-class-action-case-accusing-suffolk-police-of-bias-and-harassment.html.

84 H. Richard Lamb, Linda E. Weinberger, and Bruce H. Gross, "Mentally Ill Persons in the Criminal Justice System: Some Perspectives," *Psychiatric Quarterly* 75, no. 2 (2004); Vitale, *End of Policing*.

85 Treatment Advocacy Center, "The Treatment of Persons with Mental Illness in Prisons and Jails: A State Survey" (Arlington, VA: Treatment Advocacy Center, April 8, 2014), 6, https://www.treatmentadvocacycenter.org/storage/documents/treatment-behind-bars/treatment-behind-bars.pdf.

86 Dora M. Dumont, Scott A. Allen, Bradley W. Brockmann, Nicole E. Alexander, Josiah D. Rich, "Incarceration, Community Health, and Racial Disparities," *Journal of Health Care for the Poor and Underserved* 24, no. 1 (2013): 78–88, https://doi.org/10.1353/hpu.2013.0000; Vitale, *End of Policing*.

87 Cynthia Golembeski and Robert Fullilove, "Criminal (In)Justice in the City and Its Associated Health Consequences," supplement, *American Journal of Public Health* 98, no. S9 (September 2008): S185–90; Jennifer M. Reingle Gonzalez and Nadine M. Connell, "Mental Health of Prisoners: Identifying Barriers to Mental Health

Treatment and Medication Continuity," *American Journal of Public Health* 104, no. 12 (December 2014): 2328–33, https://doi.org/10.2105/AJPH.2014.302043; Treatment Advocacy Center, "Treatment of Persons with Mental Illness in Prisons and Jails."

88   Saheed Vassell, shot and killed by NYPD officers in Crown Heights in April 2018, was said to be the tenth person killed by the NYPD since June 2015 and up to that point. Cindy Rodriguez, "City Convenes Task Force on Police Response to Mentally Ill in Crises," *WNYC*, April 18, 2018, https://www.wnyc.org/story/city -convenes-task-force-police-response-mentally-ill-crises/. Also see Carolyn Gorman, "The System Is Failing the Mentally Ill-Not the Cops," *New York Post*, August 14, 2018, https://nypost.com/2018/08/14/the-system-is-failing-the-mentally -ill-not-the-cops/.

89   Matt Ford, "America's Largest Mental Hospital Is a Jail," *Atlantic*, June 8, 2015, 201, https://www.theatlantic.com/politics/archive/2015/06/americas-largest-mental -hospital-is-a-jail/395012/.

90   Examples include Michael Schwirtz, "Rikers Island Struggles With a Surge in Violence and Mental Illness," *New York Times*, January 19, 2018, https://www.nytimes .com/2014/03/19/nyregion/rise-in-mental-illness-and-violence-at-vast-jail-on -rikers-island.html; Alisa Roth, *Insane: America's Criminal Treatment of Mental Illness* (New York: Basic Books, 2018); Jan Ransom and Bianca Pallaro, "Behind the Violence at Rikers, Decades of Mismanagement and Dysfunction," *New York Times*, December 31, 2021, https://www.nytimes.com/2021/12/31/nyregion/rikers -island-correction-officers.html.

91   Jacques Baillargeon, Joseph V. Penn, Kevin Knight, Amy Jo Harzke, Gwen Baillargeon, Emilie A. Becker, "Risk of Reincarceration Among Prisoners with Co-occurring Severe Mental Illness and Substance Use Disorders," *Administration and Policy in Mental Health and Mental Health Services Research* 37, no. 4 (July 2010): 367–74, https://doi.org/10.1007/s10488-009-0252-9; Roger H. Peters, Harry K. Wexler, and Arthur J. Lurigio, "Co-occurring Substance Use and Mental Disorders in the Criminal Justice System: A New Frontier of Clinical Practice and Research," *Psychiatric Rehabilitation Journal* 38, no. 1 (2015): 1–6, https://doi.org /10.1037/prj0000135; Sewell, Jefferson, and Lee, "Living under Surveillance"; Allen Keller, Amy Joscelyne, Megan Granski, and Barry Rosenfeld, "Pre-migration Trauma Exposure and Mental Health Functioning among Central American Migrants Arriving at the US Border," ed. Ignacio Correa-Velez, *PLOS ONE* 12, no. 1 (January 10, 2017): e0168692, https://doi.org/10.1371/journal.pone.0168692; Guy J. Coffey, Ida Kaplan, Robyn C. Sampson, Maria Montagna Tucci, "The Meaning and Mental Health Consequences of Long-Term Immigration Detention for People Seeking Asylum," *Social Science & Medicine* 70, no. 12 (June 1, 2010): 2070–79, https://doi.org/10.1016/j.socscimed.2010.02.042; María Dolores París and Pérez Perez Duperou, "Deported to Tijuana: Social Networks and Religious Communities," in *Immigration Policy in the Age of Punishment: Detention, Deportation, and Border Control*, ed. David C. Brotherton and Philip Kretsedemas (New York: Columbia University Press, 2018), 167–86.

92 "Detention, Deportation, and Devastation: The Disproportionate Effect of Deportations on the Latino Community," (Los Angeles: Mexican American Legal
Defense and Educational Fund, National Day Laborer Organizing Network,
and National Hispanic Leadership Agenda, 2014), https://www.maldef.org/wp
-content/uploads/2019/01/Deportation_Brief_MALDEF-NHLA-NDLON.pdf;
Kevin R. Johnson, "Doubling Down on Racial Discrimination: The Racially
Disparate Impacts of Crime-Based Removals," *Case Western Reserve Law Review*
66, no. 4 (2016): 46; Jynna Radford and Abby Budiman, "Immigrants in America:
Key Charts and Facts," Pew Research Center, September 14, 2018, http://www
.pewhispanic.org/2018/09/14/facts-on-u-s-immigrants/.

93 Juan Manuel Pedroza, "Deportation Discretion: Tiered Influence, Minority
Threat, and 'Secure Communities' Deportations," special issue, *Policy Studies
Journal* 47, no. 3 (2018), https://doi.org/10.1111/psj.12300.

94 Juliana Morgan-Trostle, Kevin Zheng, and Carl Lipscombe, "The State of Black
Immigrants" (New York: Black Alliance for Just Immigration, 2016), http://www
.stateofblackimmigrants.com/assets/sobi-fullreport-jan22.pdf; Jeremy Raff, "The
'Double Punishment' for Black Undocumented Immigrants," *Atlantic*, December 30, 2017, https://www.theatlantic.com/politics/archive/2017/12/the-double
-punishment-for-black-immigrants/549425/; Monica Anderson and Gustavo Lopez, "Key Facts about Black Immigrants in the U.S.," *Pew Research Center* (blog),
January 24, 2018, http://www.pewresearch.org/fact-tank/2018/01/24/key-facts
-about-black-immigrants-in-the-u-s/.

95 Marc Rosenblum and Kristen McCabe, "Deportation and Discretion: Reviewing
the Record and Options for Change" (Washington, DC: Migration Policy Institute, October 2014).

96 Eithne Luibheid and Karma R. Chavez, *Queer and Trans Migrations: Dynamics
of Illegalization, Detention, and Deportation* (Urbana: University of Illinois Press,
2020); Megan Collier and Meghan Daniel, "The Production of Trans Illegality:
Cisnormativity in the U.S. Immigration System," *Sociology Compass* 13, no. 4
(April 2019), https://doi.org/10.1111/soc4.12666.

97 See DeGenova, "The Deportation Regime"; and Golash-Boza, *Deported*.

98 Sarah Mehta, "Deportation by Default: Mental Disability, Unfair Hearings, and
Indefinite Detention in the US Immigration System" (New York: Human Rights
Watch, 2010); Aimee L. Mayer-Salins, "Fast-Track to Injustice: Rapidly Deporting
the Mentally Ill," *Cardozo Public Law Policy & Ethics* 14 (2016): 29.

99 TRAC Immigration, "State and County Details on Deportation Proceedings
in Immigration Court," TRAC, Syracuse University, 2020, https://trac.syr.edu
/phptools/immigration/nta/.

100 Also see Tanya Golash-Boza, "Structural Racism, Criminalization, and Pathways
to Deportation for Dominican and Jamaican Men in the United States," *Social
Justice* 44, no. 2/3 (2017): 137–61.

101 Tamara K. Nopper, "Why Black Immigrants Matter: Refocusing the Discussion
on Racism and Immigration Enforcement," in *Keeping out the Other: A Critical*

Introduction to Immigration Enforcement Today, ed. David C. Brotherton and Kretsedemas Philip (New York: Columbia University Press, 2008), 205–37; Golash-Boza, "Structural Racism, Criminalization, and"; Tanya Maria Golash-Boza, "Forced Transnationalism: Transnational Coping Strategies and Gendered Stigma among Jamaican Deportees," *Global Networks* 14, no. 1 (January 1, 2014): 63–79, https://doi.org/10.1111/glob.12013; Brotherton and Barrios, *Banished to the Homeland*.

102 Jennifer Stave, Peter Markowitz, Karen Berberich, Tammy Cho, Danny Dubbaneh, Laura Simich, Nina Siulc, and Noelle Smart, "Evaluation of the New York Immigrant Family Unity Project" (New York: Vera Institute of Justice, 2017).

103 See Delgado and Stefancic, *Critical Race Theory*; Haney-López, *White by Law*.

104 Liz Robbins, "New Yorkers Facing Deportation Lose Their (Physical) Day in Court," *New York Times*, June 28, 2018, https://www.nytimes.com/2018/06/27/nyregion/new-york-immigrants-deportation-video-hearings.html.

105 See Emily Ryo, "Detained: A Study of Immigration Bond Hearings," *Law & Society Review* 50, no. 1 (2016): 117–53; and Emily Ryo, "Predicting Danger in Immigration Courts," *Law & Social Inquiry* 44, no. 1 (February 2019): 227–56, https://doi.org/10.1017/lsi.2018.20.

106 Mehta, "Deportation by Default."

107 Caleb Korngold, Kristen Ochoa, Talia Inlender, Dale McNiel, and Renée Binder, "Mental Health and Immigrant Detainees in the United States: Competency and Self-Representation," *Journal of the American Academy of Psychiatry and the Law* 43, no. 3 (2015): 5.

108 Legal Action Center, "Representing Clients with Mental Competency Issues Under Matter of M-A-M," Practice Advisory (Washington, DC: American Immigration Council, November 30, 2011), 5.

109 See Brotherton and Barrios, *Banished to the Homeland*; Golash-Boza, "Forced Transnationalism"; Yolanda C. Martín, "The Syndemics of Removal: Trauma and Substance Abuse," in *Outside Justice: Immigration and the Criminalizing Impact of Changing Policy and Practice*, ed. David C. Brotherton, Daniel L. Stageman, and Shirley P. Leyro (New York: Springer, 2013), 91–107, https://doi.org/10.1007/978-1-4614-6648-2_5; París and Duperou, "Deported to Tijuana."

110 Stumpf, "The Crimmigration Crisis"; Jiang and Erez, "Immigrants as Symbolic Assailants"; García Hernández, "Deconstructing Crimmigration," 2018.

111 Pham, "287(g) Agreements in the Trump Era"; Arriaga, "Relationships between the Public and Crimmigration Entities"; Armenta, *Protect, Serve, and Deport*; Coleman, "'Local' Migration State."

112 Stumpf, "Crimmigration Crisis."

113 Spitzer, "Toward a Marxian Theory of Deviance"; Wacquant, "Deadly Symbiosis"; Leo Chavez, *The Latino Threat: Constructing Immigrants, Citizens, and the Nation, Second Edition* (Stanford, CA: Stanford University Press, 2013); Alexander, *New Jim Crow*; Tosh, "Drugs, Crime, and Aggravated Felony Deportations."

4. THE "WILD WEST OF LAW"

1 Antonio Gramsci, *Selections from the Prison Notebooks of Antonio Gramsci* (New York: International Publishers, 1971); Kitty Calavita, *Invitation to Law and Society: An Introduction to the Study of Real Law* (Chicago: University of Chicago Press, 2010).

2 Examples include Mindie Lazarus-Black and Susan F. Hirsch, *Contested States: Law, Hegemony, and Resistance* (London: Psychology Press, 1994); Richard L. Abel, *Politics by Other Means: Law in the Struggle Against Apartheid, 1980–1994* (Abingdon, UK: Routledge, 1994); Boaventura de Sousa Santos and César A. Rodríguez-Garavito, *Law and Globalization from Below: Towards a Cosmopolitan Legality* (Cambridge: Cambridge University Press, 2005).

3 See Mark Tushnet, "The Critique of Rights," *SMU Law Review* 47 (1994): 15; Robert Gordon, "Some Critical Theories of Law and Their Critics," in *The Politics of Law: A Progressive Critique*, ed. David Kairys, 3rd ed. (New York: Basic Books, 1998), 641–61.

4 See Patricia J. Williams, *The Alchemy of Race and Rights* (Cambridge, MA: Harvard University Press, 1991); Michael W. McCann, *Law and Social Movements* (Farnham, UK: Ashgate, 2006); Richard Delgado, "The Ethereal Scholar: Does Critical Legal Studies Have What Minorities Want?," *Harvard Civil Rights–Civil Liberties Law Review* 22, no. 2 (Spring 1987): 301–22.

5 See Sameer Ashar, "Public Interest Lawyers and Resistance Movements," *California Law Review* 95 (2007): 1879–1926; Austin Sarat and Stuart Scheingold, *Cause Lawyering: Political Commitments and Professional Responsibilities* (New York: Oxford University Press, 1998); Austin Sarat and Stuart A. Scheingold, *Cause Lawyers and Social Movements* (Stanford, CA: Stanford University Press, 2006); Anna-Maria Marshall and Daniel Crocker Hale, "Cause Lawyering," *Annual Review of Law and Social Science* 10, no. 1 (November 3, 2014): 301–20, https://doi .org/10.1146/annurev-lawsocsci-102612-133932.

6 See Leila Kawar, *Contesting Immigration Policy in Court: Legal Activism and Its Radiating Effects in the United States and France* (Cambridge: Cambridge University Press, 2015).

7 Susan Bibler Coutin, "Cause Lawyering in the Shadow of the State: A U.S. Immigration Example," in *Cause Lawyering and the State in the Global Era* (Oxford, UK: Oxford University Press, 2001), 117–40; Kawar, *Contesting Immigration Policy in Court*; Jennifer Gordon, *Suburban Sweatshops: The Fight for Immigrant Rights* (Cambridge, MA: Belknap Press: An Imprint of Harvard University Press, 2007).

8 Examples include Aaron Lang, "An Opportunity for Change? Aggravated Felonies in Immigration Proceedings and the Effect of *Moncrieffe v. Holder*," *Boston University Law Journal* 33 (2015): 102–37; Yolanda Vazquez, "Advising Noncitizen Defendants on the Immigration Consequences of Criminal Convictions: The Ethical Answer for the Criminal Defense Lawyer, the Court, and the Sixth Amendment," *Berkeley La Raza Law Journal* 20 (2010): 31–65; Alina Das, "The Immigration

Penalties of Criminal Convictions: Resurrecting Categorical Analysis in Immigration Law," *SSRN Electronic Journal*, 2010, https://doi.org/10.2139/ssrn.1692891; Alina Das, *No Justice in the Shadows: How America Criminalizes Immigrants* (New York: Bold Type Books, 2020).

9 Some exceptions include Ingrid V. Eagly, "Criminal Justice in an Era of Mass Deportation: Reforms from California," *New Criminal Law Review: An International and Interdisciplinary Journal* 20, no. 1 (February 2017): 21, https://doi.org/10.1525 /nclr.2017.20.1.12; Annie Lai and Christopher N. Lasch, "Crimmigration Resistance and the Case of Sanctuary City Funding," *Santa Clara Law Review* 57 (2018): 539–610; and Robin Pomerenke, "Intersectional Resistance: A Case Study on Crimmigration and Lessons for Organizing in the Trump Era," *Hastings Women's Law Journal* 29, no. 2 (2018): 241–60.

10 Ashar, "Public Interest Lawyers"; Sarat and Scheingold, *Cause Lawyering*; Sarat and Scheingold, *Cause Lawyers and Social Movements*; Marshall and Crocker Hale, "Cause Lawyering."

11 Hamel Vyas, "Ethical Issues for Immigration Lawyers," in *Navigating the Fundamentals of Immigration Law: Guidance and Tips for Successful Practice—2018–19 Edition*, ed. John M. Area (Washington, DC: American Immigration Lawyers Association, 2018), 16.

12 See Elizabeth Keyes, "Zealous Advocacy: Pushing Against the Borders in Immigration Litigation," *Seton Hall Law Review* 45 (2015): 69; Nina Rabin, "Searching for Humanitarian Discretion in Immigration Enforcement: Reflections on a Year as an Immigration Attorney in the Trump Era," *University of Michigan Journal of Law Reform* 53 (2019): 139, https://doi.org/10.36646/mjlr.53.1.searching.

13 J. C. Salyer, *Court of Injustice: Law Without Recognition in U.S. Immigration* (Stanford, CA: Stanford University Press, 2020), 22.

14 The NYIFUP program works by funding immigration removal defense units within existing public defense organizations, namely The Legal Aid Society of New York, Brooklyn Defender Services, and The Bronx Defenders.

15 Jeff Sessions was US attorney general under Trump from February 2017 to November 2018.

16 Rabin, "Searching for Humanitarian Discretion," 143.

17 Noah Klug, "Preface," in *Navigating the Fundamentals of Immigration Law: Guidance and Tips for Successful Practice—2018–19 Edition*, ed. John M. Area (Washington, DC: American Immigration Lawyers Association, 2018), x.

18 Executive Office for Immigration Review, "Statistics Yearbook Fiscal Year 2017" (Department of Justice, 2018).

19 Ingrid V. Eagly and Steven Shafer, "A National Study of Access to Counsel in Immigration Court," *University of Pennsylvania Law Review* 164 (2015).

20 Das, "Immigration Penalties of Criminal Convictions"; Lang, "An Opportunity for Change?"; Sara Salem, "Should They Stay or Should They Go: Rethinking the Use of Crimes Involving Moral Turpitude in Immigration Law," *Florida Law Review* 70, no. 1 (2018): 225–50.

21 Rebecca Sharpless, "Toward a True Elements Test: Taylor and the Categorical Analysis of Crimes in Immigration Law," *University of Miami Law Review* 62 (2008): 979–1035.

22 Das, "Immigration Penalties of Criminal Convictions."

23 Rebecca Sharpless, "Finally, a True Elements Test," *Brooklyn Law Review* 82 (2017): 1303.

24 Adam Liptak, "Supreme Court Refuses for Now to Restore Biden Plan on Immigration Enforcement," *New York Times*, July 21, 2022, https://www.nytimes.com /2022/07/21/us/politics/supreme-court-biden-immigration.html.

25 Das, "Immigration Penalties of Criminal Convictions."

26 Sharpless, "Finally, a True Elements Test," 1303.

27 Lang, "An Opportunity for Change?"

28 Hylton v. Sessions (2018).

29 See Juliet Stumpf, "The Crimmigration Crisis: Immigrants, Crime, and Sovereign Power," *American University Law Review* 56, no. 2 (2006): 367–419; Katherine Beckett and Heather Evans, "Crimmigration at the Local Level: Criminal Justice Processes in the Shadow of Deportation," *Law & Society Review* 49, no. 1 (2015): 241–77; Jize Jiang and Edna Erez, "Immigrants as Symbolic Assailants: Crimmigration and Its Discontents," *International Criminal Justice Review* 28, no. 1 (March 2018): 5–24, https://doi.org/10.1177/1057567717721299; César Cuauhtémoc García Hernández, "Deconstructing Crimmigration," *University of California Davis Law Review* 52 (2018): 197–253, https://doi.org/10.2139/ssrn.3326202.

30 Exceptions include Ingrid V. Eagly, "Criminal Justice in an Era of Mass Deportation: Reforms from California," *New Criminal Law Review: An International and Interdisciplinary Journal* 20, no. 1 (February 2017): 21, https://doi.org/10.1525/nclr .2017.20.1.12; Annie Lai and Christopher N. Lasch, "Crimmigration Resistance and the Case of Sanctuary City Funding," *Santa Clara Law Review* 57 (2018): 539–610; and Robin Pomerenke, "Intersectional Resistance: A Case Study on Crimmigration and Lessons for Organizing in the Trump Era," *Hastings Women's Law Journal* 29, no. 2 (2018): 241–60.

31 Eagly, "Criminal Justice in an Era of Mass Deportation," 21.

32 Padilla v. Kentucky (2010).

33 See also Das, *No Justice in the Shadows*.

34 See The Innocence Project, "Celebrating 25 Years of Freedom and Justice: The Innocence Project 2016 Annual Report" (New York: The Innocence Project, 2016).

35 Hon Dana Leigh Marks and Hon Denise Noonan Slavin, "A View Through the Looking Glass: How Crimes Appear from the Immigration Court Perspective," *Fordham Urban Law Journal* 39, no. 1 (2016): 91–119.

36 Marks and Slavin, "View Through the Looking Glass."

37 In *Matter of Pickering* (2003:621), the BIA ruled that "If a court vacates an alien's conviction for reasons solely related to rehabilitation or immigration hardships, rather than on the basis of a procedural or substantive defect in the underlying criminal proceedings, the conviction is not eliminated for immigration purposes."

38 Sarat and Scheingold, *Cause Lawyering*; Susan Bibler Coutin, "Cause Lawyering in the Shadow of the State: A U.S. Immigration Example," in *Cause Lawyering and the State in the Global Era* (Oxford, UK: Oxford University Press, 2001), 117–40; Sarat and Scheingold, *Cause Lawyers and Social Movements*; Kawar, *Contesting Immigration Policy in Court.*

39 Lazarus-Black and Hirsch, *Contested States*, 20.

5. "THESE ARE PEOPLE FROM OUR COMMUNITY"

1 Following the success of its pilot period in New York City, NYIFUP was spread statewide in 2017, and it now provides universal representation for immigrants facing deportation throughout the New York State—including those detained at Batavia, Ulster, Fishkill, and Bedford Hills, state prisons with detained immigration courts. Representation in these cases is provided by the Volunteer Lawyers Project of the Erie County Bar Association, as well as Prisoners' Legal Services of New York. See https://www.vera.org/projects/new-york-immigrant-family-unity-project.

2 Jennifer Stave, Peter Markowitz, Karen Berberich, Tammy Cho, Danny Dubbaneh, Laura Simich, Nina Siulc, and Noelle Smart, "Evaluation of the New York Immigrant Family Unity Project" (New York: Vera Institute of Justice, 2017); See also, Alina Das, "Immigration Detention: Information Gaps and Institutional Barriers to Reform," *University of Chicago Law Review* 80 (2013); J. C. Salyer, *Court of Injustice: Law Without Recognition in U.S. Immigration* (Stanford, CA: Stanford University Press, 2020).

3 Ingrid V. Eagly and Steven Shafer, "A National Study of Access to Counsel in Immigration Court," *University of Pennsylvania Law Review* 164 (2015).

4 Eagly and Shafer.

5 Elizabeth Keyes, "Zealous Advocacy: Pushing Against the Borders in Immigration Litigation," *Seton Hall Law Review* 45 (2015): 69.

6 Eagly and Shafer, "National Study of Access."

7 Susan Bibler Coutin, "Cause Lawyering in the Shadow of the State: A U.S. Immigration Example," in *Cause Lawyering and the State in the Global Era* (Oxford, UK: Oxford University Press, 2001), 122–23; Chiarapl Galli, "Humanitarian Capital: How Lawyers Help Immigrants Use Suffering to Claim Membership in the Nation-State," *Journal of Ethnic and Migration Studies* 46, no. 11 (August 17, 2020): 2181–98, https://doi.org/10.1080/1369183X.2019.1582325; Sarah M. Lakhani, "Universalizing the U Visa: Challenges of Immigration Case Selection in Legal Nonprofits," *California Law Review* 107 (2019): 1661–72.

8 Alina Das, *No Justice in the Shadows: How America Criminalizes Immigrants* (New York: Bold Type Books, 2020).

9 Das, *No Justice in the Shadows*; Salyer, *Court of Injustice*; Stave et al., "Evaluation of the New York Immigrant Family Unity Project."

10 Stephen Manning and Juliet Stumpf, "Big Immigration Law," *University of California Davis Law Review* 52 (2018): 412.

11 Nina Rabin, "Searching for Humanitarian Discretion in Immigration Enforcement: Reflections on a Year as an Immigration Attorney in the Trump Era," *University of Michigan Journal of Law Reform* 53 (2019): 139–71, https://doi.org/10.36646/mjlr.53.1 .searching; See also, Das, *No Justice in the Shadows*; Salyer, *Court of Injustice*.

12 Salyer, *Court of Injustice*, 135.

13 See Stave et al., "Evaluation of the New York Immigrant Family Unity Project"; Salyer, *Court of Injustice*; Das, *No Justice in the Shadows*.

14 Leila Kawar, *Contesting Immigration Policy in Court: Legal Activism and Its Radiating Effects in the United States and France* (Cambridge: Cambridge University Press, 2015).

15 Salyer, *Court of Injustice*.

16 Salyer, *Court of Injustice*, 135.

17 Salyer, *Court of Injustice*, 136.

18 Stave et al., "Evaluation of the New York Immigrant Family Unity Project."

19 Salyer, *Court of Injustice*, 137.

20 Vera Institute of Justice, "Advancing Universal Representation Initiative," vera.org, 2023, https://www.vera.org/ending-mass-incarceration/reducing-incarceration /detention-of-immigrants/advancing-universal-representation-initiative.

21 In 2015, New York State awarded $8.1 million in grants to legal service providers to ensure compliance with *Padilla v. Kentucky* through the operation of "regional centers of immigration legal support, assistance, training and education for the attorneys providing mandated representation to immigrant clients in Criminal and Family Court." Joel Stashenko, "State Distributes $8.1M for Immigrant Legal Centers," *New York Law Journal*, July 9, 2015, https://www.law.com /newyorklawjournal/almID/1202731623737/.

22 See note 21 above. IDP was selected as the regional assistance center for NYC. https://www.immigrantdefenseproject.org/what-we-do/padilla-support-center/.

23 Immigrant Defense Project, "About," immigrantdefenseproject.org, 2018, https: //www.immigrantdefenseproject.org/about/.

24 The Legal Aid Society, "Historical Events Archive," The Legal Aid Society, 2021, https://legalaidnyc.org/history/.

25 Kawar, *Contesting Immigration Policy in Court*, 29.

26 The Legal Aid Society, "About Us," The Legal Aid Society, 2021, https://legalaidnyc .org/about/.

27 Brooklyn Defense Services, "Our Approach," Brooklyn Defense Services, 2023, https://bds.org/our-approach; "Policy, Advocacy, and Reform," Brooklyn Defense Services, 2023, https://bds.org/our-work/policy-advocacy-reform.

28 The Bronx Defenders, "Holistic Defense, Defined," The Bronx Defenders, 2015, https://www.bronxdefenders.org/holistic-defense/.

29 Stave et al., "Evaluation of the New York Immigrant Family Unity Project."

30 NYC Office of the Appellate Defender, "Reinvestigation Project," 2018, https: //oadnyc.org/reinvestigation-project/.

31 The Innocent Project, "Exonerate the Innocent," Innocence Project, 2021, https: //innocenceproject.org/exonerate/.

32 Liz Robbins, "New Yorkers Facing Deportation Lose Their (Physical) Day in Court," *New York Times*, June 28, 2018, https://www.nytimes.com/2018/06/27 /nyregion/new-york-immigrants-deportation-video-hearings.html.

33 "Justice Roadmap 2022" JusticeRoadmapNY.org, 2022, https://justiceroadmapny .org/wp-content/uploads/2022/03/Justice-Roadmap-2022.pdf.

34 Drug Policy Alliance, "About Us," 2022, https://drugpolicy.org/about-us.

35 Immigrant Defense Project, "Criminal Justice and Drug Reform," immigrantde-fenseproject.org, 2021, https://www.immigrantdefenseproject.org/criminal-justice -and-drug-reform.

36 Drug Policy Alliance, "Sensible Marijuana Access through Regulated Trade," Start SMART New York, 2021, http://smart-ny.com/.

37 Jeanmarie Evelly, "What NY's Marijuana Legalization Law Means for Immi-grants," *City Limits* (blog), April 1, 2021, https://citylimits.org/2021/04/01/what-nys -marijuana-legalization-law-means-for-immigrants/.

38 Angélica Cházaro, "Challenging the 'Criminal Alien' Paradigm," *University of California Los Angeles Law Review* 63 (2016); Mariela Olivares, "Resistance Strate-gies in the Immigrant Justice Movement," *Northern Illinois Law Review* 39 (2018): 47; Keyes, "Zealous Advocacy"; Grace Yukich, "Constructing the Model Immi-grant: Movement Strategy and Immigrant Deservingness in the New Sanctuary Movement," *Social Problems* 60, no. 3 (August 2013): 302–20, https://doi.org/10 .1525/sp.2013.60.3.302.

39 Stave et al., "Evaluation of the New York Immigrant Family Unity Project."

40 Alan Feuer, "Brooklyn Moves to Protect Immigrants From Deportation Over Petty Crimes," *New York Times*, December 22, 2017, https://www.nytimes.com /2017/04/24/nyregion/brooklyn-immigrants-deportation-crime.html.

41 Das, *No Justice in the Shadows*.

42 Liz Robbins, "Mayor and City Council Make Deal on Lawyers for Immigrants," *New York Times*, December 22, 2017, https://www.nytimes.com/2017/07/31 /nyregion/mayor-and-city-council-make-deal-on-lawyers-for-immigrants.html.

43 See Shannon Gleeson and Prerna Sampat, "Immigrant Resistance in the Age of Trump," *New Labor Forum* 27, no. 1 (January 2018): 86–95, https://doi.org/10 .1177/1095796017744778; Robin Pomerenke, "Intersectional Resistance: A Case Study on Crimmigration and Lessons for Organizing in the Trump Era," *Hastings Women's Law Journal* 29, no. 2 (2018): 241–60; Breanne J. Palmer, "The Cross-roads: Being Black, Immigrant, and Undocumented in the Era of #BlackLives-Matter," *Georgetown Journal of Law and Modern Critical Race Perspectives* 9, no. 1 (2017): 99–121; Kevin Escudero, *Organizing While Undocumented: Immigrant Youth's Political Activism under the Law* (New York: NYU Press, 2020).

44 Das, *No Justice in the Shadows*, 199.

45 Palmer, "Crossroads," 113.

46 Detention Watch Network and United We Dream, "Defund Police, ICE, & CBP," 2020, https://www.google.com/url?sa=t&rct=j&q=&esrc=s&source=web &cd=&ved=2ahUKEwiS6bvy-5T5AhWeMVkFHXP3CgMQFnoECAIQAQ &url=https%3A%2F%2Fwww.detentionwatchnetwork.org%2Fsites%2Fdefault %2Ffiles%2FDefund%2520Police%252C%2520ICE%252C%2520%2526%2520C BP_DWN%2520%2526%2520UWD_2020.pdf&usg=AOvVaw3FK2OcmLowjt -lF3TKd7Rw.

47 Silky Shah, "The Immigrant Justice Movement Should Embrace Abolition," *Forge*, February 21, 2021, https://forgeorganizing.org/article/immigrant-justice -movement-should-embrace-abolition.

48 Defund the Police and Abolish Ice Collective, "An Open Letter from Undocu-mented, DACAmented and Formerly Undocumented Leaders to the Immi-grant Rights Movement," *Medium* (blog), June 18, 2020, https://medium.com/@ acdpcollective/an-open-letter-from-undocumented-dacamented-and-formerly -undocumented-leaders-to-the-immigrant-42dda0052f7d.

49 Families for Freedom, "About Us," Families for Freedom, 2020, https: //familiesforfreedom.org/about.

50 Black Alliance for Just Immigration (BAJI), "One Year after George's Floyd's Murder We Continue the Call for Abolition," 2021, https://baji.org/our-work /statements/one-year-after-georges-floyds-murder-we-continue-the-call-for -abolition/.

51 Stories@Gilead, "The Translatinx Network," March 31, 2022, https://stories.gilead .com/articles/the-translatinx-network-helps-a-resilient-community-live-its-truth.

52 Das, *No Justice in the Shadows*; Juliana Morgan-Trostle, Kevin Zheng, and Carl Lipscombe, "The State of Black Immigrants" (New York: Black Alliance for Just Immigration, 2016), http://www.stateofblackimmigrants.com/assets/sobi -fullreport-jan22.pdf; "Groups Urge NYPD Inspector General to Audit the NYPD 'Gang Database,'" *Human Rights Watch* (blog), September 22, 2020, https:// www.hrw.org/news/2020/09/22/groups-urge-nypd-inspector-general-audit-nypd -gang-database; Sofia Cerda Compero and Sindy Nanclares, "These Transgender Latinas Want New York State to Decriminalize Sex Work," *Daily Beast* (blog), July 18, 2019, https://www.thedailybeast.com/these-transgender-latinas-want-new -york-state-to-decriminalize-sex-work.

53 Eithne Luibhéid and Karma R. Chavez, *Queer and Trans Migrations: Dynamics of Illegalization, Detention, and Deportation* (Urbana: University of Illinois Press, 2020); Shannon Gleeson and Prerna Sampat, "Immigrant Resistance in the Age of Trump," *New Labor Forum* 27, no. 1 (January 2018): 86–95, https://doi.org/10.1177 /1095796017744778; Kevin R. Johnson, "Bringing Racial Justice to Immigration Law," *Northwestern University Law Review* 116, no. 1 (2021), https://doi.org/10.2139 /ssrn.3771006.

54 Annie Lai and Christopher N. Lasch, "Crimmigration Resistance and the Case of Sanctuary City Funding," *Santa Clara Law Review* 57 (2018), 542.

55 Juliet Stumpf, "The Crimmigration Crisis: Immigrants, Crime, and Sovereign Power," *American University Law Review* 56, no. 2 (2006): 367–419.

CONCLUSION

1 Nick Miroff, "U.S. Arrests along Mexico Border Surpass 2 Million in a Year for First Time," *Washington Post*, September 19, 2022, https://www.washingtonpost .com/national-security/2022/09/19/us-border-patrol-arrests/.

2 Edgar Sandoval and Eliza Fawcett, "Criminal Investigation Is Opened After Migrant Flights to Martha's Vineyard," *New York Times*, September 20, 2022, https:// www.nytimes.com/2022/09/19/us/migrants-marthas-vineyard-texas-investigation .html; Eduardo Medina and Remy Tumin, "Migrants Who Were Flown to Martha's Vineyard Sue Florida Governor," *New York Times*, September 21, 2022, https: //www.nytimes.com/2022/09/20/us/desantis-migrants-lawsuit.html; Aaron Blake, "What the Law Says about DeSantis and Abbott Sending Migrants to Blue States," *Washington Post*, September 16, 2022, https://www.washingtonpost.com/politics /2022/09/15/desantis-abbott-migrants-legality/.

3 Blake Hounshell, "The Political Calculations Behind DeSantis's Migrant Flights North," *New York Times*, September 15, 2022, https://www.nytimes.com/2022/09 /15/us/politics/desantis-migrant-flights.html.

4 Andy Newman and Raúl Vilchis, "A Migrant Wave Tests New York City's Identity as the World's Sanctuary," *New York Times*, August 20, 2022, https://www .nytimes.com/2022/08/20/nyregion/nyc-migrants-texas.html; Miriam Jordan, "G.O.P. Governors Cause Havoc by Busing Migrants to East Coast," *New York Times*, August 4, 2022, https://www.nytimes.com/2022/08/04/us/migrants-buses -washington-texas.html; Hounshell, "Political Calculations."

5 Jordan, "G.O.P. Governors Cause Havoc."

6 Joseph Wilkinson and Tim Balk, "New York, Chicago Take Different Approaches to Migrant Buses Sent from Texas," *New York Daily News*, September 12, 2022, https://www.nydailynews.com/news/politics/new-york-elections-government /ny-chicago-new-york-different-approaches-texas-migrant-crisis-20220912 -7jqqk7jf7ze7lbzko3qyuiz5ym-story.html.

7 Anne Gratzer and Chris Sommerfeldt, "Heartbroken Son of Colombian Migrant Blames Himself for Mom's Suicide at NYC Shelter: 'She Was Perfect,'" *New York Daily News*, September 20, 2022, https://www.nydailynews.com/news/politics /new-york-elections-government/ny-son-colombian-migrant-suicide-nyc-shelter -blames-himself-20220920-cgkcxh45wjhe3oxkzmaykglilm-story.html; Gloria Oladipo and Ramon Antonio Vargas, "Attack on Asylum Seeker in New York Sparks Outrage over Conditions," *Guardian*, September 11, 2022, https://www.theguardian .com/us-news/2022/sep/11/new-york-asylum-seeker-attacked-officer-shelter.

8 Erin Durkin, "Adams Condemns Texas Governor for Busing Migrants to New York," *POLITICO* (blog), August 7, 2022, https://www.politico.com/news/2022/08 /07/eric-adams-texas-migrants-new-york-00050235.

9 Jeffery C. Mays, "Migrant Crisis Puts N.Y. 'Right to Shelter' Law to the Test," *New York Times*, September 15, 2022, https://www.nytimes.com/2022/09/15/nyregion/nyc-homeless-shelters-migrants.html.

10 "NYC Asylum Seekers: Migrants to Be Relocated to Randall's Island amid Backlash, Flooding Concerns over 1st Location," *ABC News 7 NY* (blog), October 4, 2022, https://abc7ny.com/asylum-seekers-nyc-immigration-humanitarian-relief-center-migrants/12293583/.

11 Andy Newman, "Tent City for Migrants to Be Moved After It Flooded from Modest Rain," *New York Times*, October 4, 2022, https://www.nytimes.com/2022/10/04/nyregion/nyc-migrant-encampment-eric-adams.html.

12 Jordan, "G.O.P. Governors Cause Havoc."

13 Will Sennott, Zolan Kanno-Youngs, Eileen Sullivan, and Patricia Mazzei, "With Faraway Migrant Drop-Offs, G.O.P. Governors Are Doubling Down," *New York Times*, September 15, 2022, https://www.nytimes.com/2022/09/15/us/desantis-abbott-migrants-immigration.html.

14 Alina Das, *No Justice in the Shadows: How America Criminalizes Immigrants* (New York: Basic Books, 2020); César Cuauhtémoc García Hernández, *Migrating to Prison: America's Obsession with Locking Up Immigrants* (New York: New Press, 2019). Adam Goodman, *The Deportation Machine: America's Long History of Expelling Immigrants* (Princeton, NJ: Princeton University Press, 2021); Jenna Loyd and Alison Mountz, "The Caribbean Roots of U.S. Migration Policy: How Deterrence, Detention, and Deportation of Caribbean Migrants and Refugees in the '70s and '80s Laid the Groundwork for the Militarization of the U.S.-Mexico Border Today," *NACLA Report on the Americas* 51, no. 1 (March 29, 2019): 78–84, https://doi.org/10.1080/10714839.2019.1593695; Kristina Shull, "Reagan's Cold War on Immigrants: Resistance and the Rise of a Detention Regime, 1981–1985," *Journal of American Ethnic History* 40, no. 2 (January 1, 2021): 5–51, https://doi.org/10.5406/jamerethnhist.40.2.0005.

15 Maria Ramirez Uribe, "Fact-Checking Claim on Venezuela Sending Prisoners to the US Border," *Austin American-Statesman*, October 4, 2022, https://www.statesman.com/story/news/politics/politifact/2022/10/04/fact-checking-claim-on-venezuela-sending-prisoners-to-the-us-border/69535375007/.

16 The Proud Boys are a far-right, white supremacist group known for anti-immigrant rhetoric and neofascist violence. MAGA refers to "Make America Great Again," a political slogan popularized by Donald Trump and his followers.

17 Kevin Rincon and Andrea Grymes, "City Relocating Orchard Beach Migrant Relief Center to Randall's Island, Mayor Adams Says," *CBS News New York* (blog), October 3, 2022, https://www.cbsnews.com/newyork/news/city-relocating-orchard-beach-migrant-relief-center-to-randalls-island-mayor-adams-says/; "NYC Asylum Seekers."

18 "NYC Asylum Seekers."

19 Juliet Stumpf, "The Crimmigration Crisis: Immigrants, Crime, and Sovereign Power," *American University Law Review* 56, no. 2 (2006): 367–419.

20 Jennifer Lee Koh, "Removal in the Shadows of Immigration Court," *Southern California Law Review* 90 (2017): 180–235; Alina Das, *No Justice in the Shadows: How America Criminalizes Immigrants* (New York: Basic Books, 2020).

21 Stumpf, "The Crimmigration Crisis."

22 Patrisia Macías-Rojas, *From Deportation to Prison: The Politics of Immigration Enforcement in Post-Civil Rights America* (New York: NYU Press, 2016).

23 Amada Armenta, *Protect, Serve, and Deport: The Rise of Policing as Immigration Enforcement* (Oakland: University of California Press, 2017); Felicia Arriaga, "Relationships between the Public and Crimmigration Entities in North Carolina: A 287(g) Program Focus," *Sociology of Race and Ethnicity* 3, no. 3 (2017): 417–31.

24 Philippe Bourbeau, "Detention and Immigration: Practices, Crimmigration, and Norms," *Migration Studies* 7, no. 1 (March 1, 2019): 83–99, https://doi.org/10.1093/migration/mnx069; César Cuauhtémoc García Hernández, *Migrating to Prison: America's Obsession with Locking Up Immigrants* (New York: New Press, 2019).

25 Dario Melossi, *Crime, Punishment and Migration* (SAGE, 2015); Leisy Abrego, Mat Coleman, Daniel E. Martínez, Cecilia Menjívar, and Jeremy Slack, "Making Immigrants into Criminals: Legal Processes of Criminalization in the Post-IIRIRA Era," *Journal on Migration and Human Security* 5, no. 3 (September 2017): 694–715, https://doi.org/10.1177/233150241700500308.

26 Robin Pomerenke, "Intersectional Resistance: A Case Study on Crimmigration and Lessons for Organizing in the Trump Era," *Hastings Women's Law Journal* 29, no. 2 (2018): 241–60; Breanne J. Palmer, "The Crossroads: Being Black, Immigrant, and Undocumented in the Era of #BlackLivesMatter," *Georgetown Journal of Law and Modern Critical Race Perspectives* 9, no. 1 (2017): 99–121.

ABOUT THE AUTHOR

SARAH TOSH is Assistant Professor in the Department of Sociology, Anthropology, and Criminal Justice at Rutgers University–Camden. She is a critical researcher focused on the punitive intersections between drug, crime, and immigration policy in the United States. She received her PhD in Sociology from the Graduate Center, City University of New York.

www.ingramcontent.com/pod-product-compliance
Lightning Source LLC
Chambersburg PA
CBHW020537030426

42337CB00013B/881